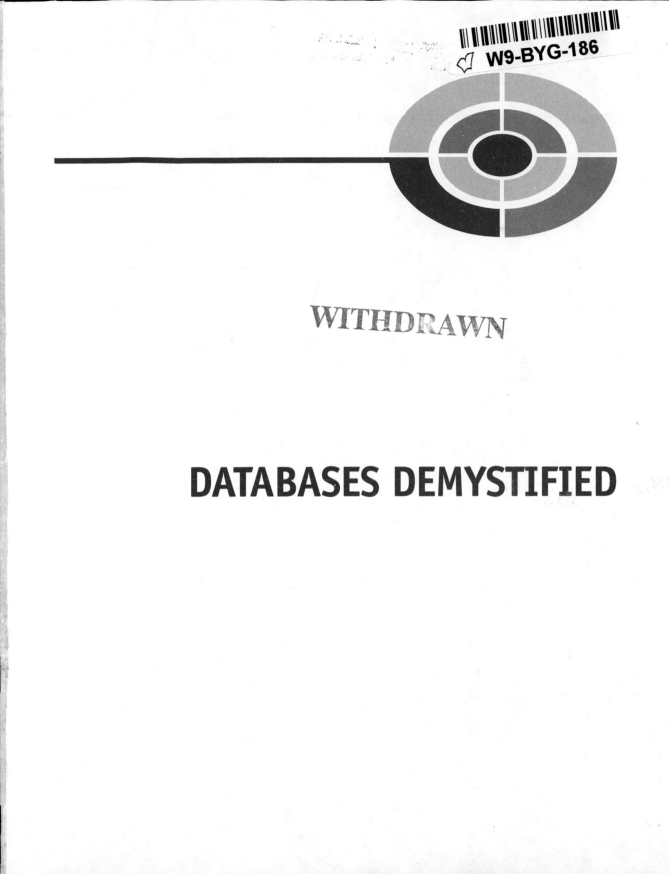

WITHDRAWN

DATABASES DEMYSTIFIED

DATABASES DEMYSTIFIED

ANDREW J. OPPEL

McGraw-Hill/Osborne

New York   Chicago   San Francisco   Lisbon   London
Madrid   Mexico City   Milan   New Delhi   San Juan
Seoul   Singapore   Sydney   Toronto

The *McGraw·Hill* Companies

McGraw-Hill/Osborne
2100 Powell Street, 10th Floor
Emeryville, California 94608
U.S.A.

To arrange bulk purchase discounts for sales promotions, premiums, or fund-raisers, please contact **McGraw-Hill**/Osborne at the above address. For information on translations or book distributors outside the U.S.A., please see the International Contact Information page immediately following the index of this book.

Databases Demystified

1234567890 CUS CUS 01987654

ISBN 007-225364-9

Publisher
Brandon A. Nordin

Vice President & Associate Publisher
Scott Rogers

Editorial Director
Wendy Rinaldi

Project Editor
Janet Walden

Acquisitions Coordinator
Athena Honore

Technical Editor
Greg Guntle

Copy Editor
Bart Reed

Proofreader
Claire Splan

Indexer
Claire Splan

Composition
Tara A. Davis, Lucie Ericksen

Illustrators
Kathleen Edwards, Melinda Lytle

Cover Series Design
Margaret Webster-Shapiro

Cover Illustrations
Lance Lekander

This book was composed with Corel VENTURA™ Publisher.

To everyone from whom I have learned so much about so many things, including the many teachers, students, and co-workers I have had the pleasure of knowing.

Andrew J. (Andy) Oppel is a proud graduate of The Boys' Latin School of Maryland and of Transylvania University (Lexington, KY) where he earned a BA in computer science in 1974. Since then he has been continuously employed in a wide variety of information technology positions, including programmer, programmer/analyst, systems architect, project manager, senior database administrator, database group manager, consultant, database designer, and data architect. In addition, he has been a part-time instructor with the University of California (Berkeley) Extension for over 20 years, and received the Honored Instructor Award for the year 2000. His teaching work has included developing two courses for UC Extension, "Concepts of Database Management Systems" and "Introduction to Relational Database Management Systems." He also earned his Oracle 9i Database Associate certification in 2003. He is currently employed as the principal data architect for Ceridian, a leading provider of human resource solutions. Aside from computer systems, Andy enjoys music (guitar and vocals), amateur radio (Pacific Division vice director, American Radio Relay League), and soccer (referee instructor, U.S. Soccer).

Andy has designed and implemented hundreds of databases for a wide range of applications, including medical research, banking, insurance, apparel manufacturing, telecommunications, wireless communications, and human resources. His database product experience includes IMS, DB2, Sybase, Microsoft SQL Server, Microsoft Access, MySQL, and Oracle (versions 7, 8, 8i, and 9i).

CONTENTS AT A GLANCE

CONTENTS

CONTENTS

xv

ACKNOWLEDGMENTS

I owe much to my parents for providing me with an excellent education and a love of both learning and teaching. I credit The Boys' Latin School of Maryland and the late Jack H. Williams, headmaster, with teaching me to write effectively. And I credit Transylvania University and Dr. James E. Miller for introducing me to the fascinating world of information systems and providing me with the tools for continuous learning. I'd like to thank the wonderful people at McGraw-Hill/Osborne for the opportunity to write my first book and for their excellent support during the writing process. Finally, my thanks to my wife Laurie and our sons Keith and Luke for their support, patience, and understanding during the long hours it took to produce this book.

INTRODUCTION

Thirty years ago, databases were found only in special research laboratories where computer scientists struggled with ways to make them efficient and useful, and published their findings in countless research papers. Today databases are a ubiquitous part of the information technology (IT) industry and business in general. We directly and indirectly use databases every day—banking transactions, travel reservations, employment relationships, web site searches, purchases, and most other transactions are recorded in and served by databases.

As with many fast-growing technologies, industry standards have lagged behind the development of database technology, resulting in a myriad of commercial products, each following a particular software vendor's vision. Moreover, a number of different database models have emerged, with the relational model being the most prevalent. *Databases Demystified* examines all of the major database models, including hierarchical, network, relational, object-oriented, and object-relational. However, *Databases Demystified* concentrates heavily upon the relational and object-relational models because these are the mainstream of the IT industry and will likely remain so in the foreseeable future.

The most significant challenge in implementing a database is designing the structure of the database correctly. Without a thorough understanding of the problem the database is intended to solve, and without knowledge of the best practices for organizing the required data, the implemented database becomes an unwieldy beast that requires constant attention. *Databases Demystified* focuses on transformation of requirements into a working database model with special emphasis on a process called *normalization*, which has proven to be an effective technique for designing relational databases. In fact, normalization can be applied successfully to other database models. And, in keeping with the notion that you cannot design an automobile if you

have never driven one, the SQL language is introduced so that the reader may "drive" a database before delving into the details of designing one.

I've drawn on my extensive experience as a database designer, administrator, and instructor to provide you with this self-help guide to the fascinating and complex world of database technology. Examples are included using both Microsoft Access and Oracle. Publicly available sample databases supplied by these vendors (the Microsoft Access Northwind database and the Oracle Human Resources database schema) are used in example figures whenever possible so that you may try the examples directly on your own computer system. A review quiz is provided at the end of each chapter along with a comprehensive exam at the end of the book.

If you have any comments, I'd like to hear from you.

Andrew J. (Andy) Oppel
andy@andyoppel.com
Honored instructor, University of California Berkeley Extension
Principal data architect, Ceridian
Certified Oracle 9*i* Database Associate

Database Fundamentals

This chapter introduces fundamental concepts and definitions regarding databases, including properties common to databases, prevalent database models, a brief history of databases, and the rationale for focusing on the relational model.

Properties of a Database

A *database* is a collection of interrelated data items that are managed as a single unit. This definition is deliberately broad because there is so much variety across the various software vendors that provide database systems. Microsoft Access places the entire database in a single data file, so an Access database can be defined as the file that contains the data items. Oracle Corporation defines their database as a collection of physical files that are managed by an instance of their database software product. An *instance* is a copy of the database software running in memory.

Microsoft SQL Server and Sybase define a database as a collection of data items that have a common owner, and multiple databases are typically managed by a single instance of the database management software. This can be quite confusing if you work with multiple products because, for example, a database as defined by Microsoft SQL Server and Sybase is exactly what Oracle Corporation calls a *schema*.

A *database object* is a named data structure that is stored in a database. The specific types of database objects supported in a database vary from vendor to vendor and from one database model to another. *Database model* refers to the way in which a database organizes its data to pattern the real world. The most common database models are presented in "Prevalent Database Models," later in this chapter.

A *file* is a collection of related records that are stored as a single unit by an operating system. Given the unfortunately similar definitions of *files* and *databases*, how can we make a distinction? A number of Unix operating system vendors call their password file a "database," yet database experts will quickly point out that, in fact, it is not. Clearly, we need a bit more rigor in our definitions. The answer lies in an understanding of certain characteristics or properties that databases possess that ordinary files do not, including the following:

- Management by a Database Management System (DBMS)
- Layers of data abstraction
- Physical data independence
- Logical data independence

These properties are discussed in the following subsections.

The Database Management System (DBMS)

The *Database Management System (DBMS)* is software provided by the database vendor. Software products such as Microsoft Access, Oracle, Microsoft SQL Server, Sybase, DB2, INGRES, and MySQL are all DBMSs. If it seems odd to you that the acronym used is DBMS instead of merely DMS, keep in mind that the term "database" was originally written as two words, and by convention has become a single compound word.

The DBMS provides all the basic services required to organize and maintain the database, including the following:

- Moving data to and from the physical data files as needed.
- Managing concurrent data access by multiple users, including provisions to prevent simultaneous updates from conflicting with one another.

- Managing transactions so that each transaction's database changes are an all-or-nothing unit of work. In other words, if the transaction succeeds, all database changes made by it are recorded in the database; if the transaction fails, none of the changes it made are recorded in the database.
- Support for a *query language,* which is a system of commands that a database user employs to retrieve data from the database.
- Provisions for backing up the database and recovering from failures.
- Security mechanisms to prevent unauthorized data access and modification.

Layers of Data Abstraction

Databases have the unique capability of presenting multiple users of the data with their own distinct views of that data while storing the underlying data only once. These are collectively called *user views.* A *user* in this context is any person or application that signs on to the database for the purpose of storing and/or retrieving data. An *application* is a set of computer programs designed to solve a particular business problem, such as an order-entry system, a payroll-processing system, or an accounting system.

When an electronic spreadsheet application such as Microsoft Excel is used, all users must share a common view of the data, and that view must match the way the data is physically stored in the underlying data file. If a user hides some columns in a spreadsheet, reorders the rows, and saves the spreadsheet, the next user who opens it will have the data presented in the manner in which the first user saved it. An alternative, of course, is for each user to save their own copy in separate physical files, but then as one user applies updates, the other users' data becomes out of date. With database systems, we can present each user a view of the same data, but the views can be *tailored* to the needs of the individual users, even though they all come for one commonly stored copy of the data. Because views store no actual data, they automatically reflect any data changes made to the underlying database objects. This is all possible through *layers of abstraction*, as shown in Figure 1-1.

The architecture shown in Figure 1-1 was first developed by ANSI/SPARC (American National Standards Institute Standards Planning and Requirements Committee) in the 1970s and quickly became a foundation for much of the database research and development efforts that followed. Most modern DBMSs follow this architecture, which is composed of three primary layers: the physical layer, the logical layer, and the external layer. The original architecture included a conceptual layer, which has been omitted here because none of the modern database vendors implemented it.

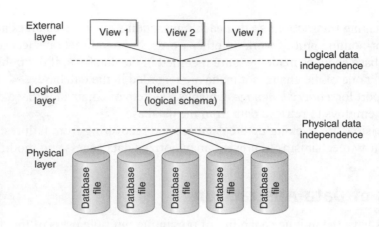

Figure 1-1 Database layers of abstraction

The Physical Layer

The *physical layer* contains the data files that hold all the data for the database. Nearly all modern DBMSs allow the database to be stored in multiple data files, which are usually spread out over multiple physical disk drives. With this arrangement, the disk drives can work in parallel for maximum performance. A notable exception is Microsoft Access, which stores the entire database in a single physical file. This arrangement limits the ability of the DBMS to scale to accommodate many concurrent users of the database, making it inappropriate as a solution for large enterprise systems, while simplifying database use on a single-user personal computer system.

The user of the database does not need to have any knowledge of how the data is actually stored within these files, or even which file contains the data item(s) of interest. In most organizations, a technician known as a *database administrator (DBA)* handles the details of installing and configuring the database software and data files and making the database available to the database users. The DBMS works with the computer's operating system to automatically manage the data files, including all file opening, closing, reading, and writing operations. The database user should not be required to refer to physical data files when using a database, which is in sharp contrast with spreadsheets and word processing, where the user must consciously save the document(s) and choose file names and storage locations. Many of the personal computer–based DBMSs are exceptions to this tenet because the user is required to locate and open a physical file as part of the process of signing on to the DBMS. In contrast, with server-based DBMSs (such as Oracle, Sybase, Microsoft SQL Server, and so on), the physical files are managed automatically and the database user never needs to refer to them when using the database.

The Logical Layer

The *logical layer* or *logical model* is the first of two layers of abstraction in the database. We say this because the physical layer has a concrete existence in the operating system files, whereas the logical layer exists only as abstract data structures assembled from the physical layer as needed. The DBMS transforms the data in the data files into a common structure. This layer is sometimes called the *schema*, a term used for the collection of all the data items stored in a particular database. Depending on the particular DBMS, this can be a set of two-dimensional tables, a hierarchical structure similar to a company's organization chart, or some other structure. The "Prevalent Database Models" section later in this chapter describes the possible structures in more detail.

The External Layer

The *external layer* or *external model* is the second layer of abstraction in the database. This layer is composed of the user views discussed earlier, which are collectively called the *subschema*. This is the layer where users and application programs that access the database connect and issue queries against the database. Ideally, only the DBA deals with the physical and logical layers. The DBMS handles the transformation of selected items from one or more data structures in the logical layer to form each user view. The user views in this layer can be predefined and stored in the database for reuse, or they can be temporary items that are built by the DBMS to hold the results of a single ad hoc database query until no longer needed by the database user. By *ad hoc*, we mean a query that was not preconceived and one that is not likely to be reused. Views are discussed in more detail in Chapter 2.

Physical Data Independence

The ability to alter the physical file structure of a database without disrupting existing users and processes is known as *physical data independence*. As shown earlier in Figure 1-1, it is the separation of the physical layer from the logical layer that provides physical data independence in a DBMS. It is essential to understand that physical data independence is not a "have or have not" property, but rather one where a particular DBMS might have more or less data independence than another. The measure, sometimes called the *degree* of physical data independence, is how much change can be made in the file system without impacting the logical layer. Prior to systems that offered data independence, even the slightest change to the way data was stored required the programming staff to make changes to every computer program that used the data, an expensive and time-consuming process.

All modern computer systems have some degree of physical data independence. For example, a spreadsheet on a personal computer will continue to work properly if copied from a hard disk to a floppy disk or if burned onto a CD. The fact that the performance (speed) of these devices varies markedly is not the point, but rather that the devices have entirely different physical construction and yet the operating system on the personal computer will automatically handle the differences and present the data in the file to the application (that is, the spreadsheet program, such as Microsoft Excel), and therefore to the user, in exactly the same way. However, on most personal systems, the user must still remember where they placed the file so they can locate it when they need it again.

DBMSs expand greatly on the physical data independence provided by the computer system in that they allow database users to access database objects (for example, tables in a relational DBMS) without having to reference the physical data files in any way. The DBMS *catalog* keeps track of where the objects are physically stored. Here are some examples of physical changes that may be made in a data-independent manner:

- Moving a database data file from one device to another or one directory to another
- Splitting or combining database data files
- Renaming database files
- Moving a database object from one data file to another
- Adding new database objects or data files

Note that we have made no mention of deleting things. It should be obvious that deleting a database object will cause anything that uses that object to fail. However, everything else should be unaffected.

Logical Data Independence

The ability to make changes to the logical layer without disrupting existing users and processes is called *logical data independence*. Figure 1-1, earlier in the chapter, shows that it is the transformation between the logical layer and the external layer that provides logical data independence. As with physical data independence, there are degrees of logical data independence. It is important to understand that most logical changes also involve a physical change. For example, you cannot add a new database object (such as a table in a relational DBMS) without physically storing the data somewhere; hence, there is a corresponding change in the physical layer. Moreover, deletion of objects in the logical layer will cause anything that uses those objects to fail but should not affect anything else.

Here are some examples of changes in the logical layer that can be safely made thanks to logical data independence:

- Adding a new database object
- Adding data items to an existing object
- Any change where a view can be placed in the external model that replaces (and processes the same as) the original object in the logical layer, such as combining or splitting existing objects

Prevalent Database Models

A *database model* is essentially the architecture that the DBMS uses to store objects within the database and relate them to one another. The most prevalent of these models are presented here in the order of their evolution. A brief history of relational databases appears in the next section to help put things in a chronological perspective.

Flat Files

Flat files are "ordinary" operating system files in that records in the file contain no information to communicate the file structure or any relationship among the records to the application that uses the file. Any information about the structure or meaning of the data in the file must be included in each application that uses the file or must be known to each human who reads the file. In essence, flat files are not databases at all because they do not meet any of the criteria previously discussed. However, it is important to understand them for two reasons. First, flat files are often used to store database information. In this case, the operating system is still unaware of the contents and structure of the files, but the DBMS has metadata that allows it to translate between the flat files in the physical layer and the database structures in the logical layer. *Metadata*, which literally means "data about data," is the term used for the information that the database stores in its catalog to describe the data stored in the database and the relationships among the data. The metadata for a customer, for example, might include a list of all the data items collected about the customer, along with the length, minimum and maximum data values, and a brief description of each data item. Second, flat files existed before databases, and the earliest database systems *evolved* from flat file systems that preceded them.

Figure 1-2 shows a sample flat file system, a subset of the data in the Microsoft Access Northwind sample database in this case. Northwind Traders is a supplier of international food items. Keep in mind that the column titles (Customer ID, Company Name, and so on) are included for illustration purposes only—only the data records

Customer File

Customer ID	Company Name	Contact Name	Address	City	Country	Phone
ALFKI	Alfreds Futterkiste	Maria Anders	Obere Str. 57	Berlin	Germany	030-007431
AROUT	Around the Horn	Thomas Hardy	120 Hanover Sq.	London	UK	(171) 555-7788

Employee File

Employee ID	Last Name	First Name	Title
3	Leverling	Janet	Sales Representative
4	Peacock	Margaret	Sales Representative
6	Suyama	Michael	Sales Representative

Product File

Product ID	Product Name	Category	Quantity Per Unit	Unit Price	Units In Stock
28	Rossle Sauerkraut	Produce	25 825 g cans	$45.60	26
39	Chartreuse verte	Beverages	750 cc per bottle	$18.00	69
41	Jack's New England Clam Chowder	Seafood	12 12 oz cans	$9.65	85
46	Spegesild	Seafood	4 450 g glasses	$12.00	95
52	Filo Mix	Grains/Cereals	16 2 kg boxes	$7.00	38
63	Vegie-spread	Condiments	15 625 g jars	$43.90	24

Order File

Order ID	Customer ID	Employee ID	Order Date	Required Date	Shipped Date	Ship Via	Freight
10643	ALFKI	6	25-Aug-1997	22-Sep-1997	02-Sep-1997	Speedy Express	$29.46
10692	ALFKI	4	30-Oct-1997	03-Oct-1997	31-Oct-1997	United Package	$61.02
10793	AROUT	3	24-Dec-1997	21-Jan-1998	08-Jan-1998	Federal Shipping	$4.52

Order Detail File

Order ID	Product ID	Unit Price	Quantity	Discount
10643	28	$46.50	15	25%
10643	39	$18.00	21	25%
10643	46	$12.00	2	25%
10692	63	$43.90	20	0%
10793	41	$9.65	14	0%
10793	52	$7.00	8	0%

Figure 1-2   Flat file order system

would be stored in the actual files. Customer data is stored in a Customer file, with each record representing a Northwind customer. Each employee of Northwind has a record in the Employee file, and each product sold by Northwind has a record in the Product file. Order data (orders placed with Northwind by its customers) is stored in two other flat files. The Order file contains one record for each customer order with data about the orders, such as the customer ID of the customer who placed the order and the name of the employee who accepted the order from the customer. The Order Detail file contains one record for each line item on an order (an order can contain multiple line items, one for each product ordered), including data such as the unit price and quantity.

An *application program* is a unit of computer program logic that performs a particular function within an application system. Northwind has an application program that prints out a listing of all the orders. This application must correlate the data between the five files by reading an order and performing the following steps:

1. Use the customer ID to find the name of the customer in the Customer file.
2. Use the employee ID to find the name of the related employee in the Employee file.
3. Use the order ID to find the corresponding line items in the Order Detail file.
4. For each line item, use the product ID to find the corresponding product name in the Product file.

This is rather complicated given that we are just trying to print a simple listing of all the orders, yet this is the best possible data design for a flat file system.

One alternative design would be to combine all the information into a single data file. Although this would greatly simplify data retrieval, consider the ramifications of repeating all the customer data on every single order line item. You might not be able to add a new customer until they have an order ready to place. Also, if someone deletes the last order for a customer, you would lose all the information about the customer. But the worst is when customer information changes because you have to find and update every record where the customer data is repeated. We will explore these issues much more deeply when we explore logical database design in Chapter 7.

Another alternative approach often used in flat file–based systems is to combine closely related files, such as the Order file and Order Detail file, into a single file, with the line items for each order following each order header record and a Record Type data item added to help the application distinguish between the two types of records. Although this approach makes correlating the order data easier, it does so by adding the complexity of mixing two different kinds of records into the same file, so there is no net gain in either simplicity or faster application development.

Overall, the worst problem with the flat file approach is that the definition of the contents of each file and the logic required to correlate the data from multiple flat files have to be included in every application program that requires those files, thus adding to the expense and complexity of the application programs. It was this very problem that provided computer scientists of the day with the incentive to find a better way to organize data.

The Hierarchical Model

The earliest databases followed the hierarchical model. The model evolved from the file systems that the databases replaced, with records arranged in a hierarchy much like an organization chart. Each file from the flat file system became a *record type*, or *node* in hierarchical terminology, but we will use the term *record* here for simplicity. Records were connected using *pointers* that contained the address of the related record. *Pointers* told the computer system where the related record was physically located, much as a street address directs us to a particular building in a city or a URL directs us to a particular web page on the Internet. Each pointer establishes a parent-child relationship, also called a *one-to-many relationship*, where one parent may have many children, but each child may have only one parent. This is similar to the situation in a traditional business organization where each manager may have many employees as direct reports, but each employee may have only one manager. The obvious problem with the hierarchical model is that there is data that does not exactly fit this strict hierarchical structure, such as an order that must have the customer who placed the order as one parent and the employee who accepted the order as another. Data relationships are presented in more detail in Chapter 2. The most popular hierarchical database was Information Management System (IMS) from IBM.

Figure 1-3 shows the hierarchical structure of the hierarchical model for the Northwind database. You will recognize the Customer, Employee, Product, Order, and Order Detail record types as they were introduced previously. Comparing the hierarchical structure with the flat file system shown in Figure 1-2, note that the Employee and Product records are shown in the hierarchical structure with dotted lines because they cannot be connected to the other records via pointers. These illustrate the most severe limitation of the hierarchical model that was the main reason for its early demise: No record may have more than one parent. Therefore, we *cannot* connect the Employee records with the Order records because the Order records already have the Customer record as their parent. Similarly, the Product records cannot be related to the Order Detail records because the Order Detail records already have the Order record as their parent. Database technicians would have to work around this shortcoming either by relating the "extra" parent records in application programs, much as was done with flat file systems, or by repeating all the records under each parent, which of course was very wasteful of then-precious disk space. Neither of these was really an acceptable solution, so IBM modified IMS to allow for multiple parents per record. The resultant database model was dubbed the "Extended Hierarchical"

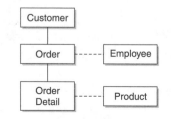

Figure 1-3   Hierarchical model structure for Northwind

model, which closely resembled the network database model in function, discussed in the next section.

Figure 1-4 shows the contents of selected records within the hierarchical model design for Northwind. Some data items were eliminated for simplicity, but a look back at Figure 1-2 should make the entire contents of each record clear, if necessary. The record for customer ALFKI has a pointer to its first order (ID 10643), and that order has a pointer to the next order (ID 10692). We know that Order 10692 is the last order for the customer because it does not have any pointers to additional orders. Looking at the next layer in the hierarchy, Order 28 has a pointer to its first Order Detail record (for Product 39), and that record has a pointer to the next detail record, and so forth. There is one additional important distinction between the flat file system and the hierarchical—the key (identifier) of the parent record is removed from the child records in the hierarchical model because the pointers handle the relationships among the records. Therefore, the customer ID and employee ID are removed from the Order record, and the product ID is removed from the Order Detail record. Leaving them in is not a good idea because this could allow contradictory information in the database, such as an order that is pointed to by one customer and yet contains the ID of a different customer.

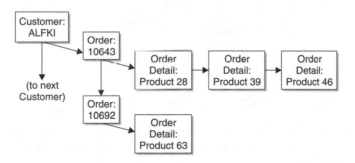

Figure 1-4   Hierarchical model record contents for Northwind

The Network Model

The network database model evolved at around the same time as the hierarchical database model. A committee of industry representatives was formed to essentially build a better mousetrap. A cynic would say that a camel is a horse that was designed by a committee, and that may be accurate in this case. The most popular database based on the network model was the Integrated Database Management System (IDMS), originally developed by Cullinane (later renamed Cullinet). The product was enhanced with relational extensions, named IDMS/R and eventually sold to Computer Associates.

As with the hierarchical model, record types (or simply "records") depict what would be separate files in a flat file system, and those records are related using one-to-many relationships, called *owner-member* relationships or *sets* in network model terminology. We'll stick with the terms *parent* and *child*, again for simplicity. As with the hierarchical model, physical address pointers are used to connect related records, and any identification of the parent record(s) is removed from each child record to avoid possible inconsistencies. In contrast with the hierarchical model, the relationships are named so the programmer can direct the database to use a particular relationship to navigate from one record to another in the database, thus allowing a record type to participate as the child in multiple relationships. The network model provided greater flexibility, but as is often the case with computer systems, at the expense of greater complexity.

The network model structure for Northwind, as shown in Figure 1-5, has all the same records as the equivalent Hierarchical Model structure that appeared in Figure 1-3. By convention, the arrowhead on the lines points from the parent to child record. Note that the Customer and Employee records now have solid lines in the structure diagram because they can be directly implemented.

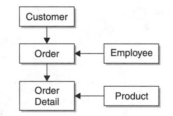

Figure 1-5   Network model structure for Northwind

In the network model contents example shown in Figure 1-6, each parent-child relationship is depicted with a different type of line, illustrating that each has a different name. This difference is important because it points out the largest downside of the network model, which is complexity. Instead of a single path that may be used for processing the records, there are now many paths. For example, if we start with the record for Employee 4 (Sales Representative Margaret Peacock) and use it to find the first order (ID 10692), we land in the middle of the chain of orders that belong to Customer ALFKI (Alfreds Futterkiste). To find all the other orders for this customer, there must be a way to work forward from where we are to the end of the chain and then wrap around to the beginning and forward from there until we return to the order from which we started. It is to satisfy this processing need that all pointer chains in network model databases are circular. As you might imagine, these circular pointer chains can easily result in an infinite loop (that is, a process that never ends) should a database user not keep careful track of where they are in the database and how they got there. The structure of the World Wide Web loosely parallels a network

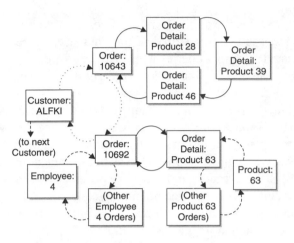

Figure 1-6   Network model record contents for Northwind

database in that each web page has links to other related web pages, and circular references are not uncommon.

The process of navigating through a network database was called "walking the set" because it involved choosing paths through the database structure much like choosing walking paths through a forest when there can be multiple ways to get to the same destination. Without an up-to-date roadmap, it is easy to get lost, or worse yet, find a dead end where you cannot get to the desired destination record. The complexity of this model and the expense of the small army of technicians required to maintain it were key factors in its eventual demise.

The Relational Model

In addition to complexity, the network and hierarchical database models share another common problem—they are inflexible. One must follow the preconceived paths through the data in order to process the data efficiently. Ad hoc queries, such as finding all the orders shipped in a particular month, require scanning the entire database to find them all. Computer scientists were still looking for a better way. There have been few times in the history of computers when a development was truly revolutionary, but the research work of Dr. E.F. Codd that led to the relational model was clearly just that.

The relational model is based on the notion that any preconceived path through a data structure is too restrictive a solution, especially in light of ever-increasing demands to support ad hoc requests for information. Database users simply cannot think of every possible use of the data before the database is created; therefore, imposing predefined paths through the data merely creates a "data jail." The relational model therefore provides the ability to relate records *as needed* rather than predefined when the records are first stored in the database. Moreover, the relational model is constructed such that queries work with sets of data (for example, all the customers who have an outstanding balance) rather than one record at a time, as with the network and hierarchical models.

The relational model presents data in familiar two-dimensional tables, much like a spreadsheet does. Unlike a spreadsheet, the data is not necessarily stored in tabular form and the model also permits combining (*joining* in relational terminology) tables to form views, which are also presented as two-dimensional tables. In short, it follows the ANSI/SPARC model and therefore provides healthy doses of physical and logical data independence. Instead of linking related records together with physical address pointers, as is done in the hierarchical and network models, a common data item is stored in each table, just as was done in flat file systems.

Figure 1-7 shows the relational model design for Northwind. A look back at Figure 1-2 will confirm that each file in the flat file system has been mapped to a table in the relational model. As you will learn in Chapter 6, this one-to-one correspondence between flat files and relational tables will not always hold true, but it is quite common. In Figure 1-7, lines are drawn between the tables to show the one-to-many relationships, with the single line end denoting the "one" side and the line end that splits into three parts (called a "crow's foot") denoting the "many" side. For example, you can see that "one" customer is related to "many" orders and that "one" order is related to "many" order details merely by inspecting the lines that connect these tables. The diagramming technique shown here, called the *entity-relationship diagram (ERD)*, will be covered in more detail in Chapter 7.

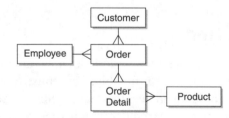

Figure 1-7   Relational model structure for Northwind

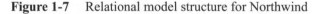

In Figure 1-8, three of the five tables have been represented with sample data in selected columns. In particular, note that the Customer ID column is stored in both the Customer table and the Order table. When the customer ID of a row in the Order table matches the customer ID of a row in the Customer table, you know that the order belongs to that particular customer. Similarly, the Employee ID column is stored in both the Employee and Order tables to indicate the employee who accepted each order.

The elegant simplicity of the relational model and the ease with which people can learn and understand it has been the main factor in its universal acceptance. The rela-

Customer Table

Customer ID	Company Name	Contact Name	Address	City	Country	Phone
ALFKI	Alfreds Futterkiste	Maria Anders	Obere Str. 57	Berlin	Germany	030-007431
AROUT	Around the Horn	Thomas Hardy	120 Hanover Sq.	London	UK	(171) 555-7788

Order
Table

Order ID	Customer ID	Employee ID	Order Date	Required Date	Shipped Date	Ship Via	Freight
10643	ALFKI	6	25-Aug-1997	22-Sep-1997	02-Sep-1997	Speedy Express	$29.46
10692	ALFKI	4	30-Oct-1997	03-Oct-1997	31-Oct-1997	United Package	$61.02
10793	AROUT	3	24-Dec-1997	21-Jan-1998	08-Jan-1998	Federal Shipping	$4.52

Employee
Table

Employee ID	Last Name	First Name	Title
3	Leverling	Janet	Sales Representative
4	Peacock	Margaret	Sales Representative
6	Suyama	Michael	Sales Representative

Figure 1-8   Relational table contents for Northwind

tional model is the main focus of this book because it is ubiquitous in today's information technology systems and will likely remain so for many years to come.

The Object-Oriented Model

The object-oriented (OO) model actually had its beginnings in the 1970s, but it did not see significant commercial use until the 1990s. This sudden emergence came from the inability of then-existing RDBMSs (Relational Database Management Systems) to deal with complex data types such as images, complex drawings, and audio-video files. The sudden explosion of the Internet and the World Wide Web created a sharp demand for mainstream delivery of complex data.

An *object* is a logical grouping of related data and program logic that represents a real world thing, such as a customer, employee, order, or product. Individual data items, such as customer ID and customer name, are called *variables* in the OO model and are stored within each object. In OO terminology, a *method* is a piece of application program logic that operates on a particular object and provides a finite function, such as checking a customer's credit limit or updating a customer's address. Among the many differences between the OO model and the models already presented, the most significant is that variables may *only* be accessed through methods. This property is called *encapsulation*.

The strict definition of *object* used here applies only to the OO model. The general term *database object,* as used earlier in this chapter, refers to any named item that might be stored in a non-OO database (for example, a table, index, or view). As OO concepts have found their way into relational databases, so has the terminology, although often with less precise definitions.

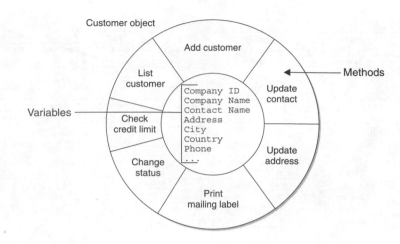

Figure 1-9   The anatomy of an object

Figure 1-9 shows the Customer object as an example of OO implementation. The circle of methods around the central core of variables is to remind us of encapsulation. In fact, you can think of an object much like an atom with an electron field of methods and a nucleus of variables. Each customer for Northwind would have its own copy of the object structure, called an *object instance,* much as each individual customer has a copy of the customer record structure in the flat file system.

At a glance, the OO model looks horribly inefficient because it seems that each instance requires that the methods and the definition of the variables be redundantly stored. However, this is not at all the case. Objects are organized into a *class hierarchy* so that the common methods and variable definitions need only be defined once and then *inherited* by other members of the same class.

OO concepts have such benefit that they have found their way into nearly every aspect of modern computer systems. For example, the Microsoft Windows Registry has a class hierarchy.

The Object-Relational Model

Although the OO model provided some significant benefits in encapsulating data to minimize the effects of system modifications, the lack of ad hoc query capability has relegated it to a niche market where complex data is required, but ad hoc query is not. However, some of the vendors of relational databases noted the significant benefits of the OO model and added object-like capability to their relational DBMS products with the hopes of capitalizing on the best of both models. The original name given to this type of database was *universal database*, and although the marketing folks loved the term, it never caught on in technical circles, so the preferred name for the model became *object-relational (OR)*. Through evolution, the Oracle, DB2, and Informix databases can all be said to be OR DBMSs to varying degrees.

To fully understand the OR model, a more detailed knowledge of the relational and OO models is required.

A Brief History of Databases

Space exploration projects led to many significant developments in the science and technology industries, including information technology. As part of the NASA Apollo moon project, North American Aviation (NAA) built a hierarchical file system named Generalized Update Access Method (GUAM) in 1964. IBM joined NAA to develop GUAM into the first commercially available hierarchical model database, called Information Management System (IMS), released in 1966.

Also in the mid 1960s, General Electric internally developed the first database based on the network model, under the direction of prominent computer scientist Charles W. Bachman, and named it Integrated Data Store (IDS). In 1967, the Conference on Data Systems Languages (CODASYL), an industry group, formed the Database Task Group (DBTG) and began work on a set of standards for the network model. In response to criticism of the "single parent" restriction in the hierarchical model, IBM introduced a version of IMS that circumvented the problem by allowing records to have one "physical" parent and multiple "logical" parents.

In June 1970, Dr. E. F. (Ted) Codd, an IBM researcher (later an IBM fellow), published a research paper titled "A Relational Model of Data for Large Shared Data Banks" in *Communications of the ACM, the Journal of the Association for Computing Machinery, Inc*. The publication can be easily found on the Internet. In 1971, the CODASYL DBTG published their standards, which were over three years in the making. This began five years of heated debate over which model was the best.

The CODASYL DBTG advocates argued the following:

- The relational model was too mathematical.
- An efficient implementation of the relational model could not be built.
- Application systems need to process data one record at a time.

The relational model advocates argued the following:

- Nothing as complicated as the DBTG proposal could possibly be the correct way to manage data.
- Set-oriented queries were too difficult in the DBTG language.
- The network model had no formal underpinnings in mathematical theory.

The debate came to a head at the 1975 ACM SIGMOD (Special Interest Group on Management of Data) conference. Ted Codd and two others debated against Charles

Bachman and two others over the merits of the two models. At the end, the audience was more confused than beforehand. In retrospect, this happened because every argument proffered by the two sides was completely correct! However, interest in the network model waned markedly in the late 1970s. It was the evolution of database and computer technology that followed that proved the relational model was the better choice, including these significant developments:

- Query languages such as SQL emerged that were not so mathematical.
- Experimental implementations of the relational model proved that reasonable efficiency could be achieved, although never as efficient as an equivalent network model database. Also, computer systems continued to drop in price, and flexibility was considered more important than efficiency.
- Provisions were added to the SQL language to permit processing of a set of data using a record-at-a-time approach.
- Advanced tools made the relational model even easier to use.
- Dr. Codd's research led to the development of a new discipline in mathematics known as *relational calculus*.

In the mid 1970s, database research and development was at full steam. A team of 15 IBM researchers in San Jose, California, under the direction of Frank King, worked from 1974 to 1978 to develop a prototype relational database called System R. System R was built commercially and became the basis for HP ALLBASE and IDMS/SQL. Larry Ellison and a company that later became known as Oracle independently implemented the external specifications of System R. It is now common knowledge that Oracle's first customer was the CIA. With some rewriting, IBM developed System R into SQL/DS and then into DB2, which remains their flagship database to this day.

A pickup team of University of California, Berkeley students under the direction of Michael Stonebraker and Eugene Wong worked from 1973 to 1977 to develop the INGRES DBMS. INGRES also became a commercial product and was quite successful. It is still available today as CA-INGRES, marketed by Computer Associates.

In 1976, Peter Chen presented the entity-relationship (ER) model. His work bolstered the modeling weaknesses in the relational model and became the foundation of many modeling techniques that followed. If Ted Codd is considered the "father" of the relational model, then we must consider Peter Chen the "father" of the ER diagram. We explore ER diagrams in Chapter 7.

Sybase, which had a successful RDBMS deployed on Unix servers, entered into a joint agreement with Microsoft to develop the next generation of Sybase (to be called System 10) with a version available on Windows servers. For reasons not publicly known, the relationship soured before the products were completed, but each party walked away with all the work developed up to that point. Microsoft finished the

Windows version and marketed the product as Microsoft SQL Server, whereas Sybase rushed to market with Sybase System 10. The products were so similar that instructors for Microsoft were known to use the Sybase manuals in class rather than first-generation Microsoft documentation. The product lines have diverged considerably over the years, but Microsoft SQL Server's Sybase roots are still evident in the product.

Relational technology took the market by storm in the 1980s. Object-oriented databases, which first appeared in the 1970s, were also commercially successful during the 1980s. In the 1990s, object-relational systems emerged, with Informix being the first to market, followed relatively quickly by Oracle and IBM.

Not only did the relational technology of the day move around, but the people did also. Michael Stonebraker left UC Berkeley to found Illustra, an object-relational database vendor, and became chief science officer of Informix when it merged with Illustra. Bob Epstein, who worked on the INGRES project with Stonebraker, moved to the commercial company along with the INGRES product. From there he went to Britton-Lee (now part of NCR) to work on early *database machines* (computer systems specialized to run only databases) and then to start up Sybase, where he was the chief science officer for a number of years. Database machines, incidentally, died on the vine because they were so expensive compared to the combination of an RDBMS running on a general-purpose computer system. The San Francisco Bay Area was an exciting place for database technologists in that era, because all the great relational products started there, more or less in parallel, with the explosive growth of "Silicon Valley." Others have moved on, but DB2, Oracle, and Sybase are still largely based in the Bay Area.

Why Focus on Relational?

The remainder of this book will focus on the relational model, with some coverage of the object-oriented and object-relational models. Aside from it being the most prevalent of all the database models in modern business systems, there are other important reasons for this focus, especially for those learning about databases for the first time:

- Definition, maintenance, and manipulation of data storage structures is easy.
- Data is retrieved through simple ad hoc queries.
- Data is well protected.
- Well-established ANSI (American National Standards Institute) and ISO (International Organization for Standardization) standards exist.
- There are many vendors from which to choose.
- Conversion between vendor implementations is relatively easy.
- RDBMSs are mature and stable products.

Quiz

Choose the correct responses in each of the multiple-choice questions. Note that there may be more than one correct response to each question.

1. Some of the properties of a database are
   a. It provides layers of database abstraction.
   b. Data items are stored exactly the way they are presented to the database user.
   c. It provides less logical data independence than the file systems it replaced.
   d. It provides both physical and logical data independence.
   e. Databases are always managed by a Database Management System.

2. User views are important because:
   a. Application programs reference them.
   b. People querying the database reference them.
   c. They provide physical data independence.
   d. They can be tailored to the needs of the database user.
   e. Data updates are shown in a delayed fashion.

3. The physical layer of the ANSI/SPARC model:
   a. Provides physical data independence
   b. Contains the physical files that comprise the database
   c. Contains files that are read and written by the DBMS independent of the computer's operating system
   d. Is normally invisible to the database user
   e. Supplies data to the logical layer

4. The logical layer of the ANSI/SPARC model:
   a. Contains database objects that are assembled by the DBMS from data in the physical layer
   b. Provides logical data independence
   c. Contains the database schema
   d. Is referenced by the external layer
   e. Lies between the physical and external layers

5. The external layer of the ANSI/SPARC model:
   a. Contains the database subschema
   b. Lies between the physical and logical layers
   c. Is directly referenced by database users
   d. Contains all the user views for the database
   e. Provides physical data independence

6. Physical data independence:
   a. Is something a database either has or does not have
   b. Is a property that all computer systems have to some degree
   c. Allows nondisruptive changes to be made to the physical layer in the ANSI/SPARC model
   d. Is achieved through the separation of the physical and logical layers of the ANSI/SPARC model
   e. Is achieved through the separation of the logical and external layers of the ANSI/SPARC model

7. Logical data independence:
   a. Is a property that all computer systems have to some degree
   b. Is achieved through the separation of the physical and logical layers of the ANSI/SPARC model
   c. Is achieved through the separation of the logical and external layers of the ANSI/SPARC model
   d. Allows data to be freely deleted from the physical database files without disrupting existing database users and processes
   e. Allows database objects to be freely added to the physical database files without disrupting existing database users and processes

8. Flat file systems:
   a. Are not really databases by themselves, even though some vendors call them that
   b. Can be used to store the database objects for a database
   c. Provide no logical data independence when used directly by application programs
   d. Require the user or application program to relate one file to another
   e. Require the user or application to know the contents of each file

9. The hierarchical database model:
   a. Was first developed by Peter Chen
   b. Stores data and methods together in the database
   c. Connects data in a hierarchical structure using physical address pointers
   d. In its pure form, permits only one parent for any given record
   e. Allows the processing of sets of database records

10. The network database model:
   a. Was first proposed by Dr. E.F. Codd
   b. Connects database records using physical address pointers
   c. Allows the processing of sets of database records
   d. Allows multiple parents for any given database record
   e. Is known for its simplicity of use

11. The relational database model:
    a. Was first proposed by Dr. E.F. Codd
    b. Does not use physical pointers to connect database records
    c. Provides superior flexibility for ad hoc queries
    d. Is difficult to understand and use
    e. Presents data as two-dimensional tables

12. The object-oriented model:
    a. Stores data as variables along with application logic modules
       called methods
    b. Provides for free-form ad hoc query of variables
    c. Was first invented in the 1980s
    d. Provides better support for complex data types than the relational model
    e. Restricts access to variables through encapsulation

13. The object-relational model:
    a. Was first proposed by Charles Bachman
    b. Combines concepts from the relational and object models in an attempt
       to get the best from each
    c. Is not supported by the mainstream (bestselling) DBMS products
    d. Overcomes the ad hoc query restrictions found in the relational model
    e. Overcomes the ad hoc query restrictions found in the object-oriented
       model

14. According to advocates of the relational model, the problems with the
    CODASYL model are
    a. It is too mathematical.
    b. It is too complicated.
    c. It lacks generally accepted standards.
    d. Set-oriented queries are too difficult.
    e. An efficient implementation cannot be built.

15. According to the advocates of the network model, the problems with the
    relational model are
    a. Record-at-a-time processing is poorly supported.
    b. It is too complicated.
    c. It has no formal mathematical underpinnings.
    d. An efficient implementation cannot be built.
    e. It lacks generally accepted standards.

16. The main reasons that the relational model became so popular are
    a. Computer systems became less expensive, so flexibility became more important than efficiency.
    b. Simple-to-use query languages such as SQL emerged.
    c. The network model saw no commercial success.
    d. Products were developed that proved reasonable efficiency could be achieved.
    e. Relational calculus was invented.

17. Important historic events in database development are
    a. GUAM was the first commercially available database.
    b. General Electric's IDS was the first known network database.
    c. Dr. E.F. Codd published his famous research paper in 1970.
    d. Early relational databases were built by both IBM and UC Berkeley.
    e. Nearly all the commercial relational databases are descendents of either System R or INGRES.

18. Currently available relational databases include
    a. Oracle
    b. Microsoft SQL Server
    c. System R
    d. IDS
    e. Sybase

19. Examples of physical changes that can be safely made in a system that has a high degree of physical data independence are
    a. Moving a file from one disk device to another
    b. Adding new user views
    c. Adding new data files
    d. Splitting or combining database objects
    e. Renaming a data file

20. Examples of logical changes that can be safely made in a system that has a high degree of logical data independence are
    a. Moving a database object from one physical file to another
    b. Deleting database objects
    c. Adding new database objects
    d. Adding data items to existing database objects
    e. Deleting data items from existing database objects

2

Exploring Relational Database Components

In this chapter we explore the conceptual, logical and physical components that comprise the relational model. *Conceptual database design* involves studying and modeling the data in a technology-independent manner. The conceptual data model that results can be theoretically implemented on any database, or even on a flat file system. The person who performs conceptual database design is often called a *data modeler*. *Logical database design* is the process of translating, or *mapping,* the conceptual design into a logical design that fits the chosen database model (relational, object-oriented, object-relational, and so on). A specialist who performs logical database design is called a *database designer*, but often the database administrator

(DBA) performs this design step. The final design step is *physical database design,* which involves mapping the logical design to one or more physical designs—each tailored to the particular DBMS that will manage the database and the particular computer system on which the database will run. The person who performs physical database design is usually the DBA. The processes involved in database design are covered in Chapter 5.

In the sections that follow, we explore the components of a conceptual database design, then the components of a logical and physical design.

Conceptual Database Design Components

Figure 2-1 shows the conceptual design for Northwind. This diagram is similar to Figure 1-7 in Chapter 1, but a few items have been added for the illustration of key points. The labeled items (Entity, Attribute, Relationship, Business Rule, and Intersection Data) are the basic components that make up a conceptual database design. Each is presented in sections that follow, except for intersection data, which is presented in "Many-to-Many Relationships."

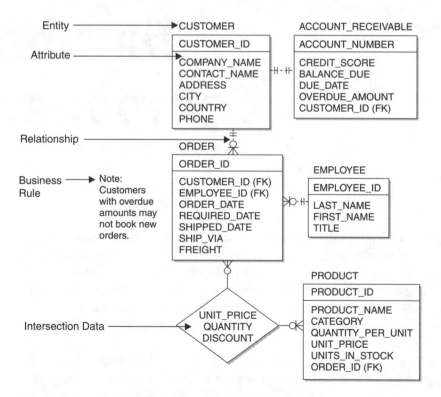

Figure 2-1 Conceptual database design for Northwind

Entities

An *entity* is a person, place, thing, event, or concept about which data is collected. In other words, entities are the real world things in which we have sufficient interest to capture and store data about them in a database. An entity is represented as a rectangle on the diagram. Just about anything that can be named with a noun can be an entity. However, to avoid designing everything on the planet into our database, we restrict ourselves to entities of interest to the people who will use our database. Each entity shown in the conceptual model represents the entire class for that entity. For example, the Customer entity represents the collection of all Northwind customers. The individual customers are called *instances* of the entity.

An *external entity* is an entity with which our database exchanges data (sending data to, receiving data from, or both), but about which we collect no data. For example, most businesses that set up credit accounts for customers purchase credit reports from one or more credit bureaus. They send a customer's identifying information to the credit bureau and receive back a credit report, but all this data is about the *customer* rather than the credit bureau itself. Assuming there is no compelling reason for the database to store data about the credit bureau, such as the mailing address of their office, the credit bureau will not appear in the conceptual database design as an entity. In fact, external entities are seldom shown in database designs, but they commonly appear in data flow diagrams as a source or destination of data. These diagrams are discussed in Chapter 7.

Attributes

An *attribute* is a unit fact that characterizes or describes an entity in some way. These are represented on the conceptual design diagram shown in Figure 2-1 as names inside the rectangle that represents the entity to which they belong. The attribute (or attributes) that appears at the top of the rectangle (above the horizontal line) is the *unique identifier* for the entity. A unique identifier, as the name suggests, provides a unique value for each instance of the entity. For example, the Customer_ID attribute is the unique identifier for the Customer entity, so each customer must have a unique value for that attribute. Keep in mind that a unique identifier can be composed of multiple attributes, but when this happens, it is still considered just *one* unique identifier.

We say attributes are a *unit* fact because they should be *atomic*, meaning they cannot be broken down into smaller units in any meaningful way. An attribute is therefore the smallest named unit of data that appears in a database system. In this sense, Address should be considered a suspect entity because it could easily be broken down into Address Line 1 and Address Line 2, as is commonly done in business systems. This change would add meaning because it makes it easier to print address labels, for example. On the other hand, database design is not an exact science, and judgment calls must be made. Although it is possible to break the Contact Name attribute into component attributes, such as First Name, Middle Initial, and Last Name, we must ask ourselves whether such a change adds meaning or value. There is no right or wrong answer here, so we must rely on the people who will be using the database, or perhaps those who are funding the database project, to help us with such decisions. Always remember that an attribute *must* describe or characterize the entity in some way (for example, size, shape, color, quantity, location).

Relationships

Relationships are the associations among the entities. Because databases are all about storing related data, the relationships become the glue that holds the database together. Relationships are shown on the conceptual design diagram (refer to Figure 2-1) as lines connecting one or more entities. Each end of a relationship line shows the *maximum cardinality* of the relationship, which is the maximum number of instances of one entity that can be associated with the entity on the opposite end of the line. The maximum cardinality may be *one* (where the line has no special symbol on its end) or *many* (where the line has a crow's foot on the end). Just short of the end of the line is another symbol that shows the *minimum cardinality,* which is the minimum number of instances of one entity that can be associated with the entity on the opposite end of the line. The minimum cardinality may be *zero,* denoted with a circle drawn on the line, or *one,* denoted with a short vertical line or tick mark drawn across the relationship line. Many data modelers use two vertical lines to mean "one and *only* one."

Learning to read relationships takes practice, and learning to define and draw them correctly takes a *lot* of practice. The trick is to think about the association between the entities in one direction, and then reverse your perspective to think about it in the opposite direction. For the relationship between Customer and Order, for example, we must ask two questions: "Each customer can have how many orders?" followed by "Each order can have how many customers?" Relationships may thus be classified into three types: *one-to-one*, *one-to-many*, and *many-to-many*, as discussed in the following sections. Some people will say many-to-one is also a relationship type, but in reality, it is only a one-to-many relationship looked at with a reverse perspective. Relationship types are best learned by example. Getting the relationships right is *essential* to a successful design.

One-to-One Relationships

A *one-to-one relationship* is an association where an instance of one entity can be associated with *at most* one instance of the other entity, and vice versa. In Figure 2-1, the relationship between the Customer and Account Receivable entities is one-to-one. This means that a customer can have *at most* one associated account receivable, and an account can have *at most* one associated customer. The relationship is also *mandatory* in both directions, meaning that a customer must have *at least* one account receivable associated with it, and an account receivable must have *at least* one customer associated with it. Putting this all together, we can read the relationship between the Customer and Account Receivable entities as "one customer has one and only one associated account receivable, and one account receivable has one and only one associated customer."

One-to-one relationships are surprisingly rare among entities. In practice, one-to-one relationships that are mandatory in both directions represent a design flaw that should be corrected by combining the two entities. After all, isn't an account receivable merely more information about the customer? We're not going to collect data *about* an account receivable, but rather the information in the Account Receivable entity is data we collect *about* the customer. On the other hand, if we buy our financial software from an independent software vendor (a common practice), the software would almost certainly come with a predefined database that it supports, so we may have no choice but to live with this situation. We won't be able to modify the vendor's database design to add additional customer data of interest to us, and at the same time, we won't be able to get the vendor's software to recognize anything that we store in our own database.

Figure 2-2 shows a different "flavor" of one-to-one relationship, one that is *optional* (some say *conditional*) in both directions. Suppose we are designing the database for an automobile dealership. The dealership issues automobiles to some employees, typically sales staff, for them to drive for a finite period of time. They obviously don't issue *all* the automobiles to employees (if they did, they would have none to sell). We can read the relationship between the Employee and Automobile entities as follows: "At any point in time, each employee can have zero or one automobiles issued to him or her, and each automobile can be assigned to zero or one employee." Note the clause "At any point in time." If an automobile is taken back from one employee and then reassigned to another, this would still be a one-to-one relationship. This is because when we consider relationships, we are always thinking in terms of a snapshot taken at an arbitrary point in time.

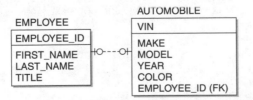

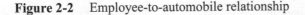
Figure 2-2 Employee-to-automobile relationship

One-to-Many Relationships

A *one-to-many relationship* is an association between two entities where any instance of the first entity may be associated with one or more instances of the second, and any instance of the second entity may be associated with at most one instance of the first. Figure 2-1, shown earlier in this chapter, has two such relationships: the one between the Customer and Order entities, and the one between the Employee and Order entities. The relationship between Customer and Order, which is mandatory in only one direction, is read as follows: "At any point in time, each customer can have zero to many orders, and each order must have one and only one owning customer."

One-to-many relationships are quite common. In fact, they are the fundamental building block of the relational database model in that all relationships in a relational database are implemented as if they are one-to-many. It is rare for them to be optional on the "one" side and even more rare for them to be mandatory on the "many" side, but these situations do happen. Consider the examples shown in Figure 2-3. When a customer account closes, we record the reason it was closed using an account closure reason code. Because some accounts are open at any point in time, this is an optional code. We read the relationship this way: "At any given point in time, each account closure reason code value can have zero, one, or many customers assigned to it, and each customer can have either zero or one account closure reason code assigned to them." Let us next suppose that as a matter of company policy, no customer account can be opened without first obtaining a credit report, and that all credit reports are kept in the database, meaning that any customer may have more than one credit report in the database. This makes the relationship between the Customer and Credit Report entities one-to-many, and mandatory in both directions. We read the relationship thus: "At any given point in time, each customer can have one or many credit reports, and each credit report belongs to one and only one customer."

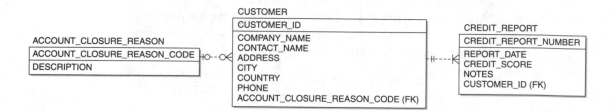

Figure 2-3   One-to-many relationships

Many-to-Many Relationships

A *many-to-many relationship* is an association between two entities where any instance of the first entity may be associated with zero, one, or more instances of the second, and vice versa. Back in Figure 2-1, the relationship between Order and Product is many-to-many. We read the relationship thus: "At any given point in time, each order contains zero to many products, and each product appears on zero to many orders."

This particular relationship has data associated with it as shown in the diamond on the diagram. Data that belongs to a many-to-many relationship is called *intersection data*. The data doesn't make sense unless you associate it with both entities at the same time. For example, Quantity Ordered doesn't make sense unless you know *who* (which customer) ordered *what* (which product). If you look back in Chapter 1 at Figure 1-7, you will recognize this data as the Order Detail table from Northwind's relational model. So, why isn't Order Detail just shown as an entity? The answer is simple: It doesn't fit the definition of an entity. We are not collecting data about the line items on the order, but rather the line items on the order are merely more data about the order.

Many-to-many relationships are quite common, and most of them will have intersection data. The bad news is that the relational model does not directly support many-to-many relationships. There is no problem with having many-to-many relationships in a conceptual design because such a design is independent of any particular technology. However, if the database is going to be relational, some changes have to be made as we map the conceptual model to the corresponding logical model. The solution is to map the intersection data to a separate table (an *intersection table)* and the many-to-many relationship to two one-to-many relationships, with the intersection table in the middle and on the "many" side of both relationships. Figure 1-7 shows this outcome. The process for recognizing and dealing with the many-to-many problem is covered in detail in Chapter 6.

Recursive Relationships

So far we have covered relationships between entities of two different types. However, relationships can exist between entity instances of the same type. These are called *recursive relationships*. Any one of the relationship types already presented (one-to-one, one-to-many, or many-to-many) can be a recursive relationship. Figure 2-4 and the following list show examples of each:

- **One-to-one** If we were to track which employees had other employees as spouses, we would expect each to be married to either zero or one other employee.

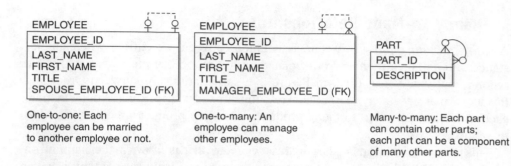

One-to-one: Each
employee can be married
to another employee or not.

One-to-many: An
employee can manage
other employees.

Many-to-many: Each part
can contain other parts;
each part can be a component
of many other parts.

Figure 2-4   Recursive relationship examples

- **One-to-many**   It is very common to track the employment "food chain"
  of who reports to whom. In most organizations, people have only one
  supervisor or manager. Therefore, we normally expect to see each employee
  reporting to zero or one other employee, and employees who are managers
  or supervisors to have one or more direct reports.
- **Many-to-many**   In manufacturing, a common relationship has to do with
  parts that make up a finished product. If you think about the CD-ROM drive
  in a personal computer, for example, you can easily imagine that it is made
  of multiple parts, and yet, it is only one part of your personal computer. So,
  any part can be made of many other parts, and at the same time, any part
  can be a component of many other parts.

Business Rules

A *business rule* is a policy, procedure, or standard that an organization has adopted.
Business rules are *very* important in database design because they dictate controls
that must be placed upon the data. In Figure 2-1, we see a business rule that states that
orders will only be accepted from customers who do not have a past-due balance.
Most business rules can be enforced through manual procedures that employees are
directed to follow or logic placed in the application programs. However, each of
these can be circumvented—employees may forget or may choose not to follow a
manual procedure, and databases can be updated directly by authorized people, bypassing the controls included in the application programs. The database can serve
nicely as the last line of defense. Business rules can be implemented in the database
as *constraints,* which are formally defined rules that restrict the data values in the
database in some way. More information on constraints can be found in the "Constraints" section later in this chapter. Note that business rules are not normally shown
on a conceptual data model diagram, as was done in Figure 2-1 for easy illustration.
It is far more common to include them in a text document that accompanies the diagram.

Logical/Physical Database Design Components

The logical database design is implemented in the logical layer of the ANSI/SPARC model discussed in Chapter 1. The physical design is implanted in the ANSI/SPARC physical layer. However, we work through the DBMS to implement the physical layer, making it difficult to separate the two layers. For example, when we create a table, we include a clause in the create table command that tells the DBMS where we wish to place it. The DBMS then automatically allocates space for the table in the requested operating system file(s). Because so much of the physical implementation is buried in the DBMS definitions of the logical structures, we have elected not to try to separate them here. During logical database design, physical storage properties (file name, storage location, and sizing information) may be assigned to each database object as we map them from the conceptual model, or they may be omitted at first and added later in a physical design step that follows logical design. For time efficiency, most DBAs perform the two design steps (logical and physical) in parallel.

Tables

The primary unit of storage in the relational model is the *table*, which is a two-dimensional structure composed of rows and columns. Each row represents one occurrence of the entity that the table represents, and each column represents one attribute for that entity. The process of mapping the entities in the conceptual design to tables in the logical design is called *normalization* and is covered in detail in Chapter 6. Often, an entity in the conceptual model maps to exactly one table in the conceptual model, but this is not always the case. For reasons you will learn with the normalization process, entities are commonly split into multiple tables, and in rare cases, multiple entities may be combined into one table. Figure 2-5 shows a listing of part of the Northwind Orders table.

It is important to remember that a relational table is a *logical* storage structure and usually does not exist in tabular form in the physical layer. When the DBA assigns a table to operating system files in the physical layer (called *tablespaces* in most RDBMSs), it is common for multiple tables to be placed in a single tablespace. However, large tables may be placed in their own tablespace or split across multiple tablespaces, which is called *partitioning*. This flexibility typically does not exist in personal computer–based RDBMSs such as Microsoft Access.

Each table must be given a unique name by the DBA who creates it. The maximum length for these names varies a lot among RDBMS products, from as little as 18 characters to as many as 255. Table names should be descriptive and should reflect

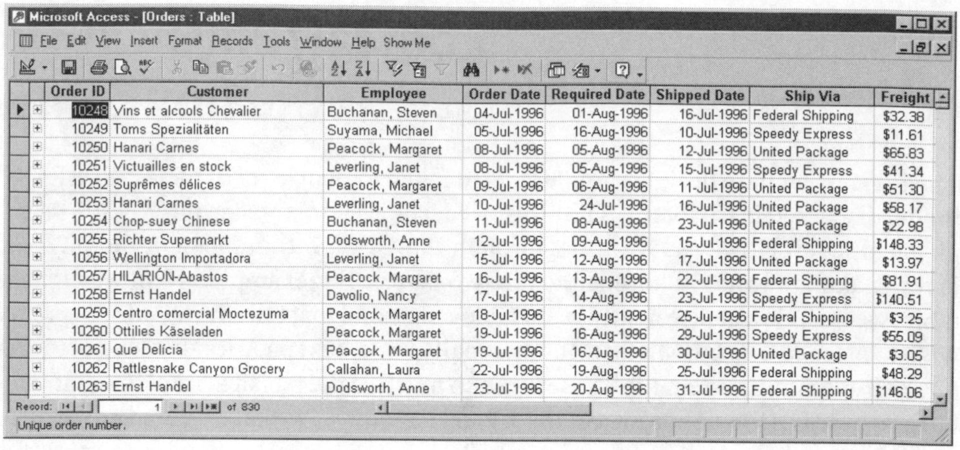

Order ID	Customer	Employee	Order Date	Required Date	Shipped Date	Ship Via	Freight
10248	Vins et alcools Chevalier	Buchanan, Steven	04-Jul-1996	01-Aug-1996	16-Jul-1996	Federal Shipping	$32.38
10249	Toms Spezialitäten	Suyama, Michael	05-Jul-1996	16-Aug-1996	10-Jul-1996	Speedy Express	$11.61
10250	Hanari Carnes	Peacock, Margaret	08-Jul-1996	05-Aug-1996	12-Jul-1996	United Package	$65.83
10251	Victuailles en stock	Leverling, Janet	08-Jul-1996	05-Aug-1996	15-Jul-1996	Speedy Express	$41.34
10252	Suprêmes délices	Peacock, Margaret	09-Jul-1996	06-Aug-1996	11-Jul-1996	United Package	$51.30
10253	Hanari Carnes	Leverling, Janet	10-Jul-1996	24-Jul-1996	16-Jul-1996	United Package	$58.17
10254	Chop-suey Chinese	Buchanan, Steven	11-Jul-1996	08-Aug-1996	23-Jul-1996	United Package	$22.98
10255	Richter Supermarkt	Dodsworth, Anne	12-Jul-1996	09-Aug-1996	15-Jul-1996	Federal Shipping	$148.33
10256	Wellington Importadora	Leverling, Janet	15-Jul-1996	12-Aug-1996	17-Jul-1996	United Package	$13.97
10257	HILARIÓN-Abastos	Peacock, Margaret	16-Jul-1996	13-Aug-1996	22-Jul-1996	Federal Shipping	$81.91
10258	Ernst Handel	Davolio, Nancy	17-Jul-1996	14-Aug-1996	23-Jul-1996	Speedy Express	$140.51
10259	Centro comercial Moctezuma	Peacock, Margaret	18-Jul-1996	15-Aug-1996	25-Jul-1996	Federal Shipping	$3.25
10260	Ottilies Käseladen	Peacock, Margaret	19-Jul-1996	16-Aug-1996	29-Jul-1996	Speedy Express	$55.09
10261	Que Delícia	Peacock, Margaret	19-Jul-1996	16-Aug-1996	30-Jul-1996	United Package	$3.05
10262	Rattlesnake Canyon Grocery	Callahan, Laura	22-Jul-1996	19-Aug-1996	25-Jul-1996	Federal Shipping	$48.29
10263	Ernst Handel	Dodsworth, Anne	23-Jul-1996	20-Aug-1996	31-Jul-1996	Federal Shipping	$146.06

Figure 2-5 Northwind Orders table (partial listing)

the name of the real-world entity they represent. By convention, some DBAs always name entities in the singular and tables in the plural, and you will see this convention used in the Northwind database. This author happens to prefer that both be named in the singular, but obviously there are other learned professionals with counter opinions. The point here is to establish naming standards at the outset so that names are not assigned in a haphazard manner, which only leads to confusion later. As a case in point, Microsoft Access permits embedded spaces in table and column names, which is counter to industry standards. Moreover, Microsoft Access, Sybase, and Microsoft SQL Server allow mixed-case names, such as OrderDetails, whereas Oracle, DB2, and others force all names to uppercase letters. Because table names such as ORDERDETAILS are not very readable, the use of an underscore to separate words per industry standards is a much better choice. You may wish to set standards that forbid the use of names with embedded spaces and names in mixed case because such names are nonstandard and make any conversion between database vendors that much more difficult.

Columns and Data Types

As already mentioned, each column in a relational table represents an attribute from the conceptual model. The *column* is the smallest named unit of data that can be referenced in a relational database. Each column must be assigned a unique name (within the table) and a data type. A *data type* is a category for the format of a particular column. Data types provide several valuable benefits:

- Restricting the data in the column to characters that make sense for the data type (for example, all numeric digits or only valid calendar dates).
- Providing a set of behaviors useful to the database user. For example, if you subtract a number from another number, you get a number as a result; but if you subtract a date from another date, you get a number representing the elapsed days between the two dates as a result.
- Assisting the RDBMS in efficiently storing the column data. For example, numbers can often be stored in an internal numeric format that saves space, compared with merely storing the numeric digits as a string of characters.

Figure 2-6 shows the table definition of the Northwind Orders table from Microsoft Access (the same table listed in Figure 2-5). The data type for each column is listed in the second column from the left. The data type names are usually self-evident, but if you find any of them confusing, you can find definitions of each in the Microsoft Access help pages.

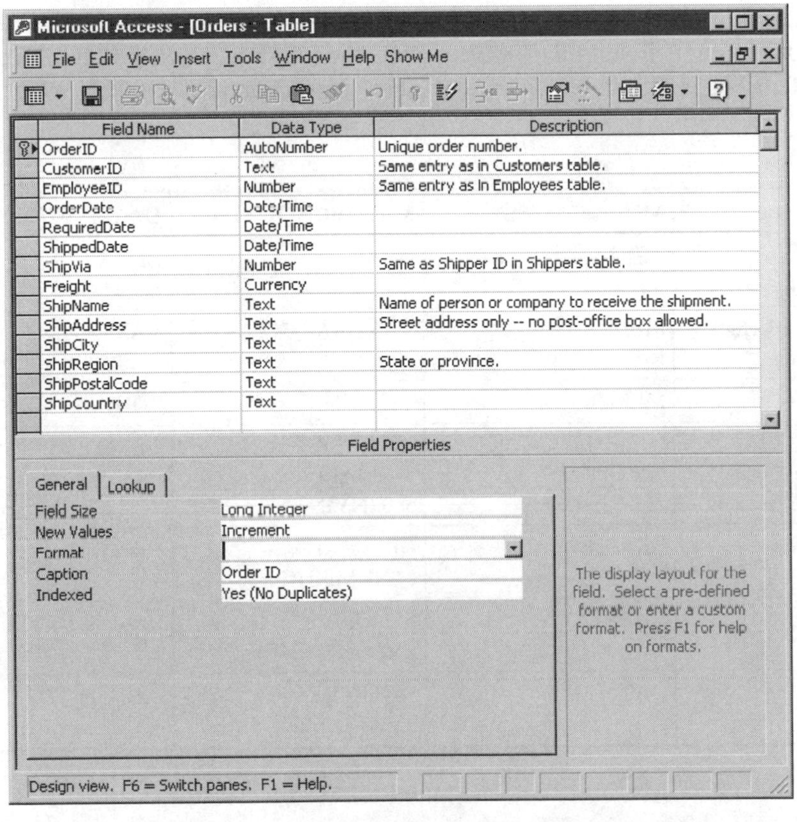

Figure 2-6   Table definition of the Northwind Orders table (Microsoft Access)

It is most unfortunate that industry standards lagged behind RDBMS development. Most vendors did their own thing for many years before sitting down with other vendors to develop standards, and this is no more evident than in the wide variation of data type options across the major RDBMS products. Today there are ANSI standards for relational data types, and the major vendors support all or most of the standard types. However, each vendor has their own "extensions" to the standards, largely in support of data types they developed before there were standards. One could say (in jest) that the greatest thing about database standards is that each vendor has their own unique set. In terms of industry standards for relational databases, Microsoft Access is probably the least compliant of the most popular products. Given the many levels of standards compliance and all the vendor extensions, the DBA must have a detailed knowledge of the data types available on the particular DBMS that is in use in order to successfully deploy the database. And, of course, great care must be taken when converting logical designs from one vendor to another.

Table 2-1 shows data types from different RDBMS vendors that are roughly equivalent. As always, the devil is in the details, meaning that these are not *identical* data types, merely equivalent. For example, the VARCHAR type in Oracle can be up to 4000 characters in length (2000 characters in versions prior to Oracle8*i*), but the equivalent MEMO type in Microsoft Access can be up to 64,000 characters.

Data Type	Microsoft Access	Microsoft SQL Server	Oracle
Fixed-Length Character	TEXT	CHAR	CHAR
Variable-Length Character	MEMO	VARCHAR	VARCHAR
Long Text	MEMO	TEXT	LONG
Integer	INTEGER or LONG INTEGER	INTEGER or SMALLINT or TINYINT	NUMBER
Decimal	NUMBER	DECIMAL or NUMERIC	NUMBER
Currency	CURRENCY	MONEY or SMALLMONEY	None, use NUMBER
Date/Time	DATE/TIME	DATETIME or SMALLDATETIME	DATE or TIMESTAMP

Table 2-1 Equivalent Data Types in Major RDBMS Products

Constraints

A *constraint* is a rule placed on a database object (typically a table or column) that restricts the allowable data values for that database object in some way. These are most important in relational databases in that constraints are the way we implement both the relationships and business rules specified in the logical design. Each constraint is assigned a unique name to permit it to be referenced in error messages and subsequent database commands. It is a good habit for DBAs to supply the constraint names because names generated automatically by the RDBMS are never very descriptive.

Primary Key Constraints

A *primary key* is a column or a set of columns that uniquely identifies each row in a table. A unique identifier in the conceptual design is thus implemented as a primary key in the logical design. The small icon that looks like a door key to the left of the Order ID field name in Figure 2-6 indicates that this column has been defined as the primary key of the Orders table. When we define a primary key, the RDBMS implements it as a *primary key constraint* to guarantee that no two rows in the table will ever have duplicate values in the primary key column(s). Note that for primary keys composed of multiple columns, each column by itself *may* have duplicate values in the table, but the *combination* of the values for the primary key columns must be unique among all rows in the table.

Primary key constraints are nearly always implemented by the RDBMS using an *index,* which is a special type of database object that permits fast searches of column values. As new rows are inserted into the table, the RDBMS *automatically* searches the index to make sure the value for the primary key of the new row is not already in use in the table, rejecting the insert request if it is. Indexes can be searched much faster than tables; therefore, the index on the primary key is essential in tables of any size so that the search for duplicate keys on every insert doesn't create a performance bottleneck.

Referential Constraints

To understand how the RDBMS enforces relationships using referential constraints, we must first understand the concept of foreign keys. When one-to-many relationships are implemented in tables, the column or set of columns that is stored in the child table (the table on the "many" side of the relationship), to associate it with the parent table (the table on the "one" side), is called a *foreign key.* It gets its name from the column(s) copied from another (foreign) table. In the Orders table shown earlier in Figure 2-6, the EmployeeID column is a foreign key to the Employees table, and the CustomerID column is a foreign key to the Customers table.

In most relational databases, the foreign key must either be the primary key of the parent table or a column or set of columns for which a unique index is defined. This again is for efficiency. Most people prefer that the foreign key column(s) have names identical to the corresponding primary key column(s), but again there are counter opinions, especially because like-named columns are a little more difficult to use in query languages. It is best to set some standards up front and stick with them throughout your database project.

Each relationship between entities in the conceptual design becomes a referential constraint in the logical design. A *referential constraint* (sometimes called a *referential integrity constraint*) is a constraint that enforces a relationship among tables in a relational database. By "enforces," we mean that the RDBMS automatically checks to ensure that each foreign key value in a child table always has a corresponding primary key value in the parent table.

Microsoft Access provides a very nice feature for foreign key columns, but it takes a bit of getting used to. When you define a referential constraint, you can define an automatic lookup of the parent table rows, as was done throughout the Northwind database. In Figure 2-6, the second column in the table is listed as CustomerID. However, in Figure 2-5, you will notice that the second column of the Orders table displays the customer name and is labeled "Customer." If you click in the Customer column for one of the rows, a pull-down menu appears to allow the selection of a valid customer (from the Customers table) to be the parent (owner) of the selected Orders table row. Similarly, the EmployeeID column of the table displays the employee name. This is a convenient and easy feature for the database user, and it prevents a nonexistent customer or employee from being associated with an order. However, it hides the foreign key in such a way that Figure 2-5 isn't very useful for illustrating how referential constraints work under the covers. Figure 2-7 lists the Orders table with the lookups removed so you can see the actual foreign key values in the EmployeeID and CustomerID columns.

When we update the Orders table, as shown in Figure 2-7, the RDBMS must enforce the referential constraints we have defined on the table. The beauty of database constraints is that they are *automatic* and therefore cannot be circumvented unless the DBA disables or deletes them. Here are the particular events that the RDBMS must handle when enforcing referential constraints:

- When we try to insert a new row into the child table, the insert request is rejected if the corresponding parent table row does not exist. For example, if we insert a row into the Orders table with an EmployeeID value of 12345, the RDBMS must check the Employees table to see if a row for EmployeeID 12345 already exists. If it doesn't exist, the insert request is rejected.

	Order ID	Customer ID	Employee ID	Order Date	Required Date	Shipped Date	Ship Via	Freight
▶ ⊞	10248	VINET	5	04-Jul-1996	01-Aug-1996	16-Jul-1996	Federal Shipping	$32.38
⊞	10249	TOMSP	6	05-Jul-1996	16-Aug-1996	10-Jul-1996	Speedy Express	$11.61
⊞	10250	HANAR	4	08-Jul-1996	05-Aug-1996	12-Jul-1996	United Package	$65.83
⊞	10251	VICTE	3	08-Jul-1996	05-Aug-1996	15-Jul-1996	Speedy Express	$41.34
⊞	10252	SUPRD	4	09-Jul-1996	06-Aug-1996	11-Jul-1996	United Package	$51.30
⊞	10253	HANAR	3	10-Jul-1996	24-Jul-1996	16-Jul-1996	United Package	$58.17
⊞	10254	CHOPS	5	11-Jul-1996	08-Aug-1996	23-Jul-1996	United Package	$22.98
⊞	10255	RICSU	9	12-Jul-1996	09-Aug-1996	15-Jul-1996	Federal Shipping	$148.33
⊞	10256	WELLI	3	15-Jul-1996	12-Aug-1996	17-Jul-1996	United Package	$13.97
⊞	10257	HILAA	4	16-Jul-1996	13-Aug-1996	22-Jul-1996	Federal Shipping	$81.91
⊞	10258	ERNSH	1	17-Jul-1996	14-Aug-1996	23-Jul-1996	Speedy Express	$140.51
⊞	10259	CENTC	4	18-Jul-1996	15-Aug-1996	25-Jul-1996	Federal Shipping	$3.25
⊞	10260	OTTIK	4	19-Jul-1996	16-Aug-1996	29-Jul-1996	Speedy Express	$55.09
⊞	10261	QUEDE	4	19-Jul-1996	16-Aug-1996	30-Jul-1996	United Package	$3.05
⊞	10262	RATTC	8	22-Jul-1996	19-Aug-1996	25-Jul-1996	Federal Shipping	$48.29
⊞	10263	ERNSH	9	23-Jul-1996	20-Aug-1996	31-Jul-1996	Federal Shipping	$146.06

Record: |◄| ◄| 1 |►|►I|►*| of 830

Enter New Value

Figure 2-7   Northwind Orders table (with foreign key values displayed)

- When we try to update a foreign key value in the child table, the update request is rejected if the new value for the foreign key does not already exist in the parent table. For example, if we attempt to change the EmployeeID for Order 10248 from 5 to 12345, the RDBMS must again check the Employees table to see if a row for EmployeeID 12345 already exists. If it doesn't exist, the update request is rejected.

- When we try to delete a row from a parent table, and that parent row has related rows in one or more child tables, either the child table rows must be deleted along with the parent row, or the delete request must be rejected. Most RDBMSs provide the option of automatically deleting the child rows, called a *cascading delete*. At first, you probably wondered why anyone would ever want automatic deletion of child rows. Consider the Orders and Order Details tables. If an order is to be deleted, why not delete the order and the line items that belong to it in one easy step? However, with the Employee table, we clearly would not want that option. If we attempt to delete Employee 5 from the Employee table (perhaps because they are no longer an employee), the RDBMS must check for rows assigned to EmployeeID 5 in the Orders table and reject the delete request if any are found. It would make no business sense to have orders automatically deleted when an employee left the company.

In most relational databases, an SQL statement is used to define a referential constraint. SQL is introduced in Chapter 4. *SQL (Structured Query Language)* is the language used in relational databases to communicate with the database. Many vendors also provide GUI (graphical user interface) panels for defining database objects such as referential constraints. In Oracle and SQL Server, these GUI panels are located within the Enterprise Manager tool. For Microsoft Access, Figure 2-8 shows the Relationships panel that is used for defining referential constraints.

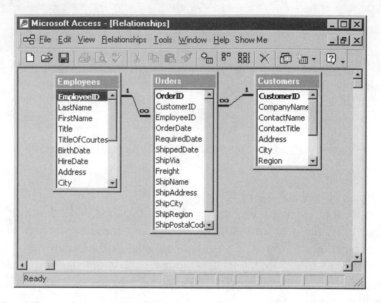

Figure 2-8   Microsoft Access Relationships panel

For simplicity, only the Orders table and its two parent tables, Employees and Customers, are shown in Figure 2-8. The referential constraints are shown as bold lines with the numeric symbol "1" near the parent table (the "one" side) and the mathematical symbol for "infinity" near the child table (the "many" side). These constraints are defined by simply dragging the name of the primary key in the parent table to the name of the foreign key in the child table. A pop-up window is then automatically displayed to allow the definition of options for the referential constraint, as shown in Figure 2-9.

At the top of the Edit Relationships panel, the two table names appear with the parent table on the left and the child table on the right. If you forget which is which, the Relationship Type field, near the bottom of the panel, should remind you. Under each table name, there are rows for selection of the column names that comprise the

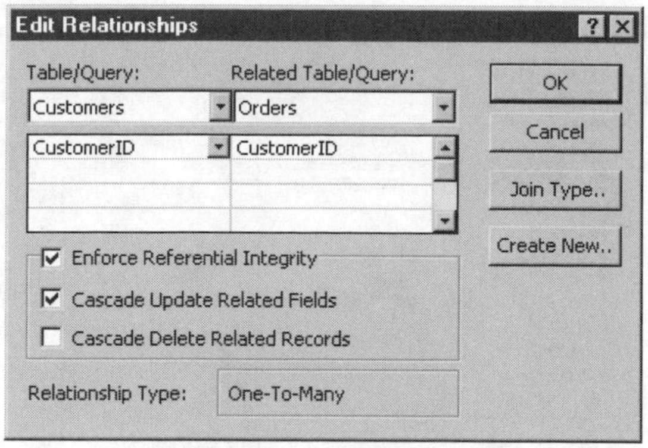

Figure 2-9   Microsoft Access Edit Relationships panel

primary key and foreign key. Figure 2-9 shows the primary key column CustomerID in the Customers table and foreign key column. The check boxes provide some options:

- **Enforce Referential Integrity**   If the box is checked, the constraint is enforced; unchecking the box turns off constraint enforcement.
- **Cascade Update Related Fields**   If the box is checked, any update to the primary key value in the parent table will cause automatic like updates to the related foreign key values. An update of primary key values is a rare situation.
- **Cascade Delete Related Records**   If the box is checked, a delete of a parent table row will cause the automatic cascading deletion of the related child table rows. Think carefully here. There are times to use this, such as the constraint between Orders and Order Details, and times when the option can lead to the disastrous unwanted loss of data, such as deleting an employee (perhaps accidentally) and having all the orders that employee handled automatically deleted from the database.

Intersection Tables

The discussion of many-to-many relationships earlier in this chapter pointed out that relational databases cannot implement these relationships directly and that an intersection table is formed to establish them. Figure 2-10 shows the implementation of the Order Details intersection table in Microsoft Access.

The many-to-many relationship between orders and products in the conceptual design becomes an intersection table (OrderDetails) in the logical design. The relationship is then implemented as two one-to-many relationships with the intersection

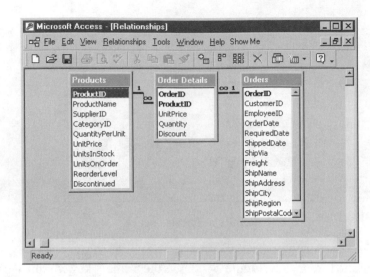

Figure 2-10   Order Details intersection table (Microsoft Access)

table on the "many" side of each. The primary key of the OrderDetails table is the combination of OrderID and ProductID, with OrderID being a foreign key to the Orders table and ProductID being a foreign key to the Products table. Take a moment to examine the contents of the intersection table and the two referential constraints. Understanding this arrangement is fundamental to understanding how relational databases work. Here are some points to consider:

- Each row in the OrderDetails intersection table belongs to the intersection of one product and one order. It would not make sense to put ProductName in this table because that name is the same every time the product appears on an order. Also, it would not make sense to put CustomerID in OrderDetails because all line items on the same order belong to the same customer.
- Each Products table row may have many related OrderDetails rows (one for each order line item on which the product was ordered), but each OrderDetails row belongs to one and only one Products table row.
- Each Orders table row may have many related OrderDetails rows (one for each line item for that particular order), but each OrderDetails row belongs to one and only one Orders table row.

Integrity Constraints

As already mentioned, business rules from the conceptual design become constraints in the logical design. An *integrity constraint* is a constraint (as defined earlier) that promotes the accuracy of the data in the database. The key benefit is that these constraints are invoked automatically by the RDBMS and cannot be circumvented (unless you are a DBA) no matter how you connect to the database. The major types of integrity constraints are NOT NULL constraints, CHECK constraints, and constraints enforced with triggers.

NOT NULL Constraints

As we define columns in database tables, we have the option of specifying whether null values are permitted for the column. A *null value* in a relational database is a special code that can be placed in a column that indicates that the value for that column in that row is unknown. A null value is not the same as a blank, an empty string, or a zero—it is indeed a special code that has no other meaning in the database.

A uniform way to treat null values is an ANSI standard for relational databases. However, there has been much debate over the usefulness of the option because the database cannot tell you *why* the value is unknown. If we leave the value for Title null in the Northwind Employees table, for example, we don't know whether it is null because it is truly unknown (we know employees must have a title, but we do not know what it is), it doesn't apply (perhaps some employees do not get titles), or it is unassigned (they will get a title eventually, but their manager hasn't figured out which title to use just yet). The other dilemma is that null values are not equal to anything, including other null values, which introduces three-valued logic into database searches. With nulls in use, a search can return the condition *true* (the column value matches), *false* (the column value does not match), or *unknown* (the column value is null). The developers who write the application programs have to handle null values as a special case. You'll see more about nulls when SQL is introduced.

In Microsoft Access, the NOT NULL constraint is controlled by the Required option on the table design panel. Figure 2-11 shows the definition of the BirthDate column of the Employee table. Note that the column is not required because the Required option is set to No. In SQL definitions of tables, we simply include the keyword NULL or NOT NULL with the column definition. Watch out for defaults! In Oracle, if you skip the specification, the default is NULL, which means the column may contain null values. But in Microsoft SQL Server and Sybase, it is just the opposite; if you skip the specification, the default is NOT NULL, meaning the column *may not* contain null values.

CHECK Constraints

A CHECK constraint uses a simple logic statement to validate a column value. The outcome of the statement must be a logical true or false, with an outcome of true allowing the column value to be placed in the table, and a value of false causing the

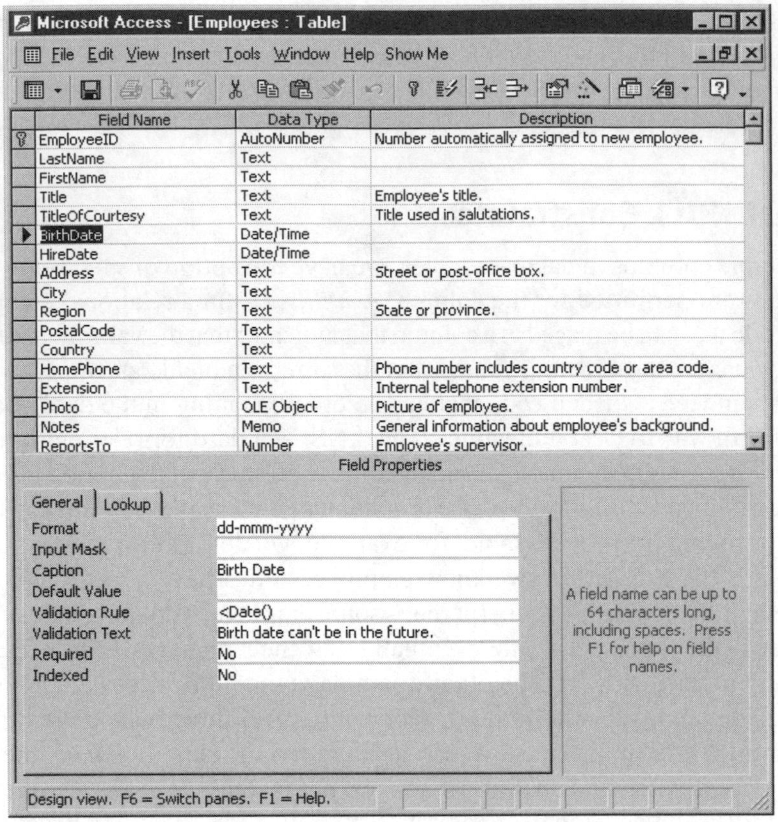

Figure 2-11   Employee table definition panel, BirthDate column

column value to be rejected with an appropriate error message. In Figure 2-11, notice that "<Date()" appears in the Validation Rule option for the BirthDate column. This rule prevents birth dates from being in the future (as the comment suggests) by making sure that the value supplied for the column is less than the current date. Although the syntax of the option will vary for other databases, the concept remains the same. In Oracle SQL, it would be written this way:

```
CHECK (BIRTH_DATE < CURRENT_DATE)
```

Constraint Enforcement Using Triggers

Some constraints are too complicated to be enforced using the declarations. For example, the business rule contained in Figure 2-1 ("Customers with overdue amounts may not book new orders") falls into this category because it involves more than one table. We need the database to prevent new rows from being added to the Orders table if the Account Receivable row for the customer has an overdue amount that is greater than zero. A *trigger* is a module of programming logic that "fires" (executes) when a particular event in the database takes place. In this example, we want the trigger to fire whenever a new row is inserted into the Orders table. The trigger obtains the overdue amount for the customer from the Account Receivable table (or wherever the column is physically stored). If this amount is greater than zero, the trigger will raise a database error that stops the insert request and causes an appropriate error message to be displayed.

In Microsoft Access, triggers may be written as macros using the Microsoft Visual Basic for Applications language. Some RDBMSs provide a special language for writing program modules such as triggers: PL/SQL in Oracle, and Transact SQL in Microsoft SQL Server and Sybase. In other RDBMSs, such as DB2, a generic programming language such as C may be used.

Views

A *view* is a stored database query that provides a database user with a customized subset of the data from one or more tables in the database. Said another way, a view is a *virtual table* because it looks like a table and for the most part behaves like a table, yet it stores no data (only the defining query is stored). The user views form the external layer in the ANSI/SPARC model. During logical design, each view is created using an appropriate method for the particular database. In many RDBMSs, a view is defined using SQL. In Microsoft Access, views are called *queries* and are created using the Query panel. Figure 2-12 shows the Microsoft Access definition of a simple view that lists active products.

The view in Figure 2-12 displays only two columns from a table that contains ten columns. Furthermore, rows for discontinued products are not displayed in the view by virtue of the "No" in the criteria row for the Discontinued column. We explore the Microsoft Access Query panel in detail in Chapter 3.

Views serve a number of useful functions:

- Hiding columns that the user does not need to see (or should not be allowed to see)
- Hiding rows from tables that a user does not need to see (or should not be allowed to see)
- Hiding complex database operations such as table joins
- Improving query performance (in some RDBMSs, such as Microsoft SQL Server)

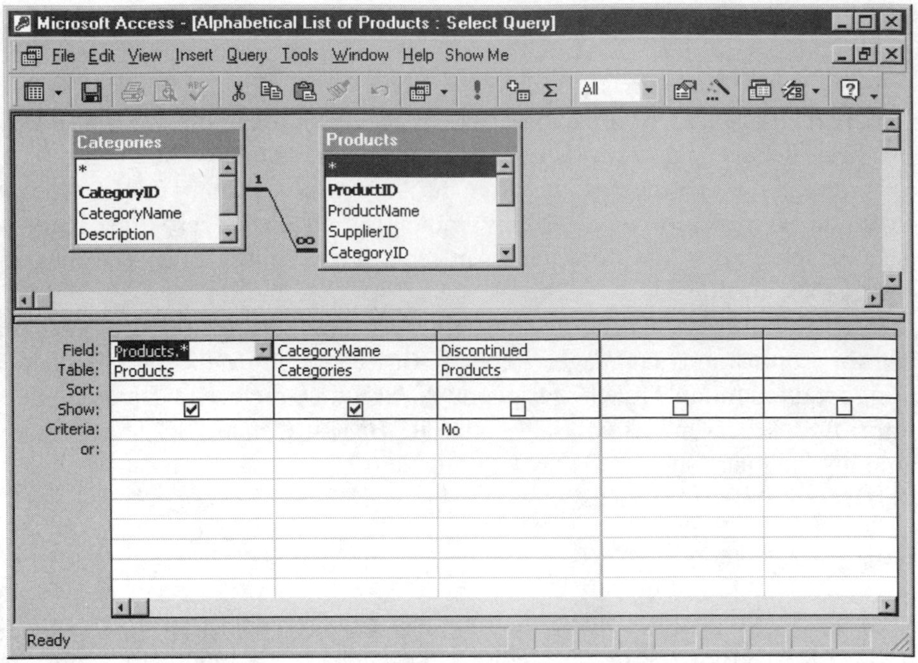

Figure 2-12 Microsoft Access view, list of active products

Quiz

Choose the correct responses to each of the multiple-choice questions. Note that there may be more than one correct response to each question.

1. Examples of an entity are
   a. A customer
   b. A alphabetical listing of products
   c. A customer order
   d. An employee's paycheck
   e. A customer's name

2. Examples of an attribute are
   a. An employee
   b. An employee's name
   c. An employee's paycheck
   d. An alphabetical listing of employees
   e. An employee's birth date

3. On a relationship line, the cardinality of "zero, one, or more" is denoted as:
   a. A vertical tick mark near the end of the line and a crow's foot at the line end
   b. A circle near the end of the line and a crow's foot at the end of the line
   c. Two vertical tick marks near the end of the line
   d. A circle and a vertical tick mark near the end of the line
   e. The mathematical symbol for "infinity" above the end of the line

4. Valid types of relationships in a relational database are
   a. One-to-many
   b. None-to-many
   c. Many-to-many
   d. One-to-one
   e. One-to-many-to-one

5. If a product can be manufactured in many plants, and a plant can manufacture many products, this is an example of which type of relationship?
   a. One-to-one
   b. One-to-many
   c. Many-to-one
   d. Many-to-many
   e. Recursive

6. Which of the following are examples of recursive relationships?
   a. An organizational unit made up of other organizational units
   b. An organizational unit made up of departments
   c. An employee who manages other employees
   d. An employee who manages a department
   e. An employee who has many dependents

7. Examples of a business rule are
   a. A referential constraint must refer to the primary key of the parent table.
   b. An employee must be at least 18 years old.
   c. A database query that eliminates columns an employee should not see
   d. Employees below pay grade 6 are not permitted to modify orders.
   e. Every order may belong to only one customer, but each customer may have many orders.

8. A relational table:
   a. Is composed of rows and columns
   b. Must be assigned a data type
   c. Must be assigned a unique name
   d. Appears in the conceptual database design
   e. Is the primary unit of storage in the relational model

9. A column in a relational table:
   a. Must be assigned a data type
   b. Must be assigned a unique name within the table
   c. Is derived from an entity in the conceptual design
   d. May be composed of other columns
   e. Is the smallest named unit of storage in a relational database

10. A data type:
    a. Restricts the data that may be stored in a view
    b. Assists the DBMS in storing data efficiently
    c. Provides a set of behaviors for a column that assists the database user
    d. May be selected based on business rules for an attribute
    e. Restricts characters allowed in a database column

11. A primary key constraint:
    a. Must reference one or more columns in a single table
    b. Enforces referential integrity constraints
    c. Must be defined for every database table
    d. Is usually implemented using an index
    e. Guarantees that no two rows in a table have duplicate primary
       key values

12. A referential constraint:
    a. Must have primary key and foreign key columns that have identical
       names
    b. Ensures that a primary key does not have duplicate values in a table
    c. Defines a many-to-many relationship between two tables
    d. Ensures that a foreign key value always refers to an existing primary
       key value in the parent table
    e. Is derived from a user view in the conceptual model

13. A referential constraint is defined:
    a. Using the Relationships panel in Microsoft Access
    b. Using SQL in most relational databases
    c. In a view
    d. Using the referential data type for the foreign key column(s)
    e. Using a database trigger

14. Intersection tables:
    a. Are used to provide users with a customized view of their data
    b. Resolve a one-to-many relationship
    c. May contain intersection data
    d. Resolve a many-to-many relationship
    e. Appear only in the conceptual database design

15. Major types of integrity constraints are
    a. CHECK constraints
    b. One-to-one relationships
    c. NOT NULL constraints
    d. Constraints enforced with triggers
    e. Data types

16. An entity in the conceptual design becomes which object in the logical design?
    a. View
    b. Table
    c. Column
    d. Referential constraint
    e. Index

17. An attribute in the conceptual design becomes which object in the logical design?
    a. View
    b. Table
    c. Column
    d. Referential constraint
    e. Index

18. Items in the external level of the ANSI/SPARC model become which type of database object in the logical model?
    a. View
    b. Table
    c. Column
    d. Referential constraint
    e. Index

19. A relationship in the conceptual design becomes which object in the logical design?
    a. View
    b. Table
    c. Column
    d. Referential constraint
    e. Index

20. A primary key constraint is implemented using which type of object in the logical design?
    a. View
    b. Table
    c. Column
    d. Referential constraint
    e. Index

3

Forms-Based Database Queries

On the theory that you cannot design a car if you have never driven one, we will take a brief tour of database queries before delving into the details of database design. This chapter provides an overview of forming and running database queries using the forms-based query tool in Microsoft Access. It is not at all my intent to provide a comprehensive guide to Microsoft Access; I am merely using Microsoft Access as a vehicle to present database query concepts that will provide a foundation for the database design theory that follows later in this book. However, I will attempt to provide enough basic information about using Microsoft Access that you will be able to follow along on your own computer as we explore forms-based queries in Microsoft Access.

QBE: The Roots of Forms-Based Queries

A *forms-based* query language uses a GUI (graphical user interface) panel for the creation of a query. The database user defines queries by entering sample data values directly into a query template to represent the result that the database is to achieve. An alternative query method uses a *command-based* query language, where queries are written as text commands. SQL (Structured Query Language) is the ubiquitous command-based query language for relational databases, and it's introduced in Chapter 4. The emphasis with both forms-based and command-based query languages is on *what* the result should be rather than *how* to achieve the result. The difference between the two is only in the way the user describes the desired result, and it's similar to the difference between using Microsoft Windows Explorer to copy a file versus using the MS-DOS copy command (in the DOS Command window) to do the same thing.

The first well-known forms-based query tool was QBE (Query By Example), which was developed by IBM in the 1970s. Personal computers, Microsoft Windows, the mouse, and many other modern computing amenities were unheard of at this time, but the interface was still graphical in nature. A form was displayed, and database users typed sample data and simple commands in boxes, where today they would click a button using a mouse. SQL, also initially developed by IBM, was also new in the 1970s. IBM conducted a controlled study to determine whether QBE or SQL was preferred by database users of the day. The conclusion was that whichever one a database user learned first was the one they preferred. Human nature it seems.

Experience has shown us that both methods are useful to know. Forms-based queries lend themselves well to casual use and database users who are more accustomed to GUI environments than to touch-typing commands. However, database users familiar with command syntax and possessing reasonable typing skills can enter command-based queries more quickly than the GUI equivalents, and command-based queries can be directly used within a programming language such as Java or C.

Getting Started in Microsoft Access

The queries shown in this chapter all use the Northwind sample database provided with Microsoft Access. You will have the best learning experience if you try the queries presented in this chapter as you read. Obviously, the sample database is required, but it is relatively simple to install from the Microsoft Office CD-ROM. Please refer to Microsoft documentation if you need assistance with the installation.

Once Microsoft Access is installed, I *highly recommend* that you copy the Northwind database file, Northwind.mdb, to another directory and use that copy as you practice Microsoft Access queries. It is easy to accidentally update the database when using Microsoft Access, and there is no simple "undo" function. If you work with a copy of the database file, recovering from mistakes becomes a simple matter of copying the original file again. On most Microsoft Windows systems, you will find the Northwind.mdb file in the directory \Program Files\Microsoft Office\ Office\Samples or \Program Files\Microsoft Office\Office11\Samples, depending on the version of Microsoft Access. Note that you may also wish to copy the three files with names beginning with NWIND9 (or just the entire Samples directory, as it's not very large). These files are *not* needed to use the database, but if you decide to run any parts of the sample application or the customized help information that comes with the database, you will need them.

The simplest way to launch Microsoft Access and open the Northwind database is merely to double-click the Northwind.mdb file in Windows Explorer. However, you may also launch Microsoft Access from the Start menu and use the Open an Existing File option to navigate to the directory where you placed the copy of Northwind.mdb and double-click the filename to open the database. Figure 3-1 shows the window that opens automatically when Microsoft Access is launched from the Start menu. Note that the screen images in this chapter are from Microsoft Access 2000, but the look and feel varies from one version to another, so your screens may not look exactly like these. For instance, the Microsoft Access XP version starts with a Getting Started side window instead of the pop-up windows shown in Figure 3-1.

Figure 3-1   Microsoft Access startup window

Once you have used Microsoft Access to open one or more database files, a list of the most recently used database files will appear in a list just below the Open an Existing File option in the startup window. You may reopen a previously used database merely by clicking its filename in the list. After you have opened the database, you will see a screen similar to the one shown in Figure 3-2.

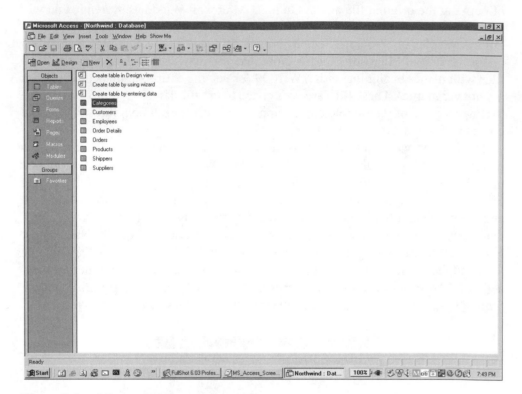

Figure 3-2   Microsoft Access main panel

This is the main panel in Microsoft Access. In a column along the left margin with the heading Objects, you can switch the type of database objects listed in the center of the panel. When you start Microsoft Access for the very first time, the default selection is Tables. However, from that point forward, Microsoft Access will remember the last type you selected for the database and always return you to that type when you subsequently reopen the database. Briefly, the types shown may be defined as follows:

- **Tables**   Relational tables. These hold the actual database data in rows and columns.

- **Queries**   Stored database queries. These are called *views* in nearly all other relational databases.

- **Forms**   GUI forms for data entry and/or display within Microsoft Access.

- **Reports**   Reports based on database queries.

- **Pages**   Web pages for data entry and/or display using a web browser.

- **Macros**   Sets of actions that each perform a particular operation, such as opening a form or printing a report.

- **Modules**   Collections of Visual Basic programming language components that are stored as a unit.

As with many personal computer–based databases, Microsoft Access is not only a database, but also a complete development environment for building and running applications. The database products that run on larger, shared computer systems commonly called *servers* typically do *not* come with application-development environments. Learning to build application programs is well outside the scope of this book, so we will not deal with the Forms, Reports, Pages, Macros, and Modules types at all. We will focus only on the Tables and Queries types in Microsoft Access.

Maintenance of the objects in the database can be performed from this panel, including the following tasks:

- To add a new object of the type displayed, click the appropriate shortcut near the top of the list. For example, the Tables object list includes a shortcut called Create Table in Design View.

- To delete an existing object, click its name so it is selected and then press DELETE.

- To display an object, double-click its name.

- To display the definition (design) of an object, click its name so that it is selected and then click the Design View button on the toolbar (the one with the ruler, pencil, and triangle on it).

The Microsoft Access Relationships Panel

Microsoft Access provides the Relationships panel, shown in Figure 3-3, for the definition and maintenance of referential constraints between the relational tables. To display this panel, either click the toolbar button (the icon with three tables and lines drawn between them on it) or select Tools | Relationships from the menu bar.

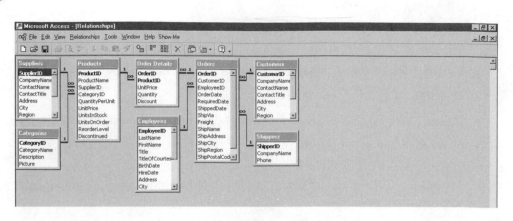

Figure 3-3   The Microsoft Access Relationships panel

The Relationships panel graphically displays tables, shown as rectangles, and one-to-many relationships, shown as lines between the rectangles. Technically, these are referential constraints (*relationships* being only a conceptual term), but because Microsoft calls them relationships on this panel, I will also for consistency. The symbol "1" shows the "one" side of each relationship, whereas the infinity symbol (similar to the number 8 laying on its side) shows the "many" side of each relationship. The relationships may be maintained as follows:

- To add tables that are not displayed, click the Show Table button on the toolbar (the one with a table and bold yellow plus sign on it), and select the tables from the pop-up window.

- To remove a table from the display, click it so that it is selected and then press DELETE. Note that this does *not* delete the table or any relationships in which the table participates; it merely removes the table from the panel.

- To add a relationship, drag the primary key in one table to the matching foreign key in another. For recursive relationships, the table must be added to the display a second time, and the relationship must be created between one displayed copy of the table and the other. This looks odd at first, but it is only to facilitate the drag-and-drop method of creating the relationship. A table shown multiple times on the panel still exists only one time in the database.

- To delete a relationship, click the narrow part of its line and press DELETE. Selecting relationships can be tricky in Microsoft Access because only the *narrow* part of the line will work, and you may have to stretch short lines by moving a table on the panel in order to even find the narrow part of the line.

- To edit a relationship, double-click the narrow part of its line. A pop-up window may be used to change various options about the relationship, including toggling enforcement of the relationship as a referential constraint on and off (that is, enabling and disabling the constraint). When a constraint is disabled, the DBMS will not prevent inserts, updates, and deletes from creating "orphan" foreign key values (foreign key values that have no matching primary key values in the parent table). The DBMS will, however, not permit a constraint to be enabled if there are orphan foreign key values in the child table.

Closing or minimizing the window will make the main panel visible once again.

The Microsoft Access Table Design View

From the main panel, a table may be selected by double-clicking its name. The default display, called the Datasheet View, is shown in Figure 3-4. The data in the table is displayed in the familiar tabular form, and the data may be updated if desired, including the insertion and deletion of rows. Be careful. There is no "undo" feature—once you move the cursor from one row to another, any changes you have made cannot be easily reversed.

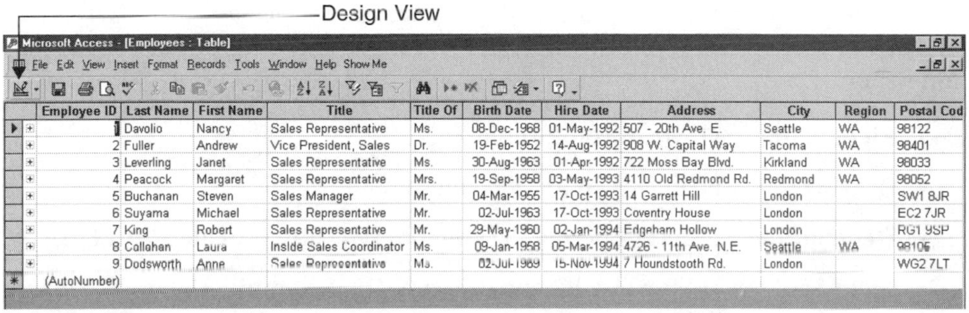

Employee ID	Last Name	First Name	Title	Title Of	Birth Date	Hire Date	Address	City	Region	Postal Cod
1	Davolio	Nancy	Sales Representative	Ms.	08-Dec-1968	01-May-1992	507 - 20th Ave. E.	Seattle	WA	98122
2	Fuller	Andrew	Vice President, Sales	Dr.	19-Feb-1952	14-Aug-1992	908 W. Capital Way	Tacoma	WA	98401
3	Leverling	Janet	Sales Representative	Ms.	30-Aug-1963	01-Apr-1992	722 Moss Bay Blvd.	Kirkland	WA	98033
4	Peacock	Margaret	Sales Representative	Mrs.	19-Sep-1958	03-May-1993	4110 Old Redmond Rd.	Redmond	WA	98052
5	Buchanan	Steven	Sales Manager	Mr.	04-Mar-1955	17-Oct-1993	14 Garrett Hill	London		SW1 8JR
6	Suyama	Michael	Sales Representative	Mr.	02-Jul-1963	17-Oct-1993	Coventry House	London		EC2 7JR
7	King	Robert	Sales Representative	Mr.	29-May-1960	02-Jan-1994	Edgeham Hollow	London		RG1 9SP
8	Callahan	Laura	Inside Sales Coordinator	Ms.	09-Jan-1958	05-Mar-1994	4726 - 11th Ave. N.E.	Seattle	WA	98105
9	Dodsworth	Anne	Sales Representative	Ms.	02-Jul-1969	15-Nov-1994	7 Houndstooth Rd.	London		WG2 7LT
(AutoNumber)										

Figure 3-4 Datasheet View (Employees table)

To see the definition of the table, click the Design View button on the toolbar (the one with the ruler, pencil, and triangle on it). Figure 3-5 shows the Design View for the Employees table.

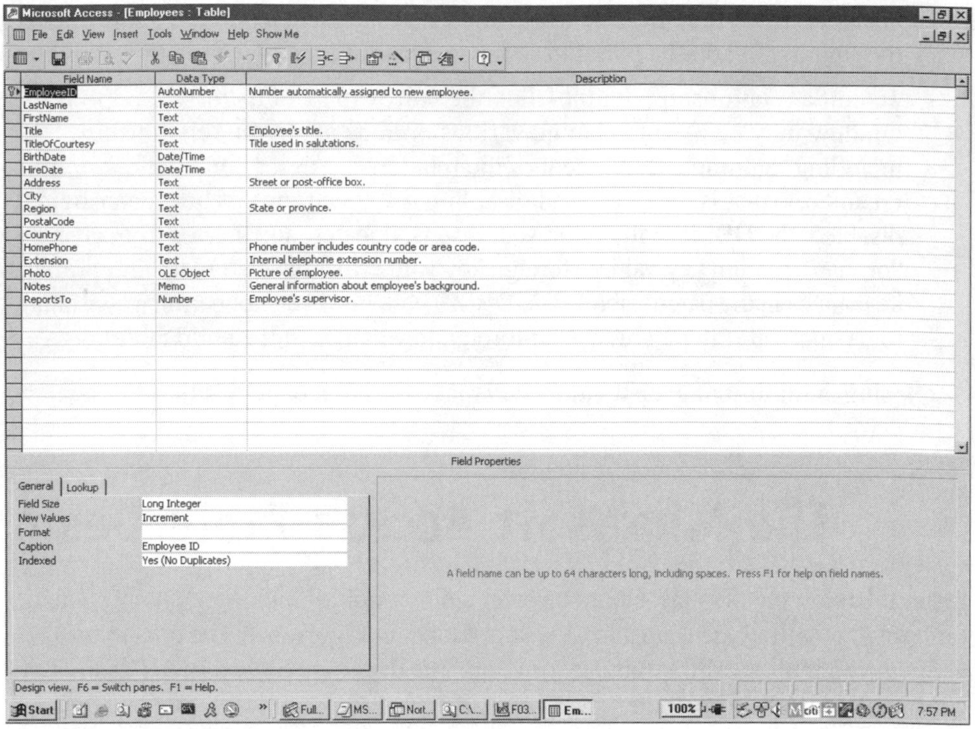

Figure 3-5 Design View (Employees table)

The Design View for a table in Microsoft Access displays information such as the following:

- **Field Name**   The name of the column.

- **Data Type**   The data type for the column.

- **Description**   A description of the column, typically provided by a DBA.

- **Field Size**   A subtype within the data type. For example, Long Integer and Short Integer apply to the more general Number data type.

- **Required**   Indicates whether the column is optional (that is, whether it may have null values).

- **Indexed**   Indicates whether the column has an index.

- **Primary Key**   Denoted with a small key icon next to the field name (or names) that comprises the primary key.

Hopefully, you recognized that everything on this panel is metadata. There are many more options than the ones noted here, and Microsoft Access is very clever about hiding and exposing options so only the applicable ones are displayed. Notice that help text in blue automatically displays in the lower-right part of the panel as you move the cursor from one option to another.

Creating Queries in Microsoft Access

As mentioned earlier, stored queries are called *views* in most databases, but because a view is defined as a stored database query, the Microsoft Access name is technically correct. Always keep in mind that queries do not store any data; instead, the data is stored in the tables. On the main panel, clicking the Queries button (along the left margin) lists all the queries stored in this database, as shown in Figure 3-6.

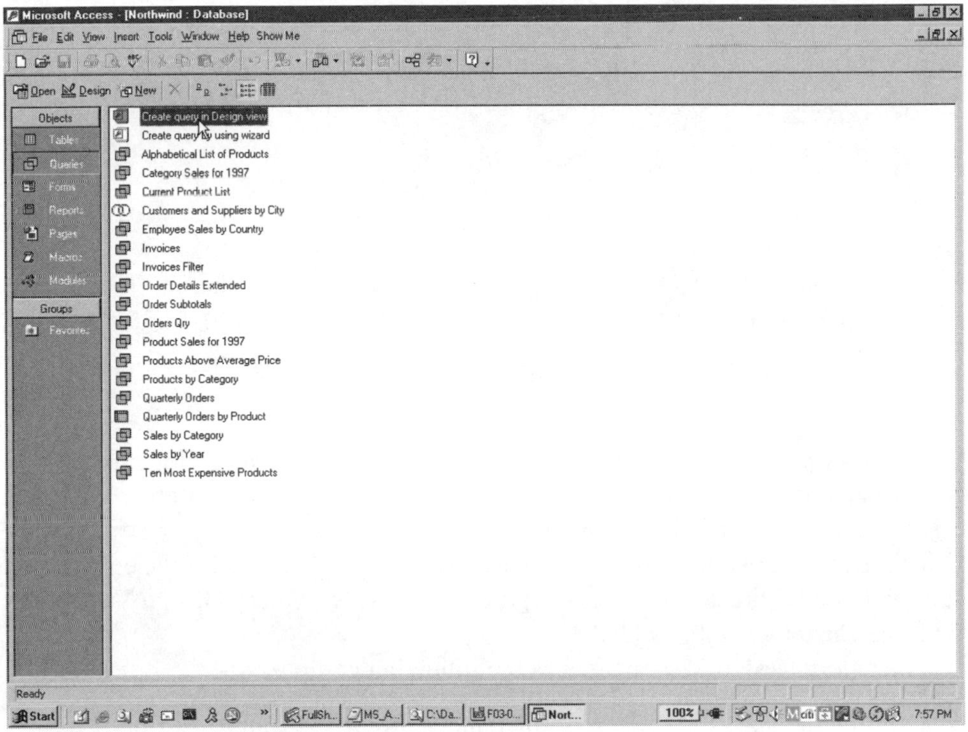

Figure 3-6   Microsoft Access Queries window

Although Microsoft Access offers several ways to create a new query, for beginners, the Create Query in Design View option is the easiest to understand. Figure 3-7 shows the Design View for a New Query panel (also called the Query Design View panel) with the Show Table dialog box open.

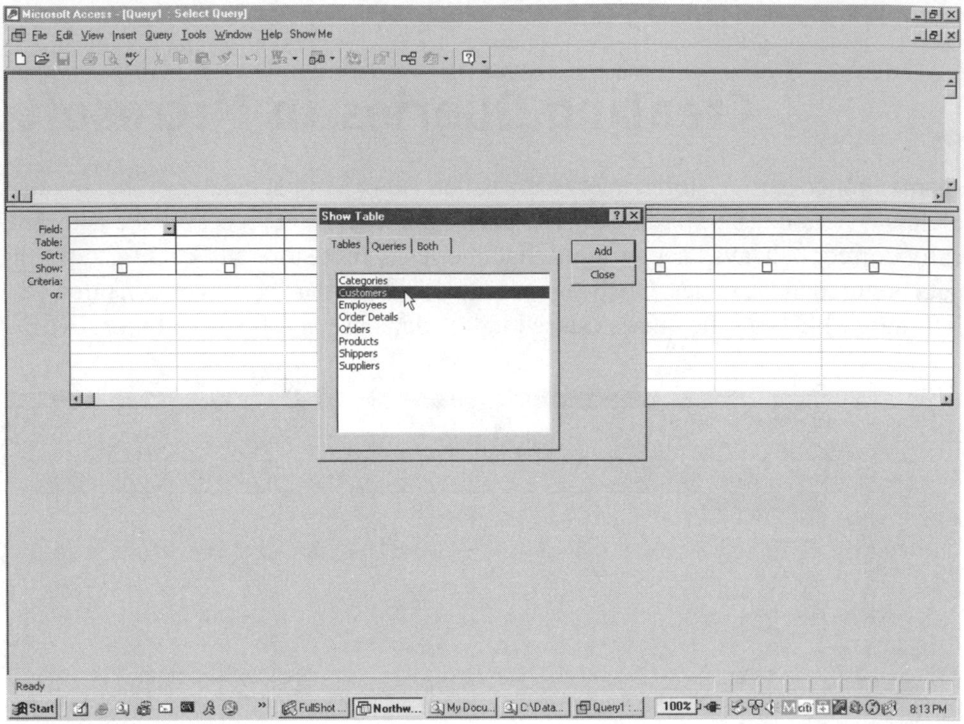

Figure 3-7   Query Design View with the Show Table dialog box visible

For every new query, Microsoft Access opens the Show Table dialog box to allow for the selection of the tables and/or queries on which the query will be based (that is, the tables or queries that are to be the source of the data that will be displayed). Once the tables are added, the Query Design View panel allows for the entry of the specification for the desired query. Figure 3-8 shows the Query Design View panel with the Customers table added.

The Query Design View panel has the following components:

- In the open area at the top of the panel (gray background), a graphical representation of the source tables and/or views and the relationships for the query are shown. Any relationships defined for the tables are automatically inherited here.

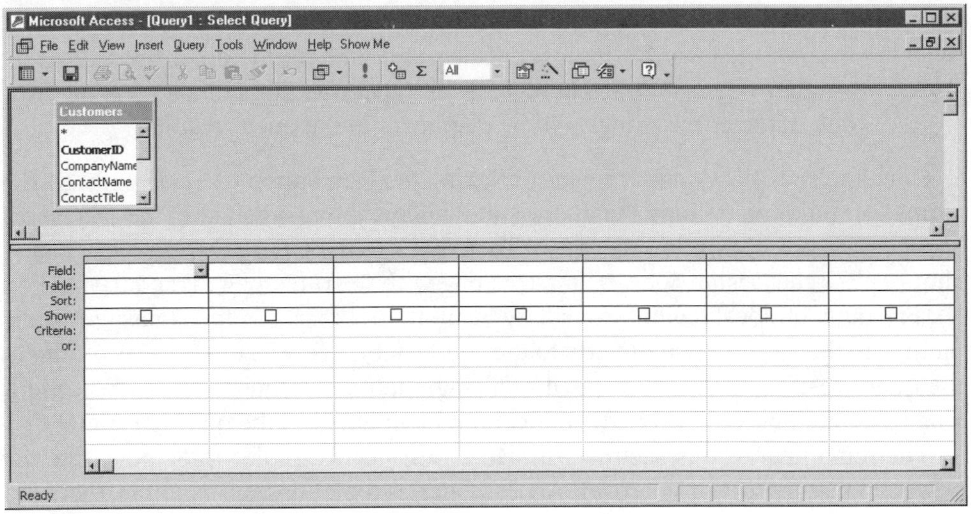

Figure 3-8   Query Design View

- In the grid area in the lower part of the panel, each column represents a
  column of data that is to be returned in the result set when the query is
  executed. Rows in the grid area define various options to be applied to the
  corresponding columns (usage examples are provided in the sections that
  follow):

  - **Field**   The specification for the source of the column. This is normally
    a table or query column name, but it can also be a constant or an
    expression similar to calculations used in spreadsheets.

  - **Table**   The source table or query name for the column.

  - **Sort**   The specification for any sort sequencing for the column
    (Ascending, Descending, or None).

  - **Show**   A check box that controls display of the column. If the box
    is not checked, the column may be used in forming the query, but does
    not appear in the query results.

  - **Criteria**   The specification that determines which rows of data are to
    appear in the query results. All conditions placed on the same line must
    be met for a row of data to be displayed in the query results. Conditions
    placed on subsequent lines (labeled "or" on the panel) are alternative sets
    of conditions that will also cause a matching data row to be displayed in
    the results. The usage of these will likely not make sense until you see
    the examples that follow, but in short, conditions placed on one line

are connected with a logical AND operator, and each new line of criteria is connected using a logical OR operator with all the other lines. Said another way, any row that matches the specifications that appear on any one of the criteria lines will be displayed in the query results.

Once the specification is complete, clicking the Run button (the one with the exclamation point on it) runs the query and displays the results using the Datasheet View, as already shown in Figure 3-4. To go back to the Query Design View panel, simply click the Design View button (the one with the ruler, pencil, and triangle on it). For most queries, data updates may be applied directly in the Datasheet View table, and they are applied directly to the source tables for the query. If a column in the query results cannot be mapped to a single table column—perhaps because it was calculated in some way—then it cannot be updated in the query results.

The remainder of this section will use a series of examples to demonstrate the powerful features of the Microsoft Access Queries tool. For each example, there is a description of the result desired and the steps required to create the specification for the query on the Query Design View panel. This is followed by a figure showing the completed Design View panel, and another figure showing the results when the query is executed.

Example 3-1: List All Customers

To list the entire Customers table (all rows and all columns), follow these steps:

1. From the main panel with Queries selected in the left margin, double-click the link Create Query in Design View.

2. Perform the following actions in the Show Table dialog box:

   • Click Customers to select the Customers table.

   • Click the Add button.

   • Click the Close button.

3. On the Design View panel, double-click the asterisk in the Customers table template (near the top of the panel).

The completed panel is shown at the top of Figure 3-9 with the query results shown below.

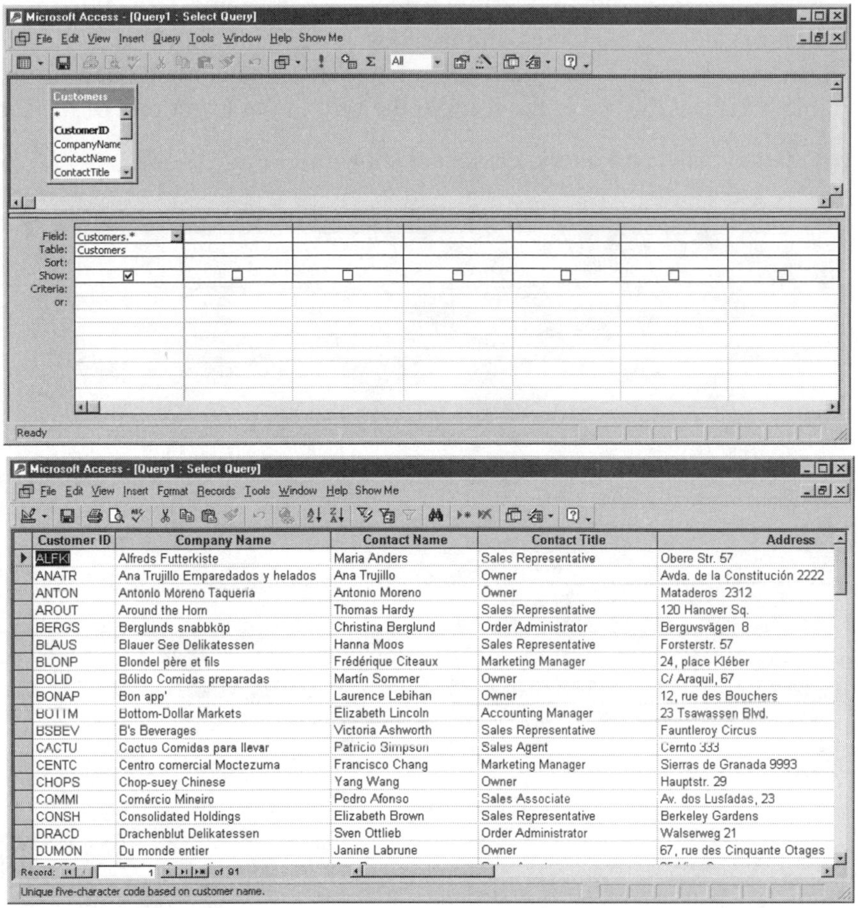

Figure 3-9   Example 3-1, "List All Customers" (Query Design View) (top), and the query results (bottom)

Example 3-2: Choosing Columns to Display

Instead of displaying all columns, we now specify only the ones that we wish to see. To list the CustomerID, CompanyName, City, Region, and Country columns for all customers (all rows and all columns), follow the steps outlined in this section.

Using the Design View from Example 3-1 as a starting point, modify the query as follows:

1. Remove the existing specification that displays all columns by clicking the small gray rectangle above field name "Customers.*" (which changes the entire column to a black background). Then press DELETE to remove the column.

2. For each desired column (CustomerID, CompanyName, City, Region, and Country), double-click the column name in the table shown at the top of the form. An alternative method is to drag and drop the column name from the table shown at the top of the form to the grid in the lower part of the form.

The completed panel and query results are shown in Figure 3-10.

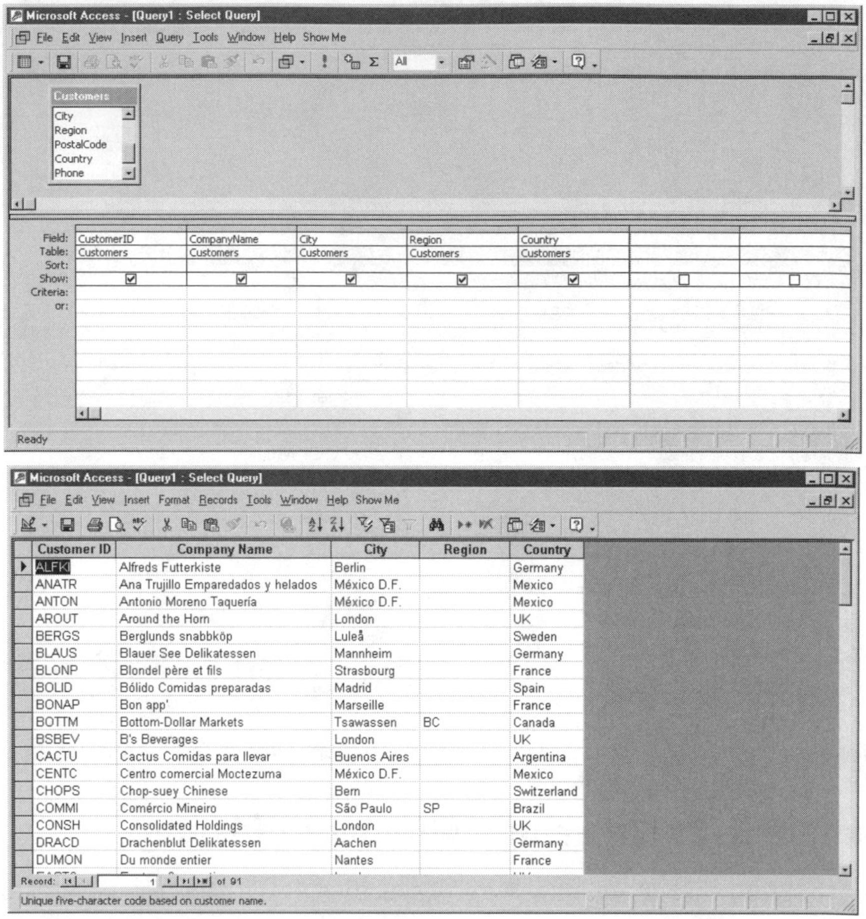

Figure 3-10   Example 3-2, "Choosing Columns to Display" (top), and the query results (bottom)

Example 3-3: Sorting Results

In any RDBMS, rows are returned in no particular order unless you request one. Microsoft Access uses the Sort specification to determine the order in which rows are returned in query results.

To modify Example 3-2 so that rows are sorted in ascending order by city, region, and country, follow these steps:

1. On the line labeled Sort in the column for City, click in the blank space and select Ascending from the pull-down list.

2. Do the same for the Region column. A simple alternative method is to type **A** in the sort specification and press ENTER.

3. Do the same for the Country column.

The completed panel and query results are shown in Figure 3-11.

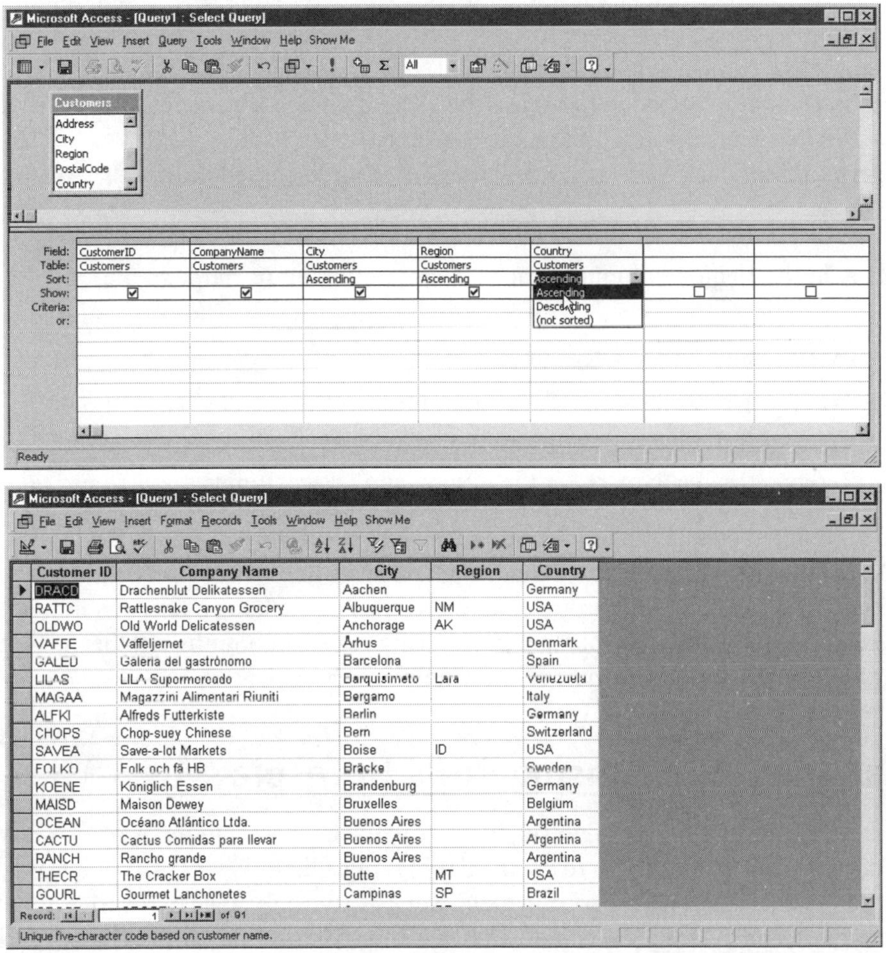

Figure 3-11   Example 3-3, "Sorting Results" (top), and the query results (bottom)

Example 3-4: Advanced Sorting

Looking at the results of Example 3-3, you can see that all the cities are listed in ascending sequence and that sorting by region and then by country had little effect and would matter only if two cities with the same name existed in different regions and countries. Spoken language not always being logically precise, this is unlikely to be what we meant when we said we wanted the data sorted by city, region, and country. Instead, we likely wanted all the rows for a country to be together, and for each country, all the rows in a region to be together, and for each region, all the cities to be listed in ascending sequence by name. If we had said sort by city *within* region *within* country, our intent would have been clearer. Now we need a way to sort by country first, region second, and city last, but city is displayed before region, and region before country. Microsoft Access sorting works on the columns in the query from left to right. How can we accomplish our goal? We can place the Region and City columns in the query a second time, use the second copies for sorting, but omit them from the query results using the Show check box.

To modify Example 3-3 so that rows are sorted as discussed, follow these steps:

1. Remove the sort specifications on the existing City and Region columns.

2. Add the Region column again by double-clicking its name in the Customers table.

3. Do the same for the City column.

4. Add the ascending sort specification to the Region and City columns that you just added (the ones to the *right* of the Country column).

5. Remove the check mark for the Region and City columns that you just added.

The completed panel and query results are shown in Figure 3-12.

Note that most languages are read from left to right, so we naturally expect tabular listings to be sorted moving from left to right, starting with the leftmost column. It is unusual, and perhaps poor human engineering, to sort columns another way. But should you ever need to, you now know how.

Example 3-5: Choosing Rows to Display

Thus far we have been displaying all 91 rows in the Customer table in every query. If we do not wish to see all the rows, displaying all of them is wasteful of system resources, especially if we are sorting them. Suppose we only wish to see rows for customers in London, UK. We can do so using the Criteria line on the Query Design View panel.

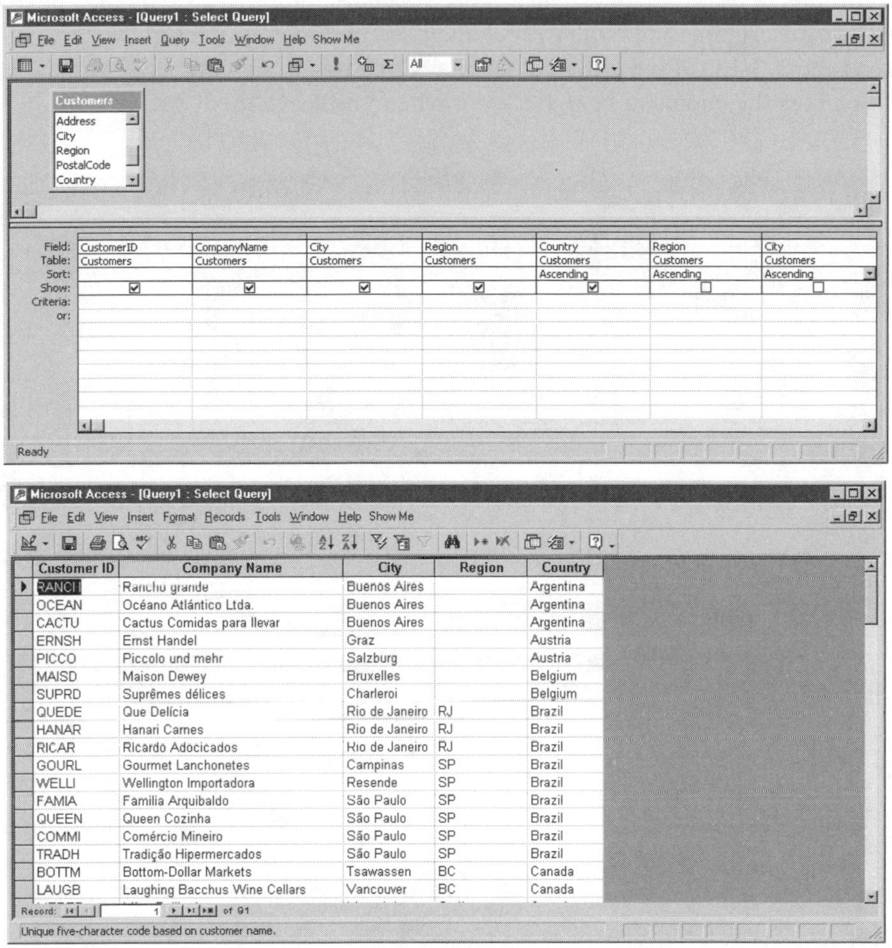

Figure 3-12 Example 3-4, "Advanced Sorting" (top), and the query results (bottom)

To modify Example 3-4 to limit the rows displayed:

1. On the line labeled Criteria, type **London** in the leftmost City column. Note that Microsoft Access pays no attention to case when selecting data in queries, so you can also enter **LONDON** or **london** and achieve the same result.

2. On the same line, type **UK** in the Country column. It is important to enter the City and Country criteria on the same line because we only want rows returned where the City is "London" *and* the Country is "UK."

The completed panel and query results are shown in Figure 3-13. You may have noticed that the criteria for Country is not enclosed in double-quotes in the panel at the top of Figure 3-13. Microsoft Access knows that this is a character format column and assumes the quotes to be there, even when you leave them out.

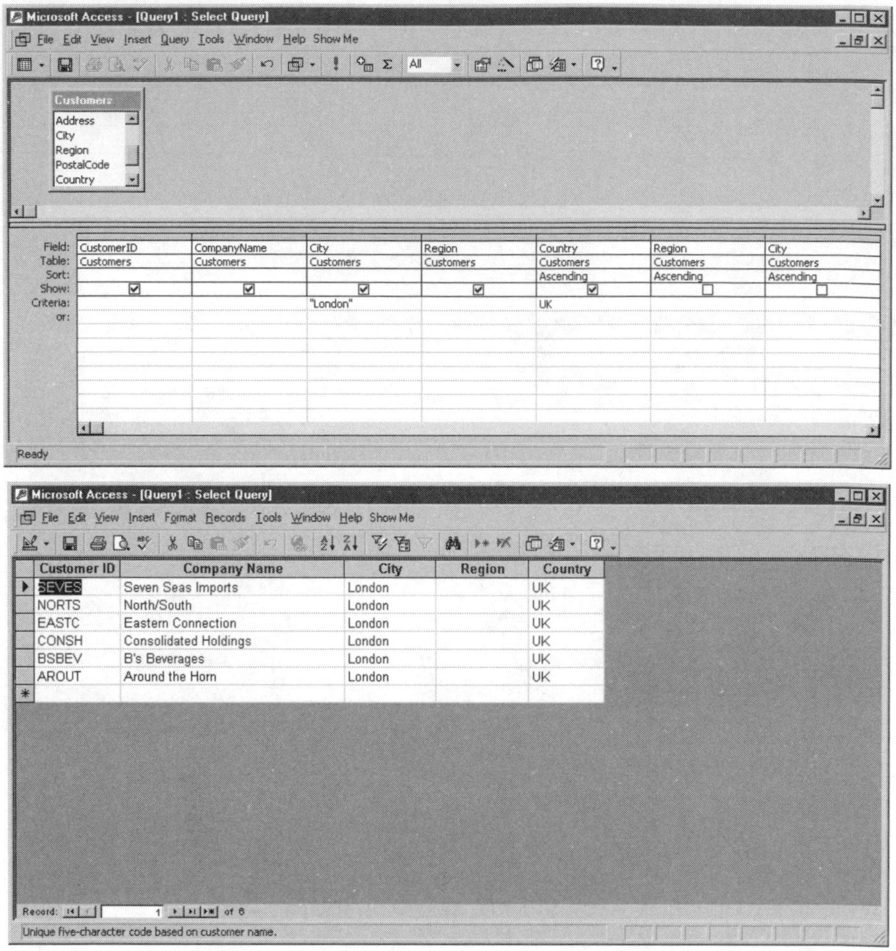

Figure 3-13 Example 3-5, "Choosing Rows to Display" (top), and the query results (bottom)

Example 3-6: Compound Row Selection

Suppose we now want to select all customers in the state of Washington in the U.S. in addition to those in London. We must add the new criteria or a *different* line of the Query View panel.

Follow these steps to modify Example 3-5 to include the additional customers:

1. On a new line in the Criteria area of the panel, enter **WA** in the leftmost Region column.

2. On the *same* line, enter **USA** in the Country column. Note that the criteria is interpreted this way: Select all rows where the City equals "London" and the Country equals "UK"; in addition, select all rows where the Region equals "WA" and the County equals "USA."

The completed panel and query results are shown in Figure 3-14.

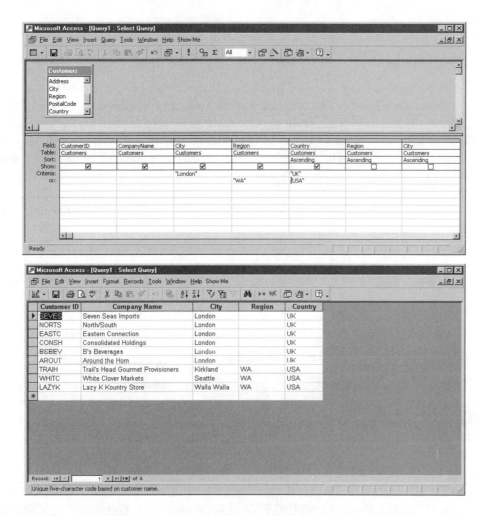

Figure 3-14   Example 3-6, "Compound Row Selection" (top), and the query results (bottom)

Example 3-7: Using Not Equal

Thus far we have looked at search criteria that assumes the "equal" (=) comparison operator. However, several other comparison operators can be used, as shown in the following table:

Operator	Description
<	Less than
<=	Less than or equal
>	Greater than
>=	Greater than or equal
<>	Not equal (ANSI standard form)

For example, suppose we need to find all the customers who are not from either the USA or the UK. Note that we have run into another situation where spoken language isn't logically precise. If we use OR as the logical operator (that is, <>"USA" OR <>"UK"), we will select all rows in the table, for no matter what data value is in the row, it won't be equal to one or the other of those two values. Therefore, we must use AND as the relational operator because we want rows that are not equal to one value *and also* not equal to the other value.

To modify Example 3-6 to find all the customers who are not in the USA and not in the UK, do the following:

1. Remove all the criteria from the previous example.
2. In the Criteria line for the Country column, enter <>"USA" AND <>"UK".

Figure 3-15 shows the completed panel and query results.

Example 3-8: Joining Tables

In relational databases, combinining data from more than one table is called *joining*. In this example, we wish to display three columns from the Customers table along with three columns from the Orders table for each order the customer has placed with Northwind. Because the relationship between orders and customers is one-to-many, whenever a customer has multiple orders, the same information about the customer will be repeated in the query results for each row returned.

Understanding joins is essential to understanding relational databases. Just as one-to-many relationships (implemented in the database as referential constraints)

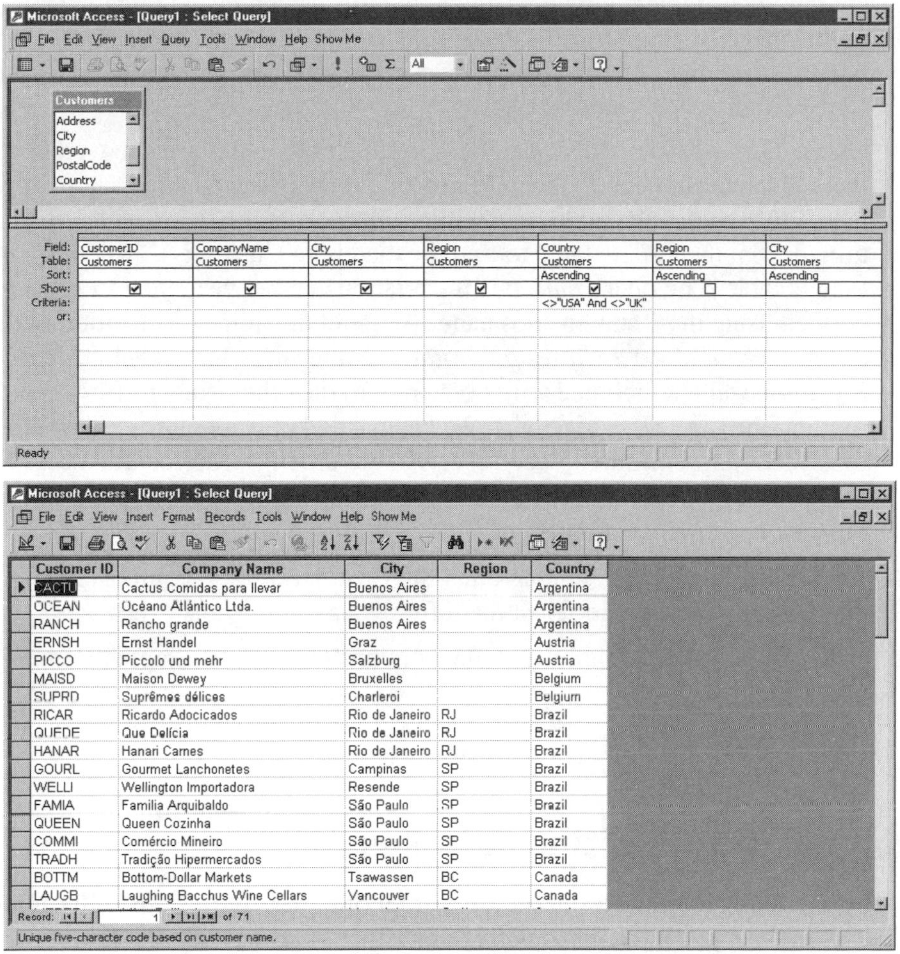

Figure 3-15   Example 3-7, "Using Not Equal" (top), and the query results (bottom)

are the fundamental building blocks for relational databases, joins arc the fundamental building blocks for relational database queries.

It is best to start with a fresh query so that you can see, from the ground up, how
queries using joins arc built. Close whatever query windows you may have open and
start on the Microsoft Access main panel with the Queries database object type selected. Exercise 3-1 can be used as a guide for getting started. To build our query, follow these steps:

1. Create a new query using the Create Query in Design View shortcut.

2. On the Show Table dialog box, add both the Customers and Orders tables to the query. Because queries describe *what* is to be done instead of *how* it is to be done, the order in which you add the tables is immaterial. Click the Close button when you're done.

3. On the Query Design View panel, notice that both tables are shown and there is a line connecting them. Microsoft Access already knows how to match the rows in the tables and will use the CustomerID for each row returned from the Orders table to find the matching CustomerID in the Customers table. The query *inherited* the relationship between the two tables defined using the Relationships panel. Without this join specification in the query, we would get a *Cartesian product* as a result, which would be every row in one table combined with every row in the other (the *product* of multiplying the two tables together). We clearly do not want our query results to look like every customer placed every single order, so Microsoft Access has helped us do the right thing. Properties of the join specifications are explored in some upcoming examples.

4. In the Customers table, double-click the CustomerID, CustomerName, and Country columns to select them for display in the query results.

5. In the Orders table, double-click the columns OrderDate, ShippedDate, and Freight.

The completed panel and query results are shown in Figure 3-16.

Example 3-9: Limiting Join Results

The row count in the query results at the bottom of Figure 3-16 shows 830 rows returned. A look at the Orders table will confirm that there are indeed 830 rows in it. Obviously, that is more information than a person would likely want to see, but from the earlier examples we know that we can limit the rows returned using the Criteria lines on the panel. Also, because we are joining rows from two tables, we can provide search criteria for the rows returned from either table or both tables. When the criteria eliminates a customer, no orders for that customer will show in the results, and when we eliminate orders from the results, we will see no customer information for those orders either. This is because the join we are using is by default an *inner join* (also known as an *exclusive* or *standard* join), which means that rows appear in the query results *only* when matching rows are found in all the tables we are joining together. In Example 3-10, you will see alternatives to this behavior.

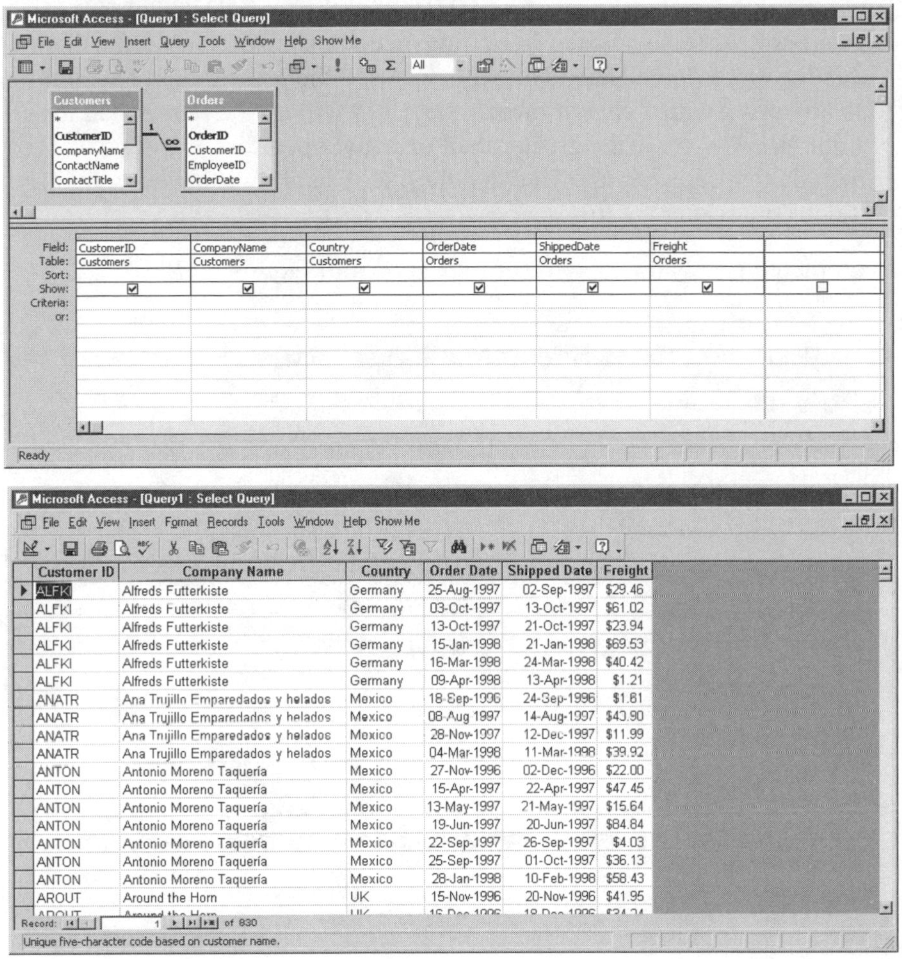

Figure 3-16   Example 3-8, "Joining Tables" (top), and the query results (bottom)

Let's assume we only want to see rows for customers in Spain and orders dated after January 1, 1998. To modify Example 3-8 to do this, follow these steps:

1. On the Criteria line in the Country column, enter **Spain**. Character strings in relational databases should be enclosed in quotes (actually, double quotes in Microsoft Access), but Microsoft Access knows the column is in character format, so it will add the quotes for you automatically (or "automagically" in IT slang).

2. On the same criteria line, enter **>1/1/1998** in the OrderDate column. Microsoft Access encloses date strings with hash marks (#) and will do this for you automatically. Note that we used the greater-than operator (>), so any order with a date of *exactly* 1/1/1998 will not be returned in the results. We would use the greater-than-or-equal operator (>=) if we want to include that date, but knowing that the 1st of January is always a holiday, it does not matter for this query.

The completed panel and query results are shown in Figure 3-17.

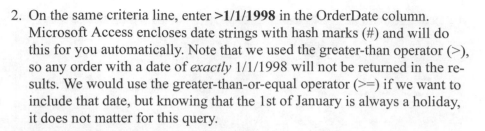

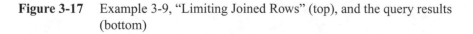

Figure 3-17 Example 3-9, "Limiting Joined Rows" (top), and the query results (bottom)

Example 3-10: Outer Joins

As described in Example 3-9, the join technique we have used so far is the *inner join*. Note that there is a customer in Spain who has no orders, so that customer's data did not appear in the Example 3-9 results. If we wish to include all customers in Spain in the results, regardless of whether they have placed orders or not, we need to use an *outer join* (also called an *inclusive* join). An outer join returns all rows from one (or both) of the tables, regardless of whether matching rows are found in the joined tables. Any data to be displayed from the table where no matching row is found is set to NULL in the query results. For example, for the customer who has no orders, all the columns from the Orders table would display as NULL in the results. Keep in mind that the returned data rows are still filtered by other search criteria (for example, only customers from Spain; only orders with dates greater than 1/1/98), but whether the filtering occurs before, during, or after the join operation is immaterial, so long as the unwanted rows are eliminated from the query results. Remember, we only describe the result we want, not how to achieve it. There are three types of outer joins, and unfortunately, the industry has settled on potentially confusing names for them:

- **Left Outer Join**   An outer join for which all rows are returned from the left-hand table in the join, and data from any matching rows found in the right-hand table is also returned.

- **Right Outer Join**   An outer join for which all the rows are returned from the right-hand table in the join, and data from any matching rows found in the left-hand table is also returned.

- **Full Outer Join**   An outer join for which all rows are returned from both tables, regardless of whether matching data is found between them. Microsoft Access does not currently support this type of join.

The confusion comes from the use of *left* and *right* in the names of the join types. All you have to do is reverse the order of the tables in any existing query, and you are essentially switching it from a left outer join to a right outer join, or vice versa. However, Microsoft Access does not make this distinction, so all its joins are simply called *outer joins*.

To change Example 3-9 into an outer join, double-click the thin part of the line between the two tables. This displays the Join Properties dialog box, shown in Figure 3-18. As with the Relationships panel, it can be tricky getting the cursor in exactly the right place on the line, but practice and a bit of patience always prevails. Note that the look of this panel has changed in newer versions of Microsoft Access.

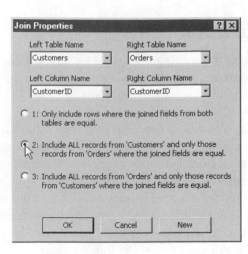

Figure 3-18   Join Properties dialog box

Here are the steps to follow to complete this example:

1. Because we want all the rows from Customers regardless of what is or is not found in the Orders table, option 2 is the one we seek. Click it to select it and then click the OK button.

2. In the criteria for the OrderDate column, add **OR IS NULL** to the entry. If we fail to do so, we will not see rows in the results for any customers who have no orders. This is because outer joins set unmatched data to NULL, and because null values are not greater than 1/1/1998 (and in fact are not greater than, less than, or equal to *anything*), the criteria as written in Example 3-9 would eliminate the row we worked so hard to include.

The completed panel and query results are shown in Figure 3-19.

Comparing the query results in Figure 3-19 with the query results in Figure 3-17, note that there is one more row in Figure 3-19. This is customer FISSA, the one who has no orders in the Orders table. For this row, the Order Date, Shipped Date, and Freight columns are null.

An interesting feature of Microsoft Access is that it generates SQL statements for all database queries. And although Microsoft Access SQL does not conform to ANSI standards, the ability to try something on the Query Design View panel and see how that action translates into SQL can be a great learning tool. SQL is carefully presented in the next chapter; so don't be intimidated by your first look at it here. To see the SQL for the Example 3-10 query, click the small downward-pointing arrow on the toolbar, next to the icon for View, and select the SQL View option from the drop-down list, as shown in the panel at the top of Figure 3-20. Note that newer

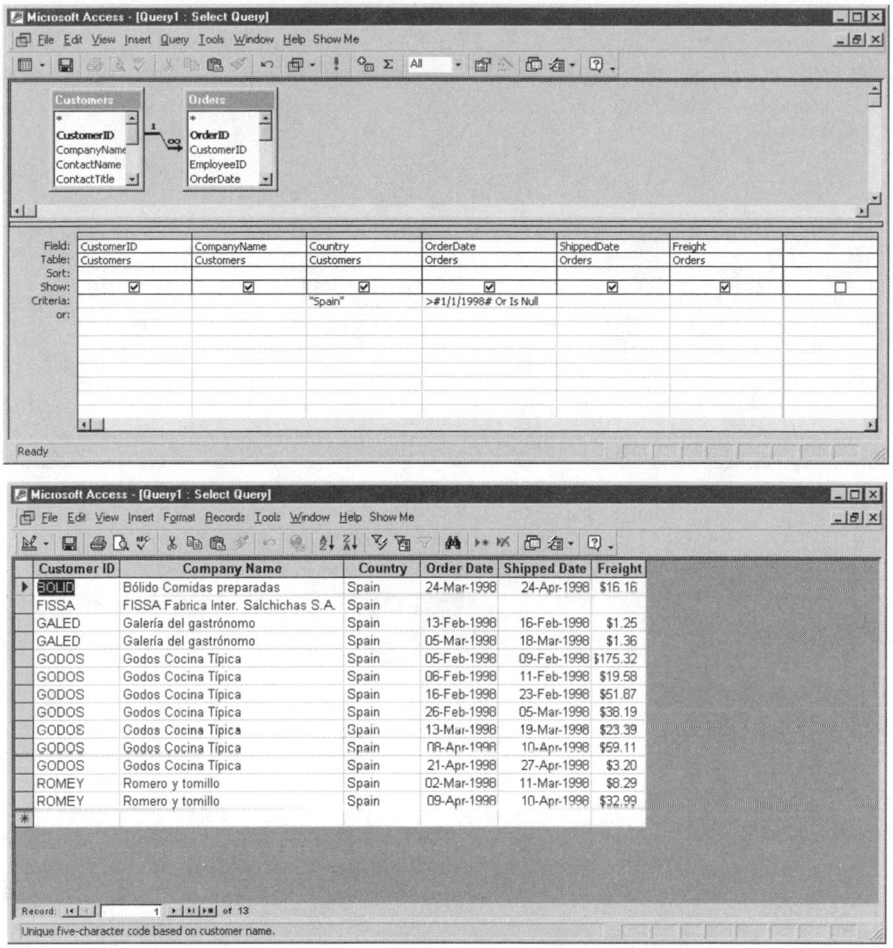

Figure 3-19   Example 3-10, "Outer Joins" (top) and the query results (bottom)

versions of Microsoft Access include additional options—PivotTable and PivotChart—in the drop-down menu. The generated SQL, as shown at the bottom of Figure 3-20, is displayed. You can even change the generated SQL and see the changes "reverse engineered" back into the Query Design View panel. This is an amazing product feature.

Example 3-11: Multiple Joins; Calculated Columns

When we need information from more than two tables in the same query result, we can simply add more tables, and therefore more join operations, to the query. The

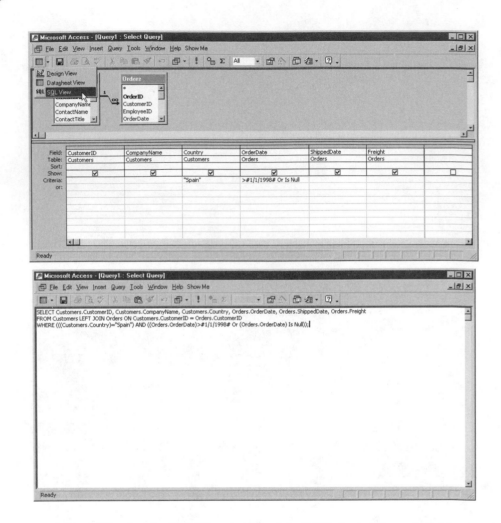

Figure 3-20 Selecting the SQL View (top), and the SQL view of Example 3-10

beauty of relational databases is that we need not be concerned with which join is best processed first and other such implementation details. We can just trust the RDBMS to make those decisions for us.

Let's consider another scenario: We want to know the total value in dollars of items ordered by our U.S. customers. Looking at the tables we have available, we realize that we need the Customers table, so we can filter by the Country column, and the Order Details table, because it contains the data we need to calculate the total value of each item ordered—namely, the quantity ordered and the unit price of each item. However, there is no way to directly join these tables in a meaningful way. If we look at the Relationships panel (refer to Figure 3-3), the solution becomes obvious: We need the Orders table. Then we can use the Customers table to find the U.S. customers, join those rows to the Orders table using CustomerID to find the orders for the U.S. customers, and finally join those rows to the Order Details table to find the line items on those orders. (Of course, there is no guarantee the RDBMS will actually process the joins in this sequence, but the end result will be the same regardless). It should be clear from this example that an overall diagram of all our tables and relationships is an *essential* document because it gives us the roadmap we need when forming queries.

This example also requires a *calculated column* (also called a *derived* column), which is formed by multiplying UnitPrice and Quantity. Just about any formula that you can use in a spreadsheet can be used in a relational database query.

Follow these steps to form the Example 3-11 query:

1. Create a new query using the Query Design View.

2. Add the tables Customers, Orders, and Order Details to the query.

3. From the Customers table, select the columns CompanyName and Country.

4. From the Order Details table, select the columns UnitPrice and Quantity.

5. To add the calculated column, enter the following into the Field line of the empty column to the right of the Quantity column: **ExtPrice: UnitPrice * Quantity**. The first part of the entry is a *label* for the new column. Every column in our results must have a unique name, and if we don't name it, Microsoft Access will. Default column names are usually not very meaningful and sometimes are just plain ugly, so it is best to *always* supply a column label (name) for calculated columns. Note that spaces in Field specifications do not matter, so we could have left them out. Chances are that Microsoft Access will rewrite your column specification by removing the spaces and placing square brackets around the column names, so don't be surprised if you see what you entered change on the panel after you move the cursor to another location on the panel.

6. To limit the query to only U.S. customers, enter **USA** in the Criteria line for the Country column.

7. Add an ascending sort to the CompanyName column.

The completed panel and query results are shown in Figure 3-21.

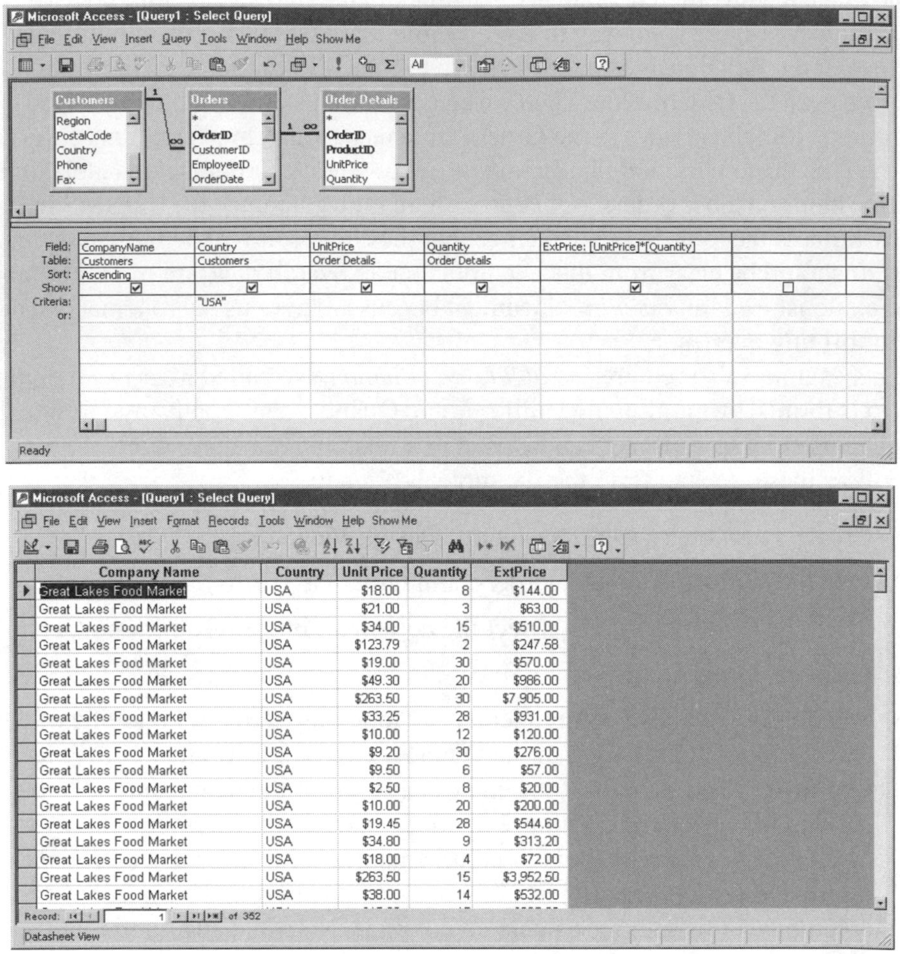

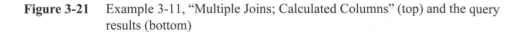

Figure 3-21   Example 3-11, "Multiple Joins; Calculated Columns" (top) and the query
results (bottom)

Example 3-12: Aggregate Functions

In reviewing the Example 3-11 results, you probably noticed that a lot of rows were
returned—352 to be exact (you may get a different number of rows if you use a version other than Microsoft Access 2000). Also, there are many rows for each customer. Not only do customers have many orders, but also each order can have many
rows. All the details are here, but at a glance, it is difficult to easily get a sense of the
total amount that each customer has ordered from Northwind. What we really need

to do is sum up the ExtPrice column for each customer. In relational databases, this is done with the SUM function.

A *function* is a special type of program that returns a single value each time it is invoked, named for the mathematical concept of a function. Because we will use the function to operate on a column, it will be invoked for each row and therefore return a single value for each row the query handles. Sometimes the term *column function* is used to remind us that the function is being applied to a table or view column. An example of an ordinary column function is ROUND, which can be used to round numbers in various ways. Special classes of functions that combine multiple rows together into one row are called *aggregate* functions. The following table shows aggregate functions that are commonly used in relational databases:

Function Name	Description
AVG	Calculates the average value for a column
COUNT	Counts the number of values found in a column
MAX	Finds the maximum value in a column
MIN	Finds the minimum value in a column
SUM	Sums (totals up) the values in a column

If we use an aggregate function by itself in a query, we get one row back for the entire query. This makes sense because there is no way for the RDBMS to know what other result we might want. So, if we want the aggregate result to be for *groups* of rows in the query, we need to include a GROUP BY specification to tell the RDBMS to group the rows by the values in one or more columns, and to apply the aggregate function to each group. This is much like asking for subtotals instead of a grand total for a list of numbers. For Example 3-12, we want the RDBMS to provide a total of the calculated column ExtPrice for each customer. In other words, we want to group the rows by customer, and for each group, display a single row containing the company name, country, and total order dollar amount.

The country is actually unnecessary because only U.S. customers are included in the query. However, it is left here to illustrate an important concept that most newcomers to relational databases have a difficult time understanding: If we select the CustomerName, Country, and calculated TotalOrders column, telling the RDBMS the formula for calculating the total orders and asking it to group the rows in the result by CustomerName, there is a hidden logic problem that will cause an error to be returned by the RDBMS. We have essentially asked it to return the value of Country for every row in the query, but to, at the same time, aggregate rows by CustomerName and provide the calculated total for each aggregate. It is illogical to ask for some rows to be aggregated and others not. To make matters worse, the resulting error message is rather cryptic. Small wonder that we often hear aggregate functions called "aggravating" functions. Remember this rule: Whenever a query includes an aggregate function, then *every* column in the query results must either be formed using an aggregate function or be named in the GROUP BY column list. In Microsoft Access, the Totals button on the toolbar toggles (hides and exposes) a line called Total on the Query View panel. It is the total line that permits us to specify aggregate functions and groupings for our query.

To create the Example 3-12 query from the Example 3-11 query, follow these steps:

1. Remove the UnitPrice and Quantity columns by clicking in the small gray rectangle above the field name and pressing DELETE.

2. Change the label on the ExtPrice column to TotalOrders. This column name will make more sense in the results.

3. Click the toolbar's Totals button (the one with the Greek letter Sigma on it) to expose the Total line in the query specification. By default, each column will initially have "Group By" specified on that line.

4. In the TotalOrders column, click in the Total line and use the pull-down menu to select the Sum function.

The completed panel and query results are shown in Figure 3-22.

Example 3-13: Self-Joins

When tables have a recursive relationship built in to them, we must use a *self-join* (joining a table to itself) in order to resolve the relationship. In the Employees table, the ReportsTo column is a foreign key to EmployeeID in the same table and shows the manager to whom each employee reports. We wish to list EmployeeID, FirstName, and LastName along with their manager's name. And, of course, there must be at least one employee in the table who has no manager listed, so we need this to be an outer join if all employees in the table are to appear in the results.

Follow these steps to create the query for Example 3-13:

1. Create a new query using the Create Query in Design View shortcut.

2. Using the Show Table dialog box, add the Employees table to the query *twice*. Notice that the second "copy" of the table will be automatically given a different name by Microsoft Access, usually Employees_1. Click Close when you are ready to proceed.

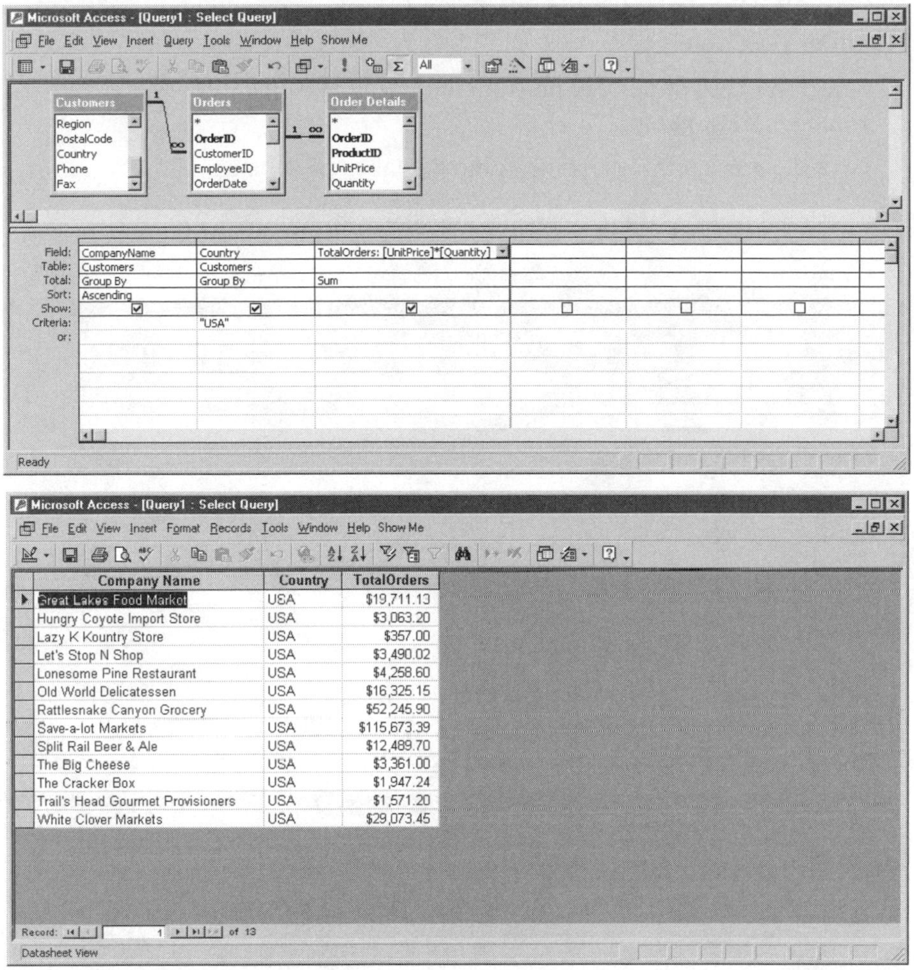

Figure 3-22 Example 3-12, "Aggregate Functions" (top), and the query results (bottom)

3. Microsoft Access is not going to know how to join this table to itself, so we must tell it which foreign key column matches the primary key. Drag the ReportsTo column from Employees and drop it on EmployeeID in the Employees_1 table. Microsoft Access will create a line, but it won't look exactly like the ones you have seen before because this one is a manual join rather than an inherited relationship.

4. To make the join an outer join, click the join line somewhere in the middle (on the thin and slanted part) and select option 2.

5. Select the EmployeeID, FirstName, and LastName columns from the Employees table.

6. Select the LastName column from the Employees_1 table. This is the *manager's* last name.

7. Give the manager's last name column a label of "Manager."

The completed panel and query results are shown in Figure 3-23.

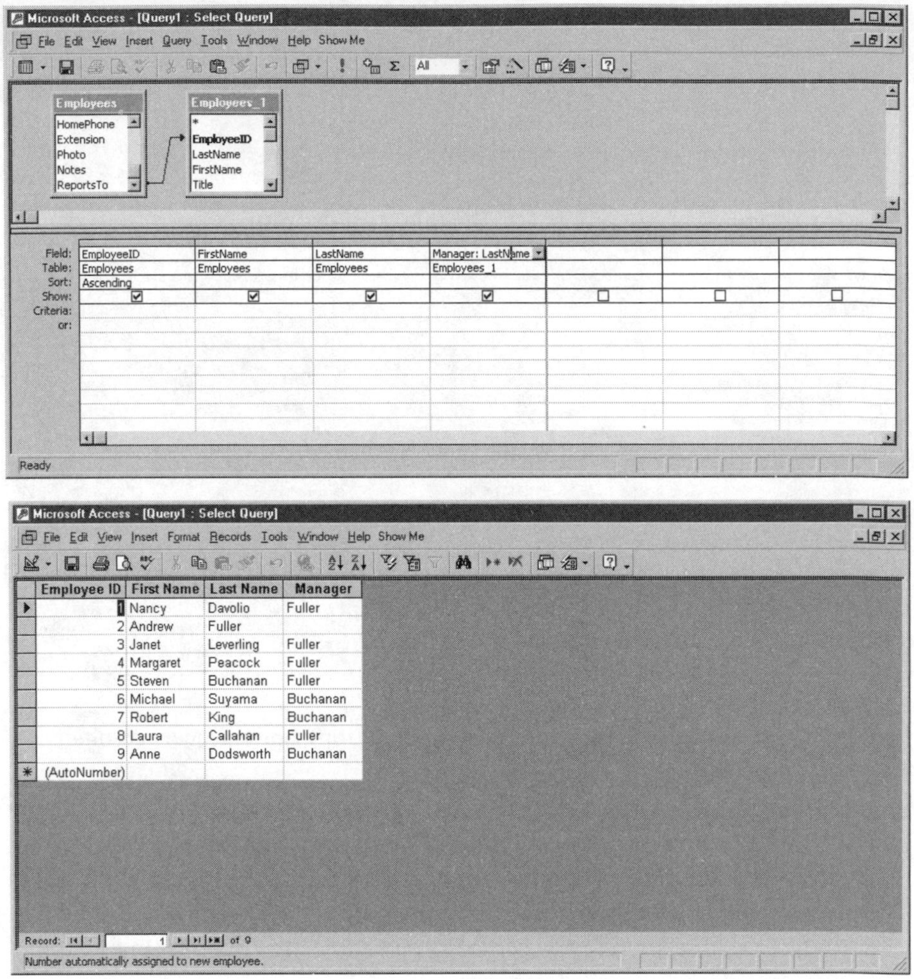

Figure 3-23   Example 3-13, "Self-Joins" (top), and the query results (bottom)

Hopefully, you have enjoyed this introduction to Microsoft Access queries. We have only scratched the surface in these examples, and there is much more to be learned from experience and experimentation. For example, once a query is saved in the Microsoft Access database, it can be included in other queries. There is no firm limit to how many levels of abstraction you can build using this method, and you will find that breaking queries into parts helps simplify the most complex ones you will encounter.

Quiz

Choose the correct responses to each of the multiple-choice questions. Note that there may be more than one correct response to each question.

1. A forms-based query language:
   a. Was first developed by IBM in the 1980s
   b. Describes how a query should be processed rather than what the results should be
   c. Resembles SQL
   d. Uses a GUI (graphical user interface)
   e. Was shown to be clearly superior in controlled studies

2. The object types in Microsoft Access that relate strictly to database management (as opposed to application development) are
   a. Tables
   b. Queries
   c. Views
   d. Forms
   e. Pages
   f. Macros
   g. Modules

3. When a table is deleted from the Microsoft Access Relationships panel:
   a. It is immediately deleted from the database.
   b. It is marked for deletion in the database.
   c. It remains in the database, but all data rows are deleted.
   d. Relationships belonging to the table are also deleted.
   e. It remains unchanged in the database and is merely removed from the Relationships panel.

4. Relationships on the Microsoft Access Relationships panel:
   a. Represent referential constraints in the database
   b. Are defined between primary keys and alternate keys

   c. Can never be recursive relationships

   d. Are inherited in queries as table joins

   e. Can be one-to-many, one-to-one, or many-to-many

5. The Microsoft Access Show Table dialog box:

   a. Lists all tables in the database and allows for the metadata about tables to be added, changed, and deleted

   b. Lists only tables stored in the database

   c. Lists tables and/or queries stored in the database

   d. Lists only queries stored the database

   e. Provides the ability to show (display) or hide (not display) tables

6. A column in the results of a Microsoft Access query can be formed from:

   a. A table column

   b. A view column

   c. A constant

   d. A calculation

   e. Anything for which a formula may be composed

7. When a query with no criteria included is executed, the result is

   a. An error message

   b. No rows being displayed

   c. All the rows in the table being displayed

   d. A Cartesian product

   e. None of the above

8. When sequencing (sorting) of rows is not included in a database query, the rows returned by the query are in:

   a. No particular sequence

   b. The order in which the rows were added to the table(s)

   c. Primary key sequence

   d. Ascending sequence by the first column in the results

   e. Ascending sequence by the first index on the table(s)

9. In a query, the search criteria REGION NOT = "CA" OR REGION NOT = "NV" will display

   a. An error message

   b. All the rows in the table

   c. Only the rows where Region is equal to "CA" or "NV"

   d. All the rows in the table except those where the Region is "CA" or "NV"

   e. No rows

10. Criteria in a Microsoft Access query are
    a. Connected with a logical AND if they are on the same line
    b. Connected with a logical OR if they are on the same line
    c. Connected with a logical AND if they are in the same field's column
    d. Connected with a logical OR if they are in the same field's column
    e. Connect by a logical AND within the same row and each line's criteria is connected with the other lines using a logical OR

11. The join connector between tables in a Microsoft Access query:
    a. May be manually created by dragging a column from one table or view to a column of another table or view
    b. May be inherited from the metadata defined on the Relationships panel
    c. May be altered to define left, right, and full outer joins
    d. Can cause a Cartesian product if defined incorrectly
    e. Will cause a Cartesian product if not defined between two tables or views in the query

12. When an outer join is used, column data from tables (or views) where no matching rows were found:
    a. Displays as zero for numeric column types
    b. Displays as blank for character column types
    c. Displays in gray
    d. Displays the text "NULL"
    e. Is set to the NULL value

13. An aggregate function:
    a. Combines data from multiple columns together
    b. Combines data from multiple rows together
    c. May be applied to table columns but not to calculated columns
    d. Is a special type of database query function
    e. Requires that every column in a query be either an aggregate function or named in the GROUP BY list for the query

14 Common aggregate functions include
    a. AVG
    b. COUNT
    c. ROUND
    d. SUM
    e. MIX

15. Self-joins:
    a. Can never produce a Cartesian product because the two data sources come from the same table
    b. Always produce a Cartesian product

   c. Are a method of resolving a recursive relationship
   d. Is the name given to any join that is manually created in
      Microsoft Access
   e. Involve joining a table to itself

16. The column name of a calculated column in the query results:
   a. Is NULL if not provided in the query definition
   b. Is automatically assigned by Microsoft Access if not provided in
      the query definition
   c. Is the first column name used in the formula if not provided in the
      query definition
   d. May be supplied using a label that appears first in the field definition
   e. May be supplied using a label that appears last in the field definition

17. Tables may be joined:
   a. Using only the primary key in one table and a foreign key in another
   b. Using any column in either table (theoretically)
   c. Only to themselves
   d. Only to other tables
   e. Only using the Cartesian product formula

18. Microsoft Access queries:
   a. Are called *views* in most other relational databases
   b. Are called *entities* in most other relational databases
   c. May be stored in the database for subsequent reuse
   d. Are highly flexible commands for retrieval of database data
   e. Provide a way to generate SQL statements

19. When a column is deleted from a Microsoft Access query:
   a. The column is only removed from the current query.
   b. The column is removed from all queries that reference it.
   c. The column is removed from the table and all queries that reference it.
   d. An error message is displayed if the column is used in any other queries.
   e. The column remains in the query but is marked so the column data will
      not be displayed in the query results.

20. A Cartesian product:
   a. Results when a join between two tables in a query is not defined
   b. Results when a join between two tables in a query is incorrectly defined
   c. Results whenever a table is joined to itself
   d. Results when each row in one table is joined to every row in another
   e. Can never happen in a Microsoft Access query

4

Introduction to SQL

This chapter introduces SQL, which has become the universal language for relational databases in that nearly every DBMS in modern use supports it. The reason for this wide acceptance is clearly the time and effort that went into the development of language features and standards, making SQL highly portable across different RDBMS products.

Oracle and its sample HR (Human Resources) schema are used to demonstrate SQL in this chapter. A free trial version of Oracle Personal Edition can be downloaded from http://otn.oracle.com, which includes the sample schemas. Except as noted in the examples, every command and feature demonstrated meets current SQL standards and therefore should work correctly in any DBMS that supports SQL. However, without the Oracle HR sample schema, you will have to create sample tables like the ones Oracle provides in order to run the exact statements included in this chapter. By convention, all the SQL statements are shown in uppercase. However, Oracle is not case sensitive for either SQL commands or database object names, so you may type the commands in upper-, lower-, or mixed case as you follow along on your own computer. But do keep in mind that data in Oracle *is* case sensitive, so whenever you type a data value that is to be stored in the database or is to be used to find data in the database, you must type it in the proper case.

As stated in the previous chapter, SQL is a command-based language. SQL statements are formed in clauses using keywords and parameters. The keywords used are usually reserved words for the DBMS, meaning they cannot be used for the names of database objects. The clauses usually have to be in a prescribed sequence. SQL statements must end with a semicolon (;). Although some RDBMSs are more forgiving, Oracle will not run an SQL statement unless it ends with a semicolon or a slash (the slash being an Oracle extension to the standard). Beyond those restrictions, the language is freeform, with one or more spaces separating language elements, and line breaks permitted between any two elements (but not in the middle of elements). SQL statements may be divided into the following categories:

- **Data Query Language (DQL)** Statements that query the database but do not alter any data or database objects. This category contains the SELECT statement. Not all vendors make a distinction here; many lump DQL into DML, as defined next.
- **Data Manipulation Language (DML)** Statements that modify data stored in database objects (that is, tables). This category contains the INSERT, UPDATE, and DELETE statements.
- **Data Definition Language (DDL)** Statements that create and modify database objects. Whereas DML and DQL work with the data in the database objects, DDL works with the database objects themselves. Said another way, DDL manages the data *containers* whereas DML manages the data *inside* the containers. This category includes the CREATE, ALTER and DROP statements.
- **Data Control Language (DCL)** Statements that manage privileges that database users have regarding the database objects. This category includes the GRANT and REVOKE statements.

Representative statements in each of these categories are presented in the sections that follow. But first, we'll cover a little bit of the history of the language.

The History of SQL

The forerunner of SQL, which was called QUEL, first emerged in the specifications for System/R, IBM's experimental relational database, in the late 1970s. However, two other products, with various names for their query language, beat IBM to the marketplace with the first commercial relational database products: Relational Software's Oracle and Relational Technology's INGRES. IBM released SQL/DS in 1982, with the query language now named SQL (System Query Language). When IBM released its next generation RDBMS, called DB2, the SQL acronym remained, but the language name had morphed into Structured Query Language. The name change was likely the result of marketing spin—*structured programming* was the mantra of the day, and although SQL has nothing to do with programming, structured or otherwise, anything with the word *structured* in its title got more attention in the marketplace.

SQL standards committees were formed by ANSI (American National Standards Institute) in 1986 and ISO (International Organization for Standardization) in 1987. Two years later, the first standard specification, known as SQL-89, was published. The standard was expanded three years later into SQL-92, which weighed in at roughly 600 pages. The third generation was called SQL-99, or SQL3. Most RDBMS products are built to the SQL-92 (now called SQL2) standard. SQL3 includes many of the object features required for SQL to operate on an object-relational database, as well as language extensions to make SQL computationally complete (adding looping, branching, and case constructs). Only a few vendors have implemented significant components of the SQL3 standard—Oracle being one of them.

Nearly every vendor has added extensions to SQL, partly because they wanted to differentiate their products, and partly because market demands pressed them into implementing features before there were standards for them. One case in point is support for the DATE and TIMESTAMP data types. Dates are highly important in business data processing, but the developers of the original RDBMS products were computer scientists and academics, not business computing specialists, so such a need was unanticipated. As a result, the early SQL dialects did not have any special support for dates. As commercial products emerged, vendors responded to pressure from their biggest customers by hurriedly adding support for dates. Unfortunately, this led to each doing so in their own way. Whenever you migrate SQL statements from one vendor to another, beware of the SQL dialect differences. SQL is highly compatible and portable across vendor products, but complete database systems can seldom be moved without some adjustments.

Getting Started with Oracle SQL

Oracle provides two different client tools for managing the formation and execution of SQL statements and the presentation of results: SQL Plus and the SQL Plus Worksheet. We call these *client* tools because they normally run on the database user's workstation and are capable of connecting remotely to databases that run on other computer systems, which are often shared servers. It is not unusual for the client tools to also be installed on the server alongside the database for easy administration, allowing the DBA logged in to the server to access the database without the need for a client workstation. Also available are the Personal and Lite editions of Oracle, where the database itself, along with the client tools, is installed on an individual user's workstation or handheld device.

The examples in this chapter focus on Oracle. However, if you are using a different RDBMS, there will be client tools for it as well, usually provided by the RDBMS vendor. For example, Sybase has a tool called iSQL, whereas Microsoft SQL Server has the GUI tools Enterprise Manager and Query Analyzer as well as a similar implementation of iSQL. Regardless of the RDBMS you are using, you may require the assistance of a DBA or system administrator in properly setting up a database account so you may access a database and run the various SQL statements demonstrated in this chapter. If you have no commercial RDBMS products available to you, several notable freeware products, such as MySQL and PostgreSQL (a derivative of INGRES), are also available. These provide reasonable implementations of many features of the SQL language.

Oracle's SQL Plus has a GUI version, which runs on Windows platforms, and a command-line version, which runs on all the platforms Oracle supports. You may start the GUI version of SQL Plus from the Windows Start menu by choosing Start | Programs | Oracle - *OraHome92* | Application Development | SQL Plus. In this example, *OraHome92* is the name of the Oracle Home on the client workstation. This value will vary from one workstation to another.

Once started, SQL Plus provides a Log On window that prompts for the username, password, and host string to be used to connect to the database. For the Oracle HR sample schema, enter **HR** into the Username field and then supply the password and host string you obtained from your DBA. The host string helps SQL Plus find the database if it is running on a remote computer system; it is normally not needed if you are running SQL Plus on the same computer that is running the database. After SQL Plus has connected to the database, a window similar to the one shown here is displayed.

Note that if you installed Oracle yourself, the demonstration accounts, such as HR, are usually locked during the installation as a security precaution. You will have to connect to the database as the SYSTEM user and do the following:

1. Unlock the HR database user account with this SQL command:

```
ALTER USER HR ACCOUNT UNLOCK;
```

2. Change the HR database user password with this SQL command (the password has been set to HRPASS here, but you may use any password you wish):

```
ALTER USER HR IDENTIFIED BY HRPASS;
```

SQL statements and SQL Plus commands may be entered at the SQL> prompt. Results display after each command, and the screen scrolls as needed. SQL Plus commands help configure SQL Plus, such as setting the width of lines on the screen and the number of lines displayed per page of output. Other SQL Plus commands control the format of the output of SQL statements, such as setting page titles, formatting columns, and adding subtotals to reports. SQL Plus commands are beyond the scope of this book, but they may be found in the *SQL Plus User's Guide and Reference* manual available (along with most other Oracle manuals) on the Oracle Technology Network website (http://otn.oracle.com).

One very useful SQL Plus command we will look at, however, is the DESCRIBE command (abbreviated DESCR or DESC). This command lists all the columns in a table or view along with the data type for each. Figure 4-1 shows the output of the DESCRIBE command for the EMPLOYEES table.

One of the common difficulties database users have with SQL Plus is that lines that are too long to display wrap to new lines. Another is that the SQL statements scroll off the screen when the results are displayed. Figure 4-2 provides an example of these issues.

SQL Plus may be run from the Windows Command Shell using the following command:

```
C:\>sqlplus hr/hrpass
```

When run this way, SQL Plus has all the same capabilities as the Windows GUI version of SQL Plus, but is perhaps not as visually pleasing. In fact, it is exactly the same utility program with only the user interface changed. An example of a command run from the Windows Command Shell version of SQL Plus is shown in Figure 4-3. This screen is quite similar to the one used when SQL Plus is run on other platforms such as VMS VAX, Unix, and Linux.

Recognizing the need for a better user interface, Oracle developed SQL Plus Worksheet as part of Oracle Enterprise Manager and started shipping it with

```
Oracle SQL*Plus                                                         _ □ ×
File  Edit  Search  Options  Help

SQL*Plus: Release 9.2.0.1.0 - Production on Sat Oct 11 11:30:48 2003

Copyright (c) 1982, 2002, Oracle Corporation.  All rights reserved.


Connected to:
Personal Oracle9i Release 9.2.0.1.0 - Production
With the Partitioning, OLAP and Oracle Data Mining options
JServer Release 9.2.0.1.0 - Production

SQL> descr employees
 Name                                      Null?    Type
 ----------------------------------------- -------- --------------------------
 EMPLOYEE_ID                               NOT NULL NUMBER(6)
 FIRST_NAME                                         VARCHAR2(20)
 LAST_NAME                                 NOT NULL VARCHAR2(25)
 EMAIL                                     NOT NULL VARCHAR2(25)
 PHONE_NUMBER                                       VARCHAR2(20)
 HIRE_DATE                                 NOT NULL DATE
 JOB_ID                                    NOT NULL VARCHAR2(10)
 SALARY                                             NUMBER(8,2)
 COMMISSION_PCT                                     NUMBER(2,2)
 MANAGER_ID                                         NUMBER(6)
 DEPARTMENT_ID                                      NUMBER(4)

SQL>
```

Figure 4-1   DESCRIBE command output for the EMPLOYEES table

```
Oracle SQL*Plus                                                         _ □ ×
File  Edit  Search  Options  Help
SQL> select * from employees;

EMPLOYEE_ID FIRST_NAME           LAST_NAME
----------- -------------------- -------------------------
EMAIL                     PHONE_NUMBER         HIRE_DATE JOB_ID        SALAR'
------------------------- -------------------- --------- ---------- ----------
COMMISSION_PCT MANAGER_ID DEPARTMENT_ID
-------------- ---------- -------------
        100 Steven               King
SKING                     515.123.4567         17-JUN-87 AD_PRES        2400(
                                        90

        101 Neena                Kochhar
NKOCHHAR                  515.123.4568         21-SEP-89 AD_VP          1700(
                      100             90

EMPLOYEE_ID FIRST_NAME           LAST_NAME
----------- -------------------- -------------------------
EMAIL                     PHONE_NUMBER         HIRE_DATE JOB_ID        SALAR'
------------------------- -------------------- --------- ---------- ----------
COMMISSION_PCT MANAGER_ID DEPARTMENT_ID
-------------- ---------- -------------
        102 Lex                  De Haan
LDEHAAN                   515.123.4569         13-JAN-93 AD_VP          1700(
                      100             90
```

Figure 4-2   SQL Plus window with wrapped lines

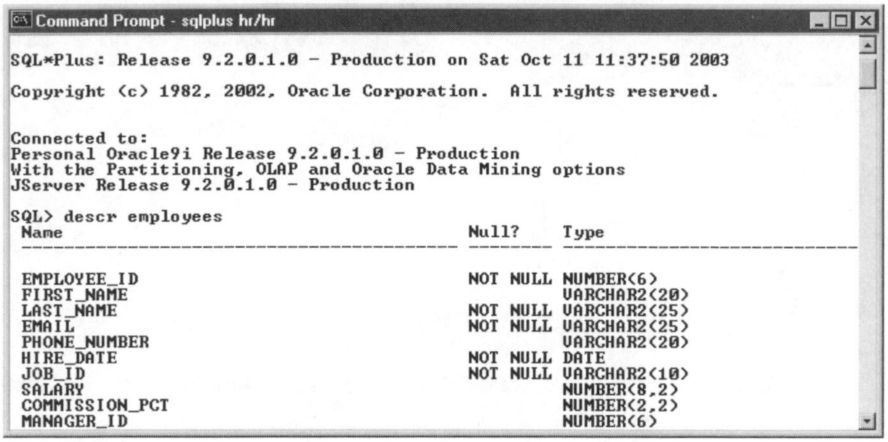
Command Prompt - sqlplus hr/hr
SQL*Plus: Release 9.2.0.1.0 - Production on Sat Oct 11 11:37:50 2003
Copyright (c) 1982, 2002, Oracle Corporation. All rights reserved.
Connected to:
Personal Oracle9i Release 9.2.0.1.0 - Production
With the Partitioning, OLAP and Oracle Data Mining options
JServer Release 9.2.0.1.0 - Production
SQL> descr employees
Name Null? Type
EMPLOYEE_ID NOT NULL NUMBER(6)
FIRST_NAME VARCHAR2(20)
LAST_NAME NOT NULL VARCHAR2(25)
EMAIL NOT NULL VARCHAR2(25)
PHONE_NUMBER VARCHAR2(20)
HIRE_DATE NOT NULL DATE
JOB_ID NOT NULL VARCHAR2(10)
SALARY NUMBER(8,2)
COMMISSION_PCT NUMBER(2,2)
MANAGER_ID NUMBER(6)

Figure 4-3 SQL Plus window, command-line version

Oracle8*i*. When SQL Plus Worksheet is started from the Windows Start menu, the login window appears, as shown here:

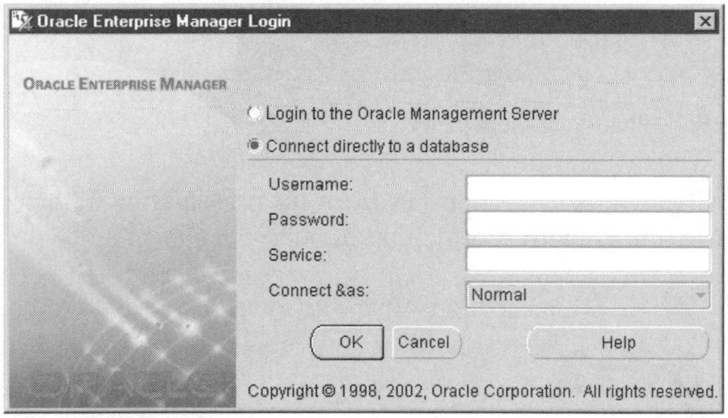
Oracle Enterprise Manager Login
ORACLE ENTERPRISE MANAGER
Login to the Oracle Management Server
Connect directly to a database
Username:
Password:
Service:
Connect &as:
Normal
OK
Cancel
Help
Copyright © 1998, 2002, Oracle Corporation. All rights reserved.

The Username and Password fields should be familiar from the SQL Plus discussion, and the Connect String field from SQL Plus is now called Service instead. The Connect As field is for use by DBAs who require a special *role* (a named set of privileges) when they connect.

Once connected, the SQL Plus Worksheet panel appears, as shown in Figure 4-4. SQL statements may be typed in the upper window, and the results are shown in the lower window. The icons in the toolbar at the top of the left margin provide various control functions, including disconnecting from the database, executing the current SQL statement, scrolling back and forth through a history of recent statements, and accessing the help facility.

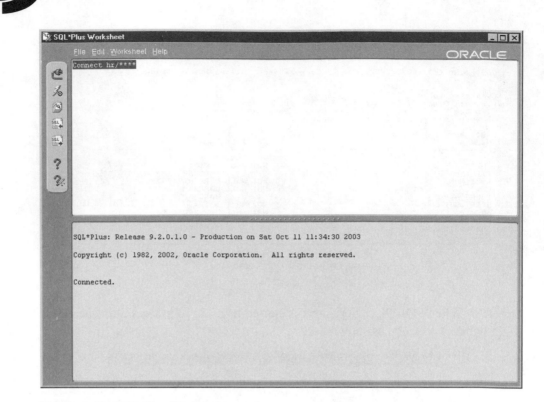

Figure 4-4   SQL Plus Worksheet panel

The SQL Plus Worksheet panel is used for the presentation of the examples that follow because of its superior formatting of query results.

Where's the Data?

You probably noticed that although SQL Plus and SQL Plus Worksheet help you format and run SQL statements, they don't provide an easy way for you to see the names and definitions of the database objects available to you. This is a typical arrangement for an RDBMS. If you are not familiar with the database schema you are using, you can obtain some basic information in one of two ways: through catalog views or a tool such as the Oracle Enterprise Manager. *Catalog views* are special views provided by the RDBMS that present database metadata that documents the database contents.

Finding Database Objects Using Catalog Views

Oracle provides a comprehensive set of catalog views that may be queried to show the names and definitions of all database objects available to a database user. Most other RDBMSs have a similar capability, but of course the names of the views vary. By issuing a SELECT statement against any of these views, you may display information about your database objects. Consult the *Oracle Server Reference* manual (available from Oracle Technology Network website) for complete information on the available catalog views. Here are two of the most useful ones:

- **USER_TABLES**   Contains one row of information for each table in the user schema. This view contains a lot of columns, but the one of most interest, TABLE_NAME, is the first column in the view. Once you know the table names, the DESCRIBE command (already introduced) can be used on each to show more information about the table definitions. Figure 4-5 shows an example of selecting everything from the USER_TABLES view.

  The SQL SELECT statement, shown in Figure 4-5, is described in more detail a little further along in this chapter.

- **USER_VIEWS**   Contains one row of information for each view in the user schema, containing, among other things, the name of the view and the text of the SQL statement that forms the view.

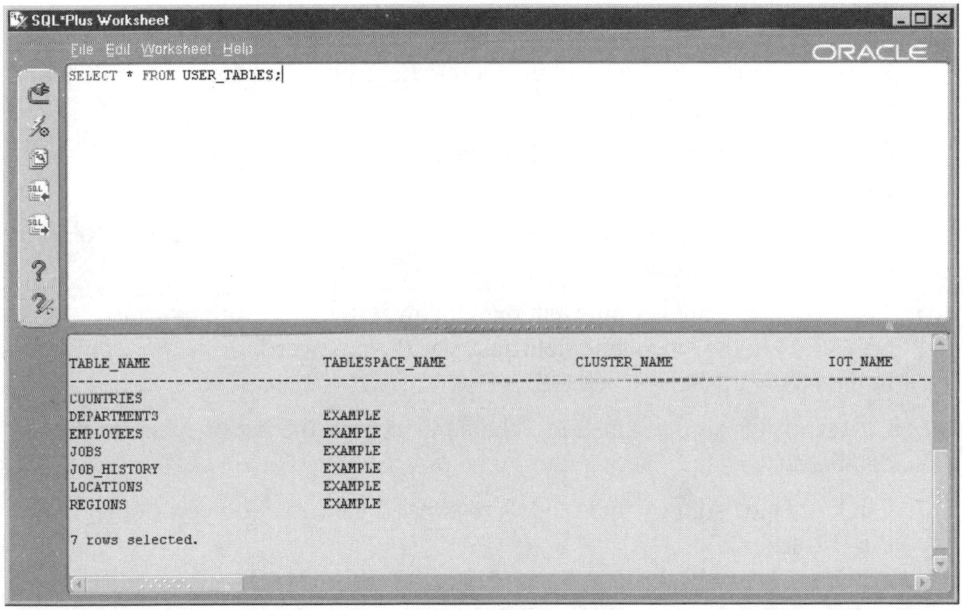

Figure 4-5   Selecting from the USER_TABLES view

Viewing Database Objects Using Oracle Enterprise Manager

For those less inclined to type SQL commands, Oracle provides a GUI tool known as Oracle Enterprise Manager (OEM). Other RDBMS vendors provide similar tools, such as the Enterprise Manager tool that comes with Sybase and Microsoft SQL Server.

The Oracle Enterprise Manager Console can be started from the Windows Start menu, by choosing Start | Programs | Oracle - *OraHome92* | Enterprise Manager Console.

Once started, OEM presents a window asking whether it should be launched in standalone mode or if instead you wish to log in to the Oracle management server. Unless directed otherwise by your DBA, you should always launch OEM in standalone mode. Next, the Oracle Enterprise Manager login window will be displayed, as already shown in a previous illustration. For OEM to work perfectly, you should connect to the database as the SYSTEM user. However, if you are working on an employer's database system, your DBA may not be very interested in handing over the keys to the database to a beginner, so you may have to settle for signing in with the Oracle database username provided by the DBA. If you do so, some error messages related to privileges may appear, and some features may not work. Once connected to OEM, you will see a panel similar to the one in Figure 4-6.

Here are the exact steps to follow to get to the EMPLOYEES table as shown in Figure 4-6:

1. Start the OEM Console from the Start menu, as described earlier.

2. Select Launch Standalone on the Oracle Enterprise Manager Console login window and then click OK.

3. Click the plus sign (+) next to Databases in the left column to expand the list of databases.

4. Click the plus sign (+) next to the name of your Oracle database (ORA9I in this example) to expand the list of database object types.

5. The Database Connect Information window will appear. In this window, type **SYSTEM** in the Username field and type the password for the SYSTEM user in the Password field. Click OK.

6. Click the plus sign (+) next to Schema to expand the list of schemas in the database.

7. Click the plus sign (+) next to HR to expand the list of objects belonging to the HR schema.

8. Click the plus sign (+) next to Tables to expand the list of tables in the HR schema.

9. Click the EMPLOYEES table to display its description in the right panel.

OEM is so full of features that describing them in detail would take an entire book of at least this size. The feature you will be most interested in is the hierarchical tree of databases and database objects that appears in the column along the left margin of the panel. Expanding the Schema item shows all the schemas in the database (each Oracle database user gets their own schema). Expanding any schema shows the object types available in that schema. Expanding any object type (as we did with the Tables type) shows a list of objects of that type in the selected schema, and clicking or expanding any individual object shows more information about that object (as we did by clicking the EMPLOYEES table object).

You've seen a little bit of the SQL SELECT statement so far. In the next section we take a detailed look at SQL.

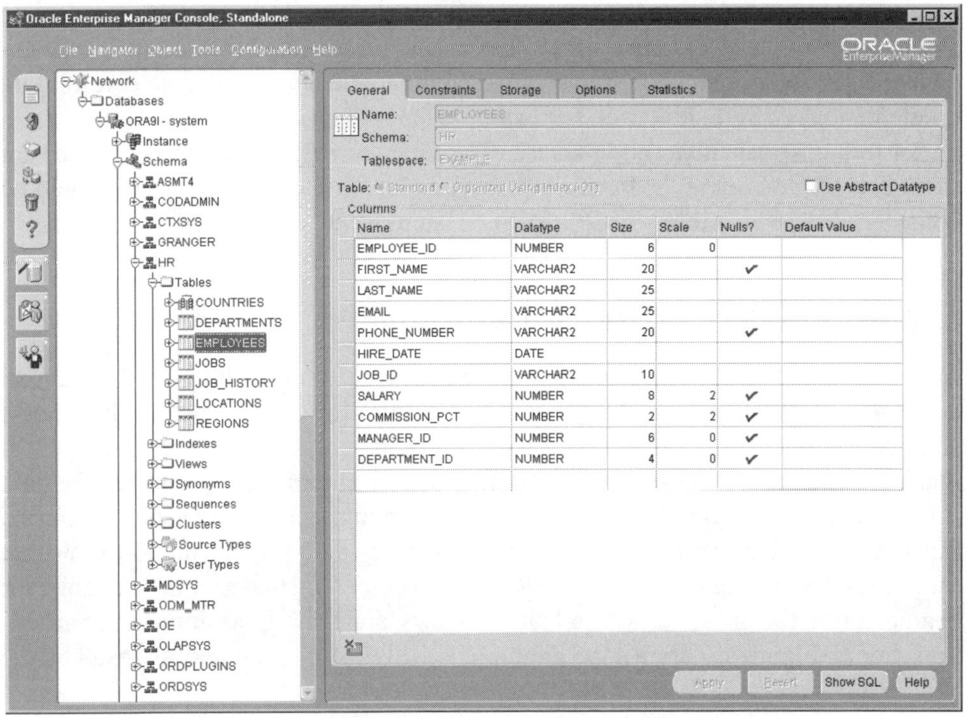

Figure 4-6   Oracle Enterprise Manager Console

Data Query Language (DQL): The SELECT Statement

The SELECT statement retrieves data from the database. The clauses of the statement, as demonstrated in the following sections, are as follows:

- **SELECT**   Lists the columns that are to be returned in the results
- **FROM**   Lists the tables or views from which data is to be selected
- **WHERE**   Provides conditions for the selection of rows in the results
- **ORDER BY**   Specifies the order in which rows are to be returned
- **GROUP BY**   Groups rows for various aggregate functions

Although it is customary in SQL to write keywords in upper case, this is not necessary in most implementations. The RDBMS SQL interpreter will usually recognize keywords written in upper, lower or mixed case. In Oracle SQL, all database object names (tables, views, synonyms, etc.) may be written in any case, but Oracle automatically changes them to upper case during processing because all Oracle database object names are stored in upper case in Oracle's metadata. Be careful with other versions of SQL, however. For example, both Sybase and MS SQL Server can be set to a case-sensitive mode where object names written in different cases are treated as *different* objects. In case-sensitive mode, the following names would be considered *different* tables: EMPLOYEES, Employees, employees.

Example 4-1: Listing All Employees

The asterisk (*) symbol may be used in place of a column list in order to select all columns in a table or view. This is a useful feature for quickly listing data, but it should be avoided in statements that will be reused because it compromises logical data independence because any new column will be automatically selected the next time the statement is run. Note also that in SQL syntax, tables, views, and *synonyms* (an alias for a table or view) are all referenced in the same way. It should follow that the names of these come for the same *namespace,* meaning that a name of a table, for example, must be unique among all tables, views, and synonyms defined in particular schema. Figure 4-7 shows the Example 4-1 SQL statement and its results.

Example 4-2: Limiting Columns to Display

To specify the columns to be selected, provide a comma-separated list following the SELECT keyword. Keep in mind that the list actually provides *expressions* that

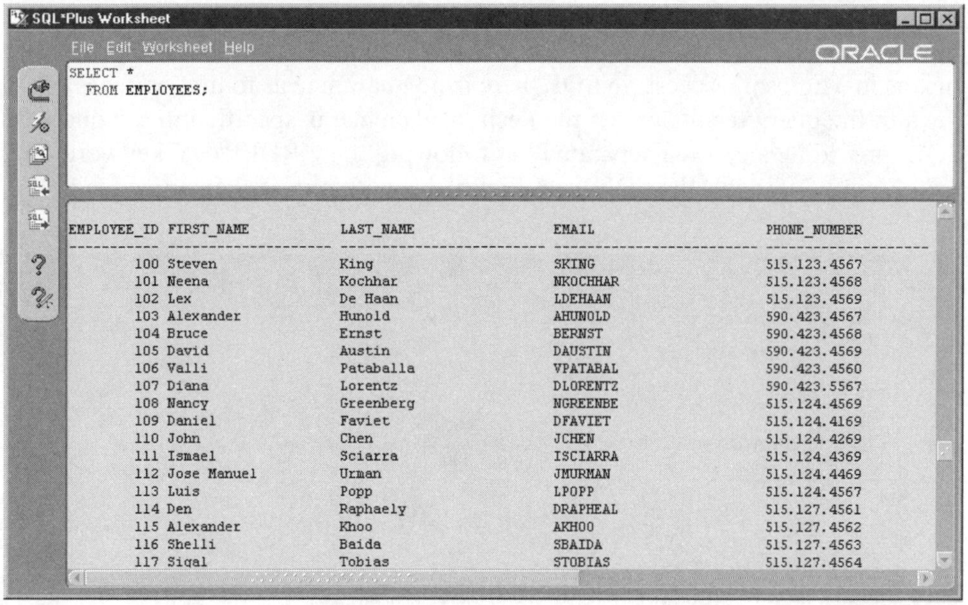


```
SELECT *
  FROM EMPLOYEES;
```

EMPLOYEE_ID	FIRST_NAME	LAST_NAME	EMAIL	PHONE_NUMBER
100	Steven	King	SKING	515.123.4567
101	Neena	Kochhar	NKOCHHAR	515.123.4568
102	Lex	De Haan	LDEHAAN	515.123.4569
103	Alexander	Hunold	AHUNOLD	590.423.4567
104	Bruce	Ernst	BERNST	590.423.4568
105	David	Austin	DAUSTIN	590.423.4569
106	Valli	Pataballa	VPATABAL	590.423.4560
107	Diana	Lorentz	DLORENTZ	590.423.5567
108	Nancy	Greenberg	NGREENBE	515.124.4569
109	Daniel	Faviet	DFAVIET	515.124.4169
110	John	Chen	JCHEN	515.124.4269
111	Ismael	Sciarra	ISCIARRA	515.124.4369
112	Jose Manuel	Urman	JMURMAN	515.124.4469
113	Luis	Popp	LPOPP	515.124.4567
114	Den	Raphaely	DRAPHEAL	515.127.4561
115	Alexander	Khoo	AKHOO	515.127.4562
116	Shelli	Baida	SBAIDA	515.127.4563
117	Sigal	Tobias	STOBIAS	515.127.4564

Figure 4-7 Example 4-1, "Listing All Employees"

describe the columns desired in the query results, and although many times these expressions are merely column names from tables or views, they may also be any constant or formula that SQL can interpret and form into data values for the column. The examples that follow show you how to use formulas and constants to form query columns. Figure 4-8 shows the SQL for selecting the LAST_NAME, FIRST_NAME, HIRE_DATE, and SALARY columns.

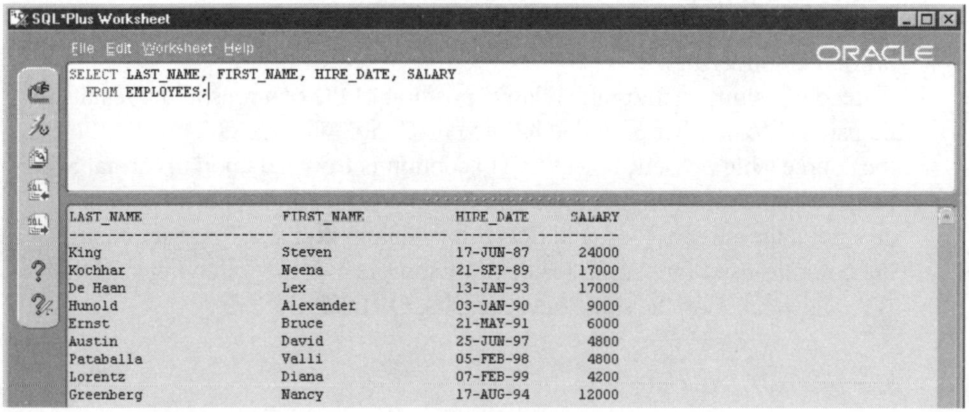


```
SELECT LAST_NAME, FIRST_NAME, HIRE_DATE, SALARY
  FROM EMPLOYEES;
```

LAST_NAME	FIRST_NAME	HIRE_DATE	SALARY
King	Steven	17-JUN-87	24000
Kochhar	Neena	21-SEP-89	17000
De Haan	Lex	13-JAN-93	17000
Hunold	Alexander	03-JAN-90	9000
Ernst	Bruce	21-MAY-91	6000
Austin	David	25-JUN-97	4800
Pataballa	Valli	05-FEB-98	4800
Lorentz	Diana	07-FEB-99	4200
Greenberg	Nancy	17-AUG-94	12000

Figure 4-8 Example 4-2, "Limiting Columns to Display"

Example 4-3: Sorting Results

Just as in Microsoft Access, in SQL there is no guarantee as to the sequence of the rows in the query results unless the desired sequence is specified in the query. In SQL, providing a comma-separated list following the ORDER BY keyword does this. Figure 4-9 shows the SQL from Figure 4-8 with row sequencing added.

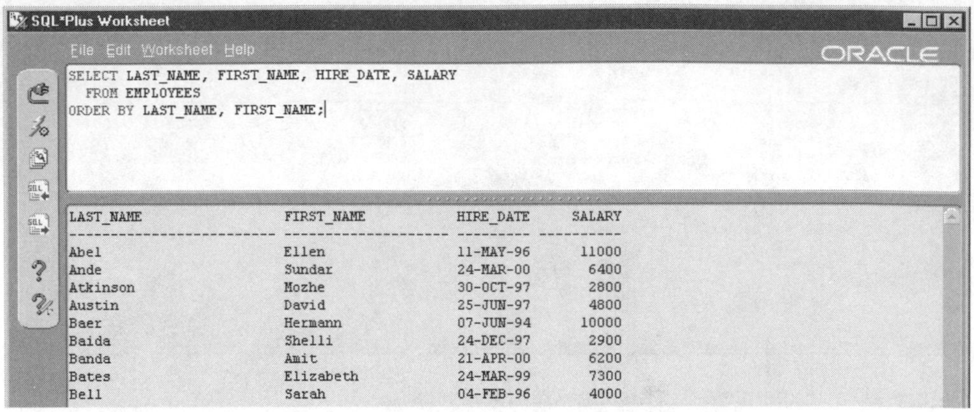

Figure 4-9   Example 4-3, "Sorting Results"

Also note the following points:

- Ascending sequence is the default for each column, but the keyword ASC may be added after the column name for ascending sequence, and DESC may be added for descending sequence.
- The column(s) named in the ORDER BY list do not have to be included in the query results (that is, the SELECT list). However, this is not the best human engineering.
- Instead of column names, the relative position of the columns in the results may be listed. The number provided has no correlation with the column position in the source table or view, however. This option is frowned upon in formal SQL because someone changing the query at a later time might shuffle columns around in the SELECT list and not realize that, in doing so, they are changing the columns used for sorting results. In Example 4-3, the following ORDER BY clause achieves the same query results: ORDER BY 1,2.

Choosing Rows to Display

SQL uses the WHERE clause for the selection of rows to display. Without a WHERE clause, all rows found in the source tables and/or views are displayed. When a WHERE clause is included, the rules of Boolean algebra, named for logician George Boole, are used to evaluate the WHERE clause for each row of data. Only rows for which the WHERE clause evaluates to a logical "true" are displayed in the query results.

As you will see in the examples that follow, individual tests of conditions must evaluate to either "true" or "false." The conditional operators supported are the same ones shown in Chapter 3 in Example 3-7 (=, <, <=, >, >=, and <>). If multiple conditions are tested in a single WHERE clause, the outcomes of these conditions can be combined together using logical operators such as AND, OR, and NOT. Parentheses may be (and should be) added to complex statements for clarity and to control the order in which the conditions are evaluated. A rather complicated order of precedence is used when multiple logical operators appear in one statement. However, it is far simpler to remember that conditions inside a pair of parentheses are always evaluated first, and to simply include enough sets of parentheses so there can be no doubt as to the order in which the conditions are evaluated.

Example 4-4: A Simple WHERE Clause

Figure 4-10 shows a simple WHERE clause that selects only rows where SALARY is equal to 11000.

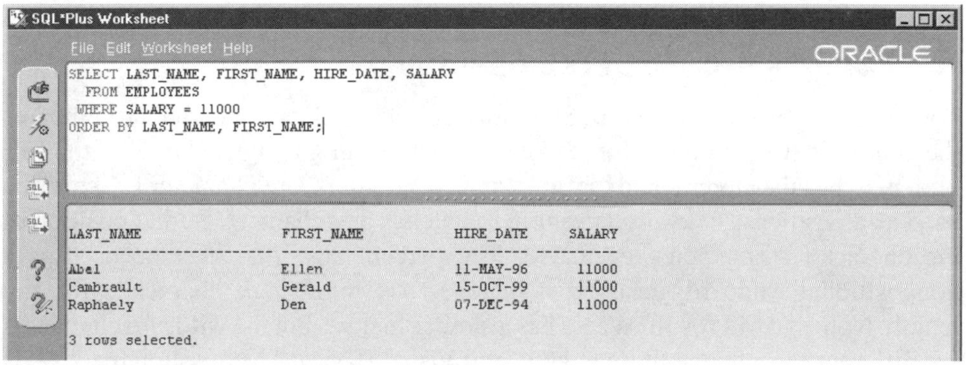

```
SELECT LAST_NAME, FIRST_NAME, HIRE_DATE, SALARY
  FROM EMPLOYEES
 WHERE SALARY = 11000
 ORDER BY LAST_NAME, FIRST_NAME;

LAST_NAME                FIRST_NAME            HIRE_DATE    SALARY
------------------------ --------------------- ---------    ----------
Abel                     Ellen                 11-MAY-96    11000
Cambrault                Gerald                15-OCT-99    11000
Raphaely                 Den                   07-DEC-94    11000

3 rows selected.
```

Figure 4-10   Example 4-4, "A Simple WHERE Clause"

Example 4-5: The BETWEEN Operator

SQL provides the BETWEEN operator to assist in finding ranges of values. The end points *are* included in the returned rows. Figure 4-11 shows the use of the BETWEEN operator to find all rows where SALARY is greater than or equal to 10000 and SALARY is less than or equal to 11000. Here's an alternative way to write the equivalent WHERE clause:

```
WHERE SALARY >= 10000
  AND SALARY <= 11000
```

```
SQL*Plus Worksheet                                                    _ □ ×
    File  Edit  Worksheet  Help                                    ORACLE
    SELECT LAST_NAME, FIRST_NAME, HIRE_DATE, SALARY
      FROM EMPLOYEES
     WHERE SALARY BETWEEN 10000 AND 11000
    ORDER BY LAST_NAME, FIRST_NAME;|


    LAST_NAME               FIRST_NAME             HIRE_DATE   SALARY
    ---------------------   --------------------   ---------   -------
    Abel                    Ellen                  11-MAY-96    11000
    Baer                    Hermann                07-JUN-94    10000
    Bloom                   Harrison               23-MAR-98    10000
    Cambrault               Gerald                 15-OCT-99    11000
    King                    Janette                30-JAN-96    10000
    Raphaely                Den                    07-DEC-94    11000
    Tucker                  Peter                  30-JAN-97    10000
    Vishney                 Clara                  11-NOV-97    10500
    Zlotkey                 Eleni                  29-JAN-00    10500

    9 rows selected.
```

Figure 4-11   Example 4-5, "The BETWEEN Operator"

Example 4-6: The LIKE Operator

For searching character columns, SQL provides the LIKE operator, which compares the character string in the column to a pattern, returning a logical "true" if the column matches the pattern, and "false" if not. The underscore character (_) may be used as a positional *wildcard,* meaning it matches any character in that position of the character string being evaluated. The percent sign (%) may be used as a nonpositional wildcard, meaning it matches any number of characters for any length. Note that Microsoft Access has a similar feature, but the wildcard characters are different (they match those in DOS and Visual Basic): The question mark (?) is the positional wildcard, and the asterisk (*) is the nonpositional wildcard. The following table provides some examples:

Pattern	Interpretation
%Now	Matches any character string that ends with "Now"
Now%	Matches any character string that begins with "Now"
%Now%	Matches any character string that contains "Now" (whether at the beginning, the end, or in the middle)
N_w	Matches any string of exactly three characters, where the first character is "N" and the third character is "w"
%N_w%	Matches any string that contains the character "N" followed by any character, which is in turn followed by the character "w" and continues with any number of characters

Figure 4-12 shows the use of the LIKE operator to display only rows where the FIRST_NAME column starts with the text "Pete".

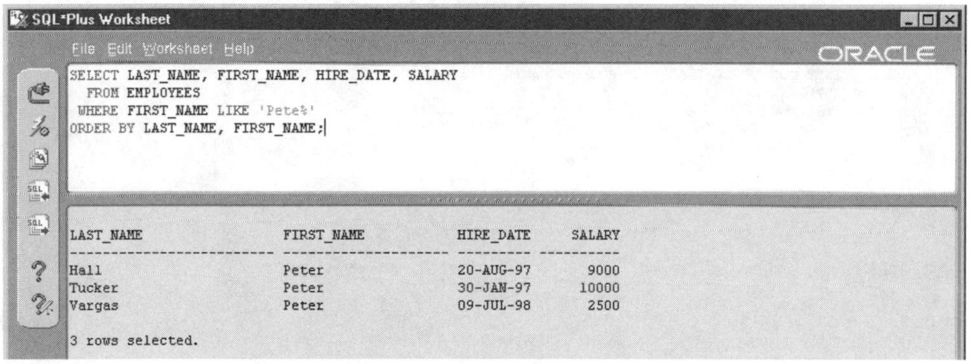

```
SQL*Plus Worksheet
File Edit Worksheet Help                                    ORACLE

SELECT LAST_NAME, FIRST_NAME, HIRE_DATE, SALARY
  FROM EMPLOYEES
  WHERE FIRST_NAME LIKE 'Pete%'
ORDER BY LAST_NAME, FIRST_NAME;


LAST_NAME                FIRST_NAME            HIRE_DATE   SALARY
------------------------ -------------------- --------- ----------
Hall                     Peter                20-AUG-97       9000
Tucker                   Peter                30-JAN-97      10000
Vargas                   Peter                09-JUL-98       2500

3 rows selected.
```

Figure 4-12 Example 4-6, "The LIKE Operator"

Example 4-7: Compound Conditions Using OR

As stated earlier, multiple conditions may be combined using the OR operator. Figure 4-13 shows a WHERE clause that selects rows having either a FIRST_NAME column beginning with "Pete" *or* a SALARY column that is between 10000 and 20000 inclusive.

Figure 4-14 changes the OR operator from Example 4-6 to the AND operator. Note that only one row is returned now because both conditions must be true for a row to appear in the query results.

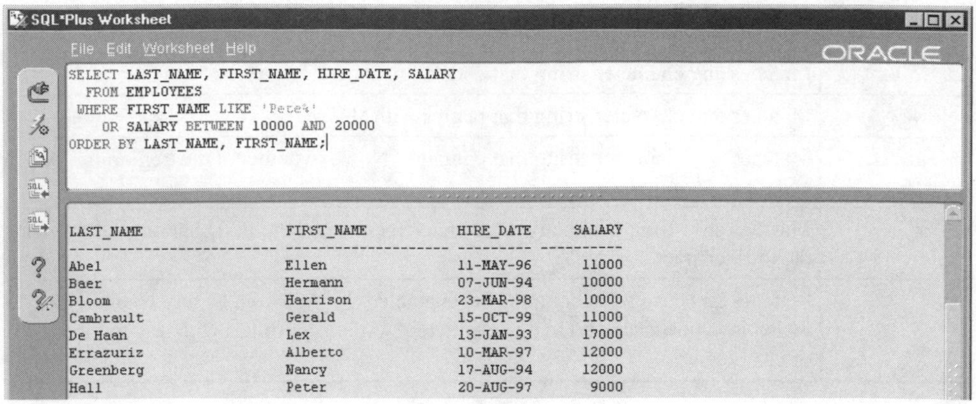

Figure 4-13 Example 4-7, "Compound Conditions Using OR"

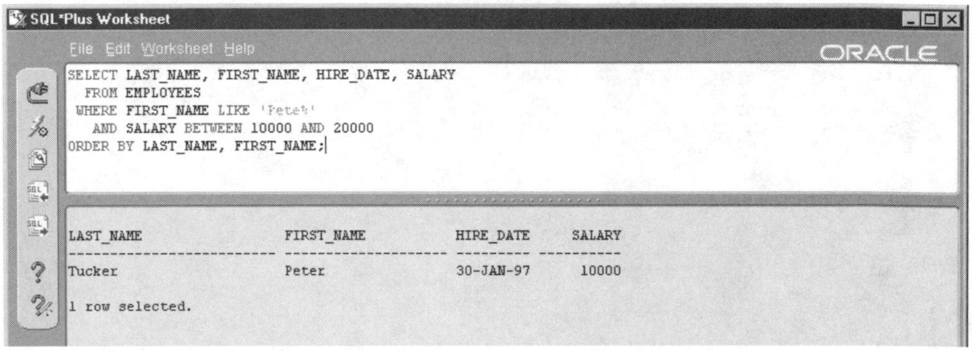

Figure 4-14 Example 4-7, "Compound Conditions Using AND"

Example 4-8: The Subselect

A very powerful feature of SQL is the *subselect* (or *subquery),* which, as the name implies, refers to a SELECT statement that contains a subordinate SELECT statement. This can be a very flexible way of selecting data.

Let's assume that we want to list all employees who work in sales. The dilemma is that the DEPARTMENTS table in the sample HR schema contains several sales departments, including Sales, Government Sales, and Retail Sales. We could place literals for those three department names or their corresponding department IDs in the WHERE clause of our SELECT statement. However, the problem we then face is maintenance of the query if a sales-related department is subsequently added or eliminated. A safer approach is to use an SQL query to find the applicable department IDs when the query is run and then use that list of IDs to find the employees. The query to find the department IDs is simple enough:

```
SELECT DEPARTMENT_ID        .
   FROM DEPARTMENTS
 WHERE DEPARTMENT_NAME LIKE '%Sales%';
```

If we place the preceding SELECT statement in the WHERE clause of a query that lists the employee information of interest, we arrive at the query shown in Figure 4-15. Note that SQL syntax requires the subselect to be enclosed in a pair of parentheses.

```
SELECT LAST_NAME, FIRST_NAME, HIRE_DATE, SALARY, DEPARTMENT_ID
   FROM EMPLOYEES
 WHERE DEPARTMENT_ID IN
       (SELECT DEPARTMENT_ID FROM DEPARTMENTS
          WHERE DEPARTMENT_NAME LIKE '%Sales%')
 ORDER BY LAST_NAME, FIRST_NAME;
```

LAST_NAME	FIRST_NAME	HIRE_DATE	SALARY	DEPARTMENT_ID
Abel	Ellen	11-MAY-96	11000	80
Ande	Sundar	24-MAR-00	6400	80
Banda	Amit	21-APR-00	6200	80
Bates	Elizabeth	24-MAR-99	7300	80
Bernstein	David	24-MAR-97	9500	80
Bloom	Harrison	23-MAR-98	10000	80
Cambrault	Gerald	15-OCT-99	11000	80
Cambrault	Nanette	09-DEC-98	7500	80

Figure 4-15   Example 4-8, "The Subselect"

The statement shown in Example 4-8 is known as a *noncorrelated* subselect because the inner SELECT (that is, the one inside the WHERE clause) can be run first and the results used when the outer SELECT is run. There also is such a thing as a *correlated* subselect (or subquery), where the outer query must be invoked multiple times, once for each row found in the inner query. Consider this example:

```
SELECT LAST_NAME, FIRST_NAME, SALARY, DEPARTMENT_ID
   FROM EMPLOYEES A
 WHERE SALARY >
       (SELECT AVG(SALARY)
          FROM EMPLOYEES B
          WHERE A.DEPARTMENT_ID = B.DEPARTMENT_ID);
```

This statement finds all employees whose salary is above the average salary for their department. The inner SELECT finds the average salary for each department. The outer SELECT is then executed for each row returned from the inner SELECT (that is, for each department) to find all employees for that department where the salary is above the average for that department. Hopefully, you recognized the AVG function, which was introduced back in Chapter 3 in Example 3-12. We will review using aggregate functions in an upcoming SQL example.

Joining Tables

Example 4-9: The Cartesian Product

As you learned previously in Example 3-8, we need to join tables (or views) whenever we need data from more than one table in our query results. In SQL, you specify joins by listing the tables or views to be joined in a comma-separated list in the FROM clause of the SELECT statement. However, SQL is not going to remind you to tell the RDBMS how to match rows in the tables (or views) being joined. If you forget, you will get a Cartesian product, as shown in Figure 4-16.

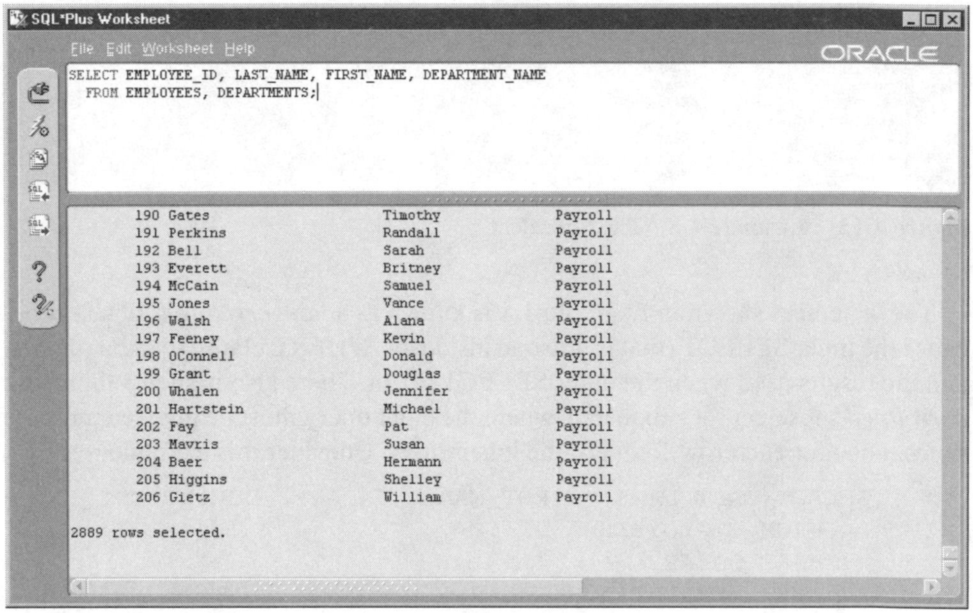

Figure 4-16   Example 4-9, "The Cartesian Product"

Whenever you write a new query, you should apply a "reasonableness" test to the results. Example 4-9 looks fine on the surface, but when you consider that there are only 107 employees, you realize something is horribly wrong. How could we possibly get 2889 rows simply by joining employees and departments? The answer: We failed to include a join specification in the WHERE clause, so the RDBMS created a Cartesian product for us, joining each employee with *every* department, and 27 departments times 107 employees yields 2889 (27 * 107) rows. Oops!

Example 4-10: The Inner Join of Two Tables

Figure 4-17 shows the correction, which involves adding a WHERE clause that tells the DBMS to match the DEPARTMENT_ID column in the EMPLOYEES table (the foreign key) to the DEPARTMENT_ID column in the DEPARTMENTS table (the primary key). Now we get a much more reasonable result with 106 rows.

```
SELECT EMPLOYEE_ID, LAST_NAME, FIRST_NAME, DEPARTMENT_NAME
  FROM EMPLOYEES, DEPARTMENTS
 WHERE EMPLOYEES.DEPARTMENT_ID = DEPARTMENTS.DEPARTMENT_ID ;


     190  Gates           Timothy      Shipping
     191  Perkins         Randall      Shipping
     192  Bell            Sarah        Shipping
     193  Everett         Britney      Shipping
     194  McCain          Samuel       Shipping
     195  Jones           Vance        Shipping
     196  Walsh           Alana        Shipping
     197  Feeney          Kevin        Shipping
     198  OConnell        Donald       Shipping
     199  Grant           Douglas      Shipping
     200  Whalen          Jennifer     Administration
     201  Hartstein       Michael      Marketing
     202  Fay             Pat          Marketing
     203  Mavris          Susan        Human Resources
     204  Baer            Hermann      Public Relations
     205  Higgins         Shelley      Accounting
     206  Gietz           William      Accounting

106 rows selected.
```

Figure 4-17   Example 4-10, "Inner Join of Two Tables"

However, if there are 107 employees, why did we only get 106 in Example 4-10? The answer lies in the fact that we performed an inner (or standard) join. Rows were returned only when a matching department row was found for an employee—and there is one employee, the owner of the company, who does not work in a department. We can correct this problem by changing our inner join to an outer join. In this case, we want all rows from the EMPLOYEES table, even if no matching row is found in the DEPARTMENTS table for some employees.

Example 4-11: Outer Joins in Oracle

The Oracle syntax for outer joins is just plain strange. It involves placing a plus sign enclosed in parentheses (+) in the WHERE clause on the side of the condition where null values are to be returned. In this case, when there is no matching DEPARTMENTS table row for an employee, we want the data from the EMPLOYEES table to display anyway, with the DEPARTMENT_NAME from the DEPARTMENTS table set to null. If you think of the symbol (+) as meaning "add nulls here," you might find it easier to remember. Here is the adjusted SQL statement:

```
SELECT EMPLOYEE_ID, LAST_NAME, FIRST_NAME, DEPARTMENT_NAME
   FROM EMPLOYEES, DEPARTMENTS
 WHERE EMPLOYEES.DEPARTMENT_ID = DEPARTMENTS.DEPARTMENT_ID(+);
```

The Oracle outer join syntax grew out of necessity, with customers demanding a solution and no standards at the time to follow. Starting with Oracle9*i* Release 2, the ANSI Standard LEFT OUTER JOIN syntax is supported. So now the preceding statement may be rewritten in a more understandable way:

```
SELECT EMPLOYEE_ID, LAST_NAME, FIRST_NAME, DEPARTMENT_NAME
   FROM EMPLOYEES
        LEFT OUTER JOIN DEPARTMENTS
          ON EMPLOYEES.DEPARTMENT_ID = DEPARTMENTS.DEPARTMENT_ID;
```

Example 4-12: Limiting Join Results

Additional conditions can easily be added to the WHERE clause to limit rows returned from a query that also involves joins. Figure 4-18 shows a modification to

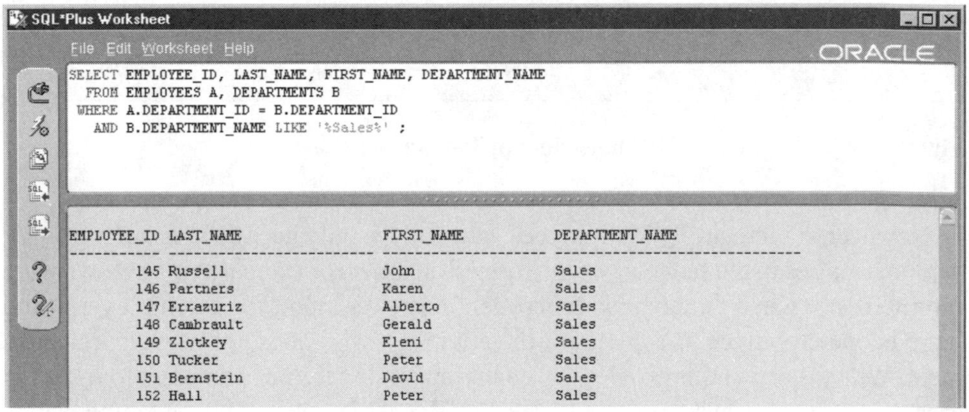

Figure 4-18   Example 4-12, "Limiting Join Results"

Example 4-10, such that only employees who work in departments with "Sales" in the department name are retuned.

Example 4-13: The Self-Join

When a table has a recursive relationship, we need to join the table to itself in order to follow the relationship in our query results. The EMPLOYEES table has such a relationship in that the MANAGER_ID column contains the EMPLOYEE_ID value of the employee to whom each employee reports. In our example, every employee has a manager in the table except for the owner of the company, as shown in Figure 4-19.

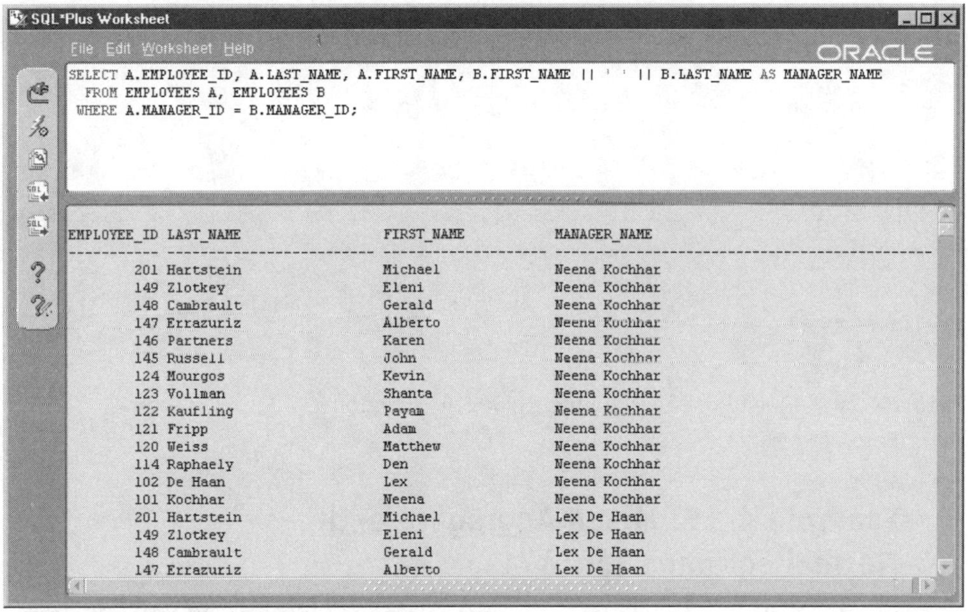

Figure 4-19   Example 4-13, "The Self-Join"

Note that we added another wrinkle to this example by concatenating the first and last names of the manager with a space in between to form the MANAGER_NAME column in the results. The column name is assigned using the keyword AS followed by the desired name. The query was coded as an inner join, so the one employee who does not have a manager will not show up in the results. As with any join, we can rewrite this one into an outer join by changing the WHERE clause. In this example, it would be written as follows:

```
WHERE A.MANAGER_ID = B.MANAGER_ID (+)
```

Aggregate Functions

Example 4-14: Simple Aggregate Functions

As you will recall from Example 3-12 in the previous chapter, aggregate functions combine multiple rows together. In Figure 4-20, aggregate functions are used to find the minimum, maximum, and average salaries for all employees along with a count of the total number of employees. Because there is no GROUP BY clause to group rows, the entire table is considered one group, so only one row is returned in the result set.

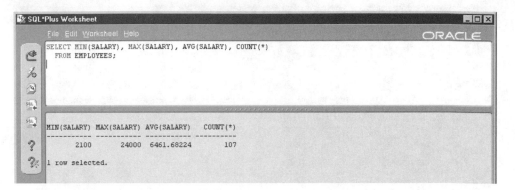

Figure 4-20   Example 4-14, "Simple Aggregate Functions"

Example 4-15: Mixed Aggregate and Normal Columns (Error)

If we add DEPARTMENT_ID to the query without adding a GROUP BY clause, the query returns an error message, as shown in Figure 4-21. The error message can be confusing, but notice the placement of the asterisk under the SQL statement. Oracle is attempting to show the particular part of the statement where the error was found. In this case, it is telling you that DEPARTMENT_ID is not a group function.

Example 4-16: Aggregate Functions with GROUP BY

The request in Example 4-15 is illogical because it essentially asks the RDBMS to display every value of DEPARTMENT_ID, but at the same time, display only one row containing the values for the other columns (those columns being formed with aggregate functions). To remedy the situation, we must tell the RDBMS that we

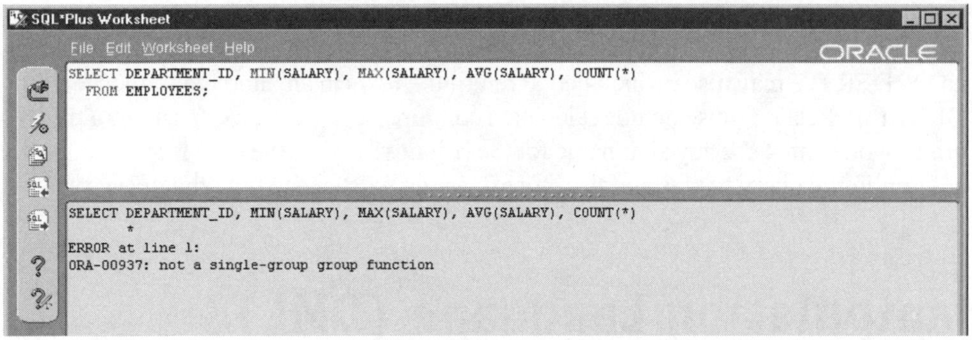
SQL*Plus Worksheet
File Edit Worksheet Help
ORACLE
SELECT DEPARTMENT_ID, MIN(SALARY), MAX(SALARY), AVG(SALARY), COUNT(*)
FROM EMPLOYEES;
SELECT DEPARTMENT_ID, MIN(SALARY), MAX(SALARY), AVG(SALARY), COUNT(*)
*
ERROR at line 1:
ORA-00937: not a single-group group function

Figure 4-21 Example 4-15, "Mixed Aggregate and Normal Columns (Error)"

wish to *group* the rows by DEPARTMENT_ID, and for each *group* display the DEPARTMENT_ID along with the aggregate column results (the minimum, maximum, and average salaries for the department and the count of the number of employees in the department). The corrected statement is shown in Figure 4-22. We add a ROUND function to the AVG(SALARY) column to round the average to two decimal places. Note that the ROUND function is *not* an aggregate function—it merely rounds a single column value. It is perfectly acceptable to apply a function to the results of another function, which is known as *nesting* functions. There seems no limit to the clever things we can do with SQL.

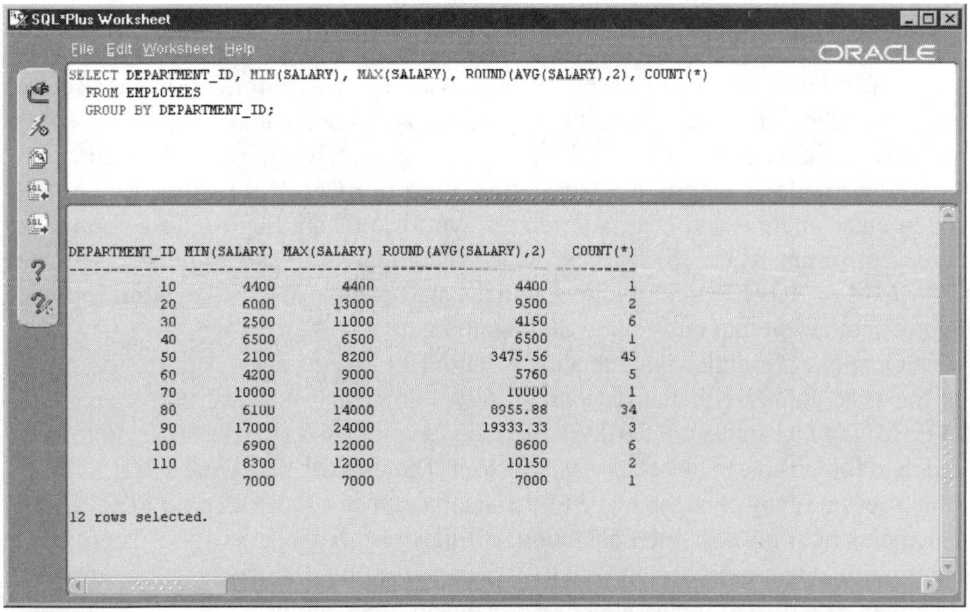
SQL*Plus Worksheet
File Edit Worksheet Help
ORACLE
SELECT DEPARTMENT_ID, MIN(SALARY), MAX(SALARY), ROUND(AVG(SALARY),2), COUNT(*)
FROM EMPLOYEES
GROUP BY DEPARTMENT_ID;
DEPARTMENT_ID MIN(SALARY) MAX(SALARY) ROUND(AVG(SALARY),2) COUNT(*)
------------- ----------- ----------- -------------------- ----------
10 4400 4400 4400 1
20 6000 13000 9500 2
30 2500 11000 4150 6
40 6500 6500 6500 1
50 2100 8200 3475.56 45
60 4200 9000 5760 5
70 10000 10000 10000 1
80 6100 14000 8955.88 34
90 17000 24000 19333.33 3
100 6900 12000 8600 6
110 8300 12000 10150 2
7000 7000 7000 1
12 rows selected.

Figure 4-22 Example 4-16, "Aggregate Functions with GROUP BY"

The GROUP BY clause causes returned rows to be automatically ordered by the columns listed because the DBMS must perform a sort in order to group the rows. However, an ORDER BY may also be included to return the rows in an alternate sequence. If the ORDER BY clause must include calculated columns, just use the expression for the column—you cannot use any alias name for the column because the alias is assigned to the column in the query results and therefore does not exist at the time the query runs.

Data Manipulation Language (DML)

The DML statement types in SQL are INSERT, UPDATE, and DELETE. These commands allow you to add, change, and remove rows of data in the tables. Before we look at each of these statement types, you first need to understand the concept of transactions and how the RDBMS supports them.

Transaction Support (COMMIT and ROLLBACK)

In terms of the RDBMS, a *transaction* is a series of one or more SQL statements that are treated as a single unit. A transaction must completely work or completely fail, meaning that any database changes a transaction makes must be made permanent when the transaction successfully completes. On the other hand, these changes must be entirely removed from the database if the transaction fails before completion. For example, we could start a transaction at the beginning of a process that creates a new order and then, at the end of the process when all the order information has been entered, completes the transaction. It is important that other database users not see fragments of an incomplete order until it has been completely entered and confirmed.

SQL provides support for transactions with the COMMIT and ROLLBACK statements. There is some variation in the syntax and handling of these commands across different RDBMS vendors. Most vendors require no argument with the COMMIT or ROLLBACK statement, so the statement is just the keyword followed by the semicolon that ends every SQL statement.

In Oracle, a transaction is automatically started for each database user session as soon as the user connects to the database. At any time, the database user can issue a COMMIT, which makes all the database changes completed up to that point permanent and therefore visible to any other database user. The user can also issue a ROLLBACK, which reverses any changes made to the database. The COMMIT and ROLLBACK statements not only end one transaction, but they also begin a new one. There is one more wrinkle to remember: In Oracle, an *automatic* commit occurs before any DDL statement. (DDL statements are covered later in this chapter.)

By contrast, in Sybase and Microsoft SQL Server, transaction support is not as automatic. The database user must issue a BEGIN TRANSACTION statement to start a transaction. Once a transaction is started, changes made to the database can be made permanent with a COMMIT TRANSACTION statement, or they can be reversed using a ROLLBACK TRANSACTION statement. Some RDBMSs, such as Microsoft Access and MySQL, do not provide transaction support at all.

The INSERT Statement

The INSERT statement in SQL is used to add new rows of data to tables. An INSERT statement may also insert rows via a view, provided the following conditions are met:

- If the view joins multiple tables, the columns referenced by the INSERT statement must all be from the same table. Said another way, an INSERT can only affect one table.
- The view must include all the mandatory table columns in the base table. If there are columns with NOT NULL constraints that do not appear in the view, it is impossible to provide values for those columns and therefore impossible to use the view to perform an insert.

The INSERT statement takes two basic forms: one where column values are provided in the statement itself, and the other where values are selected from a table or view using a subselect. Let's have a look at those two forms.

Example 4-17: INSERT with VALUES Clause

The INSERT with VALUES clause form of the INSERT statement can only create one row each time it is run because the values for that one row of data are provided in the statement itself. Figure 4-23 shows an example.

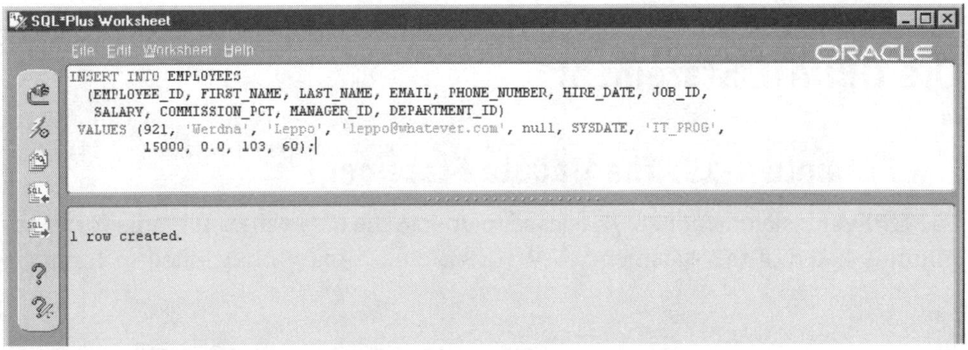

Figure 4-23   Example 4-17, "INSERT with VALUES Clause"

Note the column list following the INSERT keyword. This comma-separated list is optional, but if provided must always be enclosed in a pair of parentheses. If you omit the list, the column values must be provided in the correct order (that is, the same as the order in which the columns are physically ordered in the table), and you cannot skip any column values. The statement may malfunction if anyone adds columns to the table, even optional ones, so it is *always* a good idea to provide the column list, even though it is more work to create one. Following the column list is the keyword VALUES and then a list of the values for the columns. This comma-separated list must also be enclosed in a pair of parentheses. The items in the VALUES list have a one-to-one correspondence with the column list (if one was provided) or with the columns defined in the table or view (if a column list was not provided). With Oracle, the keyword NULL may be used to assign null values to columns in the list.

Example 4-18: INSERT with Subquery

The INSERT with subquery form of the INSERT statement creates one row in the target table for each row retrieved from the source table or view. A subquery is used to retrieve the information that will be inserted. In the example that follows, rows in an imaginary table called EMPLOYEE_INPUT are used to insert data into the EMPLOYEES table:

```
INSERT INTO EMPLOYEES
    (EMPLOYEE_ID, FIRST_NAME, LAST_NAME, EMAIL, PHONE_NUMBER,
     HIRE_DATE, JOB_ID)
   SELECT EMPLOYEE_ID, FIRST_NAME, LAST_NAME, EMAIL, PHONE_NUMBER,
          SYSDATE, JOB_ID)
     FROM EMPLOYEE_INPUT;
```

If you wish to try this INSERT statement, you can find the statements used to create the EMPLOYEE_INPUT table in the Data Definition Language (DDL) section a bit further along in this chapter.

The UPDATE Statement

Example 4-19: The Update Statement

The UPDATE statement in SQL is used to update the data values for table (or view) columns listed in the statement. A WHERE clause may be included to limit the scope of the statement to rows matching its conditions; otherwise, the statement attempts to update every row in the table (or view) named in the statement. Figure 4-24 shows an example of the UPDATE statement.

Figure 4-24   Example 4-19, "The UPDATE Statement"

For each column to be updated, a SET clause is used to name the column and the new value for the column. The new value provided may be a constant, another column name, or any other expression that SQL can resolve to a column value. If the SET clause references multiple columns, the column names and values must be in a comma-separated list. The UPDATE statement may include a WHERE clause to limit the rows affected by the statement. If the WHERE clause is omitted, the UPDATE statement will attempt to update every row in the table (or view). If you forget this key point, remember our friend the ROLLBACK statement, which can back out the results of the update.

The DELETE Statement

The DELETE statement removes one or more rows from a table. The statement may also reference a view, but only if the view is based on a single table (in other words, views that join multiple tables cannot be referenced). A DELETE statement does not reference columns because the statement automatically clears all column data for any rows deleted. A WHERE clause may be included to limit the rows affected by the DELETE statement; if the WHERE clause is omitted, the statement attempts to delete all the rows in the referenced table. Figure 4-25 shows an example of a DELETE statement.

Figure 4-25   Example 4-20, "The DELETE Statement"

Data Definition Language (DDL) Statements

Data Definition Language (DDL) statements define the database objects but do not insert or update any data stored within those objects (DML statements serve that function). In SQL, there are three basic commands within DDL:

- **CREATE**   Creates a new database object of the type named in the statement
- **DROP**   Drops (destroys) an existing database object of the type named in the statement
- **ALTER**   Changes the definition of an existing database object of the type named in the statement

In the sections that follow, we look at the most commonly used DDL statement types. There is a lot of variety in DDL statements across RDBMS vendors, so consult the vendor's documentation for more details.

The CREATE TABLE Statement

TABLE statement adds a new table to the database. Here is an example using the EMPLOYEES table:

```
CREATE TABLE EMPLOYEE_INPUT (
    EMPLOYEE_ID      NUMBER(6)      NOT NULL,
    FIRST_NAME       VARCHAR2(20)   NULL,
    LAST_NAME        VARCHAR2(25)   NOT NULL,
    EMAIL            VARCHAR2(25)   NOT NULL,
    PHONE_NUMBER     VARCHAR2(20)   NULL,
    HIRE_DATE        DATE           NOT NULL,
```

```
JOB_ID            VARCHAR2(10)    NOT NULL,
SALARY            NUMBER(8,2)     NULL,
COMMISSION_PCT    NUMBER(2,2)     NULL,
MANAGER_ID        NUMBER(6)       NULL,
DEPARTMENT_ID     NUMBER(4)       NULL)
;
```

Note that a comma-separated list of columns is provided, along with the data type and NULL or NOT NULL specification for each. You may recall that data types were discussed in Chapter 2 and that there is a wide variation in supported data types across RDBMS vendors. The data types shown here apply to Oracle. Be careful with NULL and NOT NULL specifications. In most RDBMSs, including Oracle, NULL is the default. However, in others, such as Sybase and Microsoft SQL Server, NOT NULL is the default. It is therefore safer, but of course more work, to always specify either NULL or NOT NULL. Incidentally, most RDBMSs require that primary key columns be specified as NOT NULL. You'll see how to create a primary key constraint on the EMPLOYEE_ID column of this table in the "Primary Key Constraints" section a little further along in this chapter.

This example shows the ANSI standard components of the CREATE TABLE statement. There are many vendor extensions. For example, in Oracle, the STORAGE clause may be included to specify the amount of physical space that is to be allocated to the table, and a TABLESPACE clause may be included to specify the tablespace that will hold the table's data.

The ALTER TABLE Statement

The ALTER TABLE statement may be used to change many aspects of the definition of a database table. Again, there is a wide variation in implementation across RDBMS vendors, but generally speaking, the following types of changes may be made using the ALTER TABLE statement:

- Adding columns to the table
- Removing columns from the table
- Altering the data type for existing table columns
- Changing physical storage attributes of the table
- Adding, removing, or altering constraints

Because the implementation of constraints is the way we enforce business rules in the database, we will take a closer look at them here. In Oracle, it is important to name the constraints because the names appear in any error messages generated when constraint violations take place.

Referential Constraints

Here is an example of a referential constraint definition using the ALTER TABLE statement:

```
ALTER TABLE EMPLOYEE_INPUT
   ADD CONSTRAINT EMP_DEPT_FK
   FOREIGN KEY (DEPARTMENT_ID)
   REFERENCES DEPARTMENTS (DEPARTMENT_ID);
```

In this example, a referential constraint named EMP_DEPT_FK is added to the EMPLOYEES table to define the DEPARTMENT_ID column as a foreign key to the primary key column (DEPARTMENT_ID) of the DEPARTMENTS table. This is the way we implement the relationships we've identified in the logical database design.

Primary Key Constraints

Primary key constraints ensure that the column(s) designated as the primary key for the table never have duplicate values. Most RDBMSs, Oracle included, create a unique index to assist in enforcement of primary key constraints. An *index* is a special database object containing the key value from one or more table columns and pointers to the table rows that match the key value. Indexes can be used for fast searching of a table based on the key value. Here is the definition of the primary key constraint for the EMPLOYEES table:

```
ALTER TABLE EMPLOYEE_INPUT
   ADD CONSTRAINT EMPLOYEES_PK
   PRIMARY KEY (EMPLOYEE_ID)
   USING INDEX;
```

Unique Constraints

In addition to primary keys, we can force uniqueness of other column(s) in a table using a unique constraint. A table may have only one primary key constraint, but in addition it may have as many unique constraints as necessary. Most RDBMSs, including Oracle, use a unique index to assist with the enforcement of unique constraints. For example, we can use a unique constraint to ensure that no two employees have the same e-mail address as follows:

```
ALTER TABLE EMPLOYEE_INPUT
   ADD CONSTRAINT EMPLOYEES_UNQ_EMAIL
   UNIQUE (EMAIL);
```

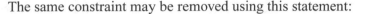
The same constraint may be removed using this statement:

```
ALTER TABLE EMPLOYEE_INPUT
  DROP CONSTRAINT EMPLOYEES_UNQ_EMAIL;
```

Check Constraints

Check constraints can be used to enforce any business rule that can be applied to a single column in a table. The condition included in the constraint must always be true whenever the column data in the table is changed or else an error message is displayed. The following example implements a check constraint that ensures that the SALARY column in the EMPLOYEES table is always greater than zero:

```
ALTER TABLE EMPLOYEES
  ADD CONSTRAINT EMPLOYEES_CHK_SALARY_MIN
  CHECK (SALARY > 0);
```

The same constraint may be removed with this statement:

```
ALTER TABLE EMPLOYEES
  DROP CONSTRAINT EMPLOYEES_CHK_SALARY_MIN;
```

The CREATE VIEW Statement

Because a view is merely a stored query, any query that can be run using a SELECT statement can be saved as a view in the database. View names must be unique among all the tables, views, and synonyms in the database schema. In Oracle, the OR REPLACE option may be included so that an existing view of the same name will be replaced. The following example creates a view for the query shown in Figure 4-18:

```
CREATE OR REPLACE VIEW SALES_EMPLOYEES AS
   SELECT EMPLOYEE_ID, LAST_NAME, FIRST_NAME, DEPARTMENT_NAME
     FROM EMPLOYEES A, DEPARTMENTS B
    WHERE A.DEPARTMENT_ID = B.DEPARTMENT_ID
      AND B.DEPARTMENT_NAME LIKE '%Sales%';
```

Running the following SQL statement will select the data from the view, which will yield the exact same results as those shown in Figure 4-18:

```
SELECT * FROM SALES_EMPLOYEES;
```

The CREATE INDEX Statement

The CREATE INDEX statement creates an index on one or more table columns. As previously mentioned, indexes provide fast searching of a table based on one or more key columns. Indexes on foreign keys can also greatly improve the performance of joins. The RDBMS automatically maintains the index when rows are added to or deleted from the database or indexed column values are updated. However, indexes take storage space and their maintenance takes processing resources. The following example creates an index on the DEPARTMENT_ID column in the EMPLOYEE_INPUT table:

```
CREATE INDEX EMPLOYEE_INPUT_IX_DEPT_ID
  ON EMPLOYEE_INPUT (DEPARTMENT_ID);
```

If the column values in the index will always be unique, the UNIQUE keyword may be placed between the CREATE and INDEX keywords. As an alternative, a unique constraint may be added to the table, which indirectly creates the unique index. Unique indexes are usually more efficient than nonunique ones.

The DROP Statement

The DROP statement is used to remove database objects from the database when they are no longer necessary. For table deletions, the CASCADE CONSTRAINTS clause may be added to automatically remove any referential constraints in which the table participates. When a table is dropped, most objects depending on the table (indexes and constraints) are also dropped. In most RDBMSs, however, views dependent on a dropped table remain but are marked invalid so they cannot be used until the table is re-created. Here are the DROP statements that remove the objects created in the preceding examples:

```
DROP VIEW SALES_EMPLOYEES;
DROP INDEX EMPLOYEE_INPUT_IX_DEPT_ID;
DROP TABLE EMPLOYEE_INPUT CASCADE CONSTRAINTS;
```

Data Control Language (DCL) Statements

A database *privilege* is the authorization to do something in the database. The database user granting the privilege is called the *grantor*, and the database user receiving the privilege is called the *grantee*. Privileges fall into two broad categories:

- **System privileges** Permit the grantee to perform a general database function, such as creating new user accounts or connecting to the database

- **Object privileges**   Permit the grantee to perform specific actions on specific objects, such as selecting from the EMPLOYEES table or updating the DEPARTMENTS table

To reduce the tedium of managing privileges, most RDBMSs support storing a group of privilege definitions as a single named object called a *role*. Roles may then be granted to individual users, who then inherit all the privileges contained in the role. RDBMSs that support roles also typically come with a number of predefined roles. Oracle, for example, has a role called DBA that contains all the high-powered system and object privileges a database user needs in administering a database.

The GRANT Statement

Privileges are given to users in SQL using the GRANT statement. The following examples show the syntax for granting a system privilege and an object privilege to database users.

The following statement grants the CONNECT privilege to user OE (one of the other Oracle sample schema users):

```
GRANT CONNECT TO OE;
```

The following statement grants the select, insert, and update privileges on the EMPLOYEES table in the IIR schema to user OE. Note that we must qualify the table name with the schema name because we are logged in as the SYSTEM user. You must always qualify objects that belong to another schema (user) when you reference them in SQL. Here's the statement:

```
GRANT SELECT, INSERT, UPDATE ON HR.EMPLOYEES TO OE;
```

Most RDBMSs that support privileges also allow for giving the grantee permission to grant the privilege to others. In Oracle, the clause for doing so is WITH ADMIN OPTION for system privileges and WITH GRANT OPTION for object privileges. However, I *strongly* recommend *against* doing so. It is simply too easy to lose control of privileges when you allow people who have a privilege to in turn grant it to others.

The REVOKE Statement

Granted privileges can be withdrawn using the REVOKE statement. For object privileges, if WITH GRANT OPTION is exercised by the user, the revoke cascades and everyone downstream loses the privilege as well. This is not necessarily true for system privileges—consult your RDBMS manuals for details. Better yet, if you never use WITH GRANT OPTION and WITH ADMIN OPTION, you will never have to worry about this problem. The privileges shown in the previous section can be revoked with these commands:

```
REVOKE DBA FROM HELEN_WHEELS;
REVOKE SELECT, INSERT, UPDATE ON DEPARTMENTS FROM BOB_THE_BOSS;
```

Quiz

Choose the correct responses to each of the multiple-choice questions. Note that there may be more than one correct response to each question.

1. SQL may be divided into the following subsets:
    a. Data Selection Language (DSL)
    b. Data Control Language (DCL)
    c. Data Purge Language (DPL)
    d. Data Query Language (DQL)
    e. Data Replication Language (DRL)

2. SQL was first developed:
    a. By IBM
    b. In 1982
    c. Based on ANSI specifications
    d. By ANSI
    e. In the 1970s

3. SQL Plus is
    a. Oracle's SQL3-compliant language
    b. Available in both GUI and command-line versions
    c. Functionally equivalent to the SQL Plus Worksheet
    d. Oracle's client software for running SQL
    e. A set of Oracle extensions to SQL

4. A SELECT without a WHERE clause:
    a. Selects all rows in the source table or view
    b. Selects all columns in the source table or view
    c. Results in an error message
    d. Always outputs results to a log file
    e. Lists only the definition of the table or view

5. In SQL, row order in query results:
    a. Is specified using the SORTED BY clause
    b. Is unpredictable unless specified in the query

    c. May be either descending or ascending for any column

    d. Defaults to descending when sequence is not specified

    e. May only be specified for columns in the query results

6. The BETWEEN operator:

    a. Includes the end-point values

    b. Selects rows added to a table during a time interval

    c. Can be rewritten using the <= and NOT = operators

    d. Can be rewritten using the <= and >= operators

    e. Is an Oracle extension to SQL

7. The LIKE operator:

    a. Uses underscores as nonpositional wildcards

    b. Uses underscores as positional wildcards

    c. Uses question marks as nonpositional wildcards

    d. Uses percent signs as positional wildcards

    e. Uses percent signs as nonpositional wildcards

8. A subselect:

    a. May be corrugated or noncorrugated

    b. Is a powerful way of calculating columns

    c. Allows for the flexible selection of rows

    d. Must not be enclosed in parentheses

    e. May be used to select values to be applied to WHERE clause conditions

9. A join without a WHERE clause or JOIN clause:

    a. Always performs an inner join

    b. Results in an error message

    c. Results in an outer join

    d. Results in a Cartesian product

    e. Returns no rows in the result set

10. An outer join:

    a. May be written using a (+) symbol in the FROM clause

    b. May be written using a (+) symbol in the WHERE clause

    c. Results in a Cartesian product

    d. Returns all rows in one of the two tables

    e. Can be a left, right, or full outer join

11. A self-join:

    a. Involves two different tables

    b. Can be either an inner or outer join

    c. Can never result in a Cartesian product

    d. Resolves recursive relationships

    e. May use a subselect to further limit returned rows

12. An SQL statement containing an aggregate function:
    a. Must contain a GROUP BY clause
    b. May also include ordinary columns
    c. May not include both GROUP BY and ORDER BY clauses
    d. May also include calculated columns
    e. May not involve joining multiple tables

13. A COMMIT in Oracle:
    a. Ends a transaction
    b. Begins a new transaction
    c. Makes changes effected by a transaction visible to all users
    d. Causes changes made by a transaction to become permanent
    e. Is automatic just before any DDL statement is run

14. An INSERT statement:
    a. Must contain a column list
    b. Must contain a VALUES list
    c. May create multiple table rows
    d. May contain a subquery
    e. Creates a new table

15. An UPDATE statement without a WHERE clause:
    a. Results in an error message
    b. Updates no rows in a table
    c. Updates every row in a table
    d. Results in a Cartesian product
    e. Updates every column in a table

16. A DELETE statement with a column list:
    a. Results in an error message
    b. Deletes every row in the table
    c. Deletes every column in the table
    d. Results in a Cartesian product
    e. Can be used to delete from a view

17. A CREATE statement:
    a. Is a form of DML
    b. Creates new user privileges
    c. Creates a database object
    d. May be corrected later using an ALTER statement
    e. May be reversed later using a DROP statement

18. An ALTER statement:
    a. May be used to add a constraint
    b. May be used to drop a constraint
    c. May be used to add a view
    d. May be used to drop a view
    e. May be used to drop a table column

19. A check constraint:
    a. Enforces referential integrity
    b. Enforces a business rule
    c. Creates an index to assist with the constraint
    d. Restricts a database user's privileges
    e. Validates data in an index

20. Database privileges:
    a. May be changed with an ALTER PRIVILEGE statement
    b. May be either system or object privileges
    c. Must be granted using roles
    d. Are best managed when assembled into groups using GROUP BY
    e. Are managed using GRANT and REVOKE

5

The Database Life Cycle

Before we delve into the particulars of database design, it is useful to understand the framework in which the design takes place. The *life cycle* of a database (or computer system) is the term we use for all the events that take place between the time we first recognize a need for a database, continuing through its development and deployment, and finally ending with the day it is retired from service.

Most businesses that develop computer systems have a formal process they follow. The process ensures that development runs smoothly, is cost effective, and that the outcome is a complete computer system that meets expectations. Databases are never designed and implemented in a vacuum—there are always other components of the complete system, such as the user interface, application programs, and reports, that are developed along with the database. All the work to be accomplished over the long term is typically divided into projects, with each project having its own finite list of goals (sometimes called *deliverables*), an expected timeframe for completion, and a project manager or leader who will be held accountable for delivery of the project. In order to understand the database life cycle, you must also understand the life cycle of the entire systems-development effort and the way projects are organized and managed. In this chapter, we take a look at both traditional and nontraditional systems-development processes.

Not all databases are built by businesses using formal projects and funding. However, the disciplines outlined in this chapter can assist you in thinking through your database project, asking the tough questions, before you embark on an extended effort.

The Traditional Method

The traditional method for developing computer systems follows a process called the *system development life cycle (SDLC)*, which divides the work into the phases shown in Figure 5-1. There are perhaps as many variations of the SDLC as there are authors, project management software vendors, and companies that have elected to create their own methodology. However, they all have the basic components, and in that sense, are all cut from the same cloth. We could argue the merits of one variation versus another, but that would merely confuse matters when all we need is a basic overview. A good textbook on systems analysis can provide greater detail should you need it. Figure 5-1 shows the traditional SDLC steps in the left column, the basic project activities in the middle column, and the database steps that support the project activities in the right column. We will explore each step further in the sections that follow. Note that the process is not always unidirectional—there are times when missing or incomplete information is discovered that requires you to go back one phase and adjust the work done there. The dotted lines pointing back to prior phases in Figure 5-1 serve as a reminder that a certain amount of rework is normal and expected during a project following the SDLC methodology.

Planning

During the planning phase, the organization must reach an understanding at a high level of where they currently are, where they want to be, and a reasonable approach or plan for getting from one place to the other. Planning is often done over a longer time period than any one individual project, and the overall information systems plan for the organization forms the basis from which projects should be launched to achieve the overall objectives. For example, a long-range objective in the plan might be "Increase profits by 15 percent." In support of that objective, a project to develop an application system and database to track customer profitability might be proposed.

Once a particular project is proposed, a feasibility study is usually launched to determine if the project can be reasonably expected to achieve (or help achieve) the

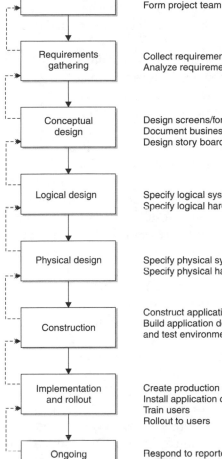

Phases	Project Activities	Database Activities
Planning	Feasibility study Form project team	Review DBMS options Assign database specialist to team
Requirements gathering	Collect requirements Analyze requirements	Collect and analyze user views Identity preliminary entities
Conceptual design	Design screens/forms/reports Document business rules Design story boards or screen flows	Develop conceptual data model Update enterprise conceptual model
Logical design	Specify logical system software Specify logical hardware	Develop logical data model Perform normalization
Physical design	Specify physical system software Specify physical hardware	Physical database design
Construction	Construct application software Build application development and test environments	Create development and test databases Test any required data conversion
Implementation and rollout	Create production environment Install application components Train users Rollout to users	Create production databases Perform required data conversion
Ongoing support	Respond to reported problems Apply mandated changes Respond to change requests	Database performance tuning Database software patches Schema changes to support application changes

Figure 5-1   Traditional system development life cycle (SDLC)

objective and if preliminary estimates of time, staff, and materials required for the project fit within the required timeframe and available budget. Often a return on investment (ROI) or similar calculation is used to measure the expected value of the proposed project to the organization. If the feasibility study meets management approval, the project is placed on the overall schedule for the organization and the project team is formed. The composition of the project team will change over the life of the project, with people added and released as particular skill and staffing levels are needed. The one consistent member of the project team will be the project manager (or project leader), who is responsible for the overall management and execution of the project.

Many organizations assign a database specialist (database administrator or data modeler) to projects at their inception, as shown in Figure 5-1. In a *data-driven* approach, where the emphasis is on studying the data in order to discover the processing that must take place to transform the data as required by the project, early assignment of someone skilled at analyzing the data is essential. In a *process-driven* approach, where the emphasis is on studying the processes required in order to discover what the data should be, a database specialist is less essential during the earliest phases of the project. Industry experience suggests that the very best results are obtained by applying *both* a process-driven and a data-driven approach. However, there is seldom time and staff to do so, so the next-best results for a project involving databases come from the data-driven approach. Processes still need to be designed, but if we study the data first, the required processes become apparent. For example, in designing our customer profitability system, if we have customer sales data and know that customers who place fewer, larger orders are more profitable, then we can conclude that we need a process to rank customers by order volume and size. On the other hand, if all we know is that we need a process that ranks customers, it may take considerably more work to arrive at the criteria we should use to rank them.

The database activities in this phase involve reviewing DBMS options and determining whether the technologies currently in use meet the overall needs of the project. Most organizations settle on one, or perhaps two, standard DBMS products that they use for all projects. At this point, the goals of the project should be compared with the current technology to ensure that the project can reasonably be expected to be successful using that technology. If a newer version of the DBMS is required, or if a completely different DBMS is required, now is the time to find out so the acquisition and installation of the DBMS can be started.

Requirements Gathering

During the requirements-gathering phase, the project team must gather and document a high-level, yet precise, description of what the project is to accomplish. The focus must be on *what* rather than *how*; the "how" is developed during the subsequent design phases. It is important for the requirements to include as much as can be known about the existing and expected business processes, business rules, and entities. The more work that is done in the early stages of a project, the more smoothly the subsequent stages will proceed. On the other hand, without some tolerance for the unknown (that is, those gray areas that have no solid answers), *analysis paralysis* may occur, wherein the entire project stalls while analysts spin their wheels looking for answers and clarifications that are not forthcoming.

From a database design perspective, the items of most interest during requirements gathering are user views. Recall that a *user view* is the method employed for presenting a set of data to the database user in a manner tailored to the needs of that person or application. At this phase of development, user views take the form of existing or proposed reports, forms, screens, Web pages, and the like.

Many techniques may be used in gathering requirements. The more commonly used ones are compared and contrasted here: conduct interviews, conduct survey, observation, and document review. No particular technique is clearly superior to another, and it is best to find a blend of techniques that works well for the particular organization rather than rely on one over the others. For example, whether it is better to conduct a survey and follow up with interviews with key people, or to start with interviews and use the interview findings to formulate a survey, is often a question of what works best given the organization's culture and operating methods. With each technique detailed in the following subsections, some advantages and disadvantages are listed to assist in decision making.

Conduct Interviews

Interviewing key individuals who have information about what the project is expected to accomplish is a popular approach. One of the common errors, however, is to interview only management. If representatives of the people who are actually going to use the new application(s) and database(s) are not included, the project may end up delivering something that is not practical, because management may not fully understand the details of what is required to run the business of the organization.

The advantages of requirements gathering using interviews include

- The interviewer can receive answers to questions that were not asked. Side topics often come up that provide additional useful information.
- The interviewer can learn a lot from the body language of the interviewee. It is far easier to detect uncertainty and attempts at deception in person rather than in written responses to questions.

The disadvantages include

- Interviews take considerably more time than other methods.

- Poorly skilled interviewers can "telegraph" the answers they are expecting by the way they ask the questions or by their reaction to the answers received.

Conduct a Survey

Another popular approach is to write a survey seeking responses to key questions regarding the requirements for a project. The survey is sent to all the decision makers and potential users of the application(s) and database(s) the project is expected to deliver, and responses are analyzed for items to be included in the requirements.

The advantages of requirements gathering using surveys include

- A lot of ground can be covered in a short time. Once the survey is written, it takes little additional effort to distribute it to a wider audience if necessary.
- Questions are presented in the same manner to every participant.

The disadvantages include

- Surveys typically have very poor response rates. Consider yourself fortunate if 10 percent respond without having to be prodding or threatened with consequences.
- Unbiased survey questions are much more difficult to compose than one would imagine.
- The project team does not get the benefit of the nonverbal clues that an interview provides.

Observation

Observing the business operation and the people who will be using the new application(s) and database(s) is another popular technique for gathering requirements.

The advantages of requirements gathering using observation include

- Assuming you watch in an unobtrusive manner, you get to see people following normal processes in everyday use. Note that these may not be the processes that management believes are being followed, or even the ones in existing documentation. Instead, you may observe adaptations that were made so that the processes actually work or so they are more efficient.
- You may observe events that people would not think (or dare) to mention in response to questionnaires or interview questions.

The disadvantages include the following:

- If the people know they are being watched, behavior changes, and you may not get an accurate picture of their business processes. This is often termed the *Hawthorne effect* after a phenomenon first noticed in the Hawthorne Plant of Western Electric, where production improved not because of improvements in working conditions but rather because management demonstrated interest in such improvements.
- Unless enormous periods of time are dedicated to observation, you may never see the exceptions that subvert existing business processes. To bend an old analogy, you end up paving the cow path while cows are wandering on the highway on the other side of the pasture due to a hole in the fence.
- Travel to various business locations can add to project expense.

Document Review

This technique involves locating and reviewing all available documents for the existing business units and processes that will be affected by the new program(s) and database(s).

The advantages of requirements gathering using document review include

- Document review is typically less time consuming than any of the other methods.
- Documents often provide an overview of the system that is better thought out compared with the introductory information you receive in an interview.
- Pictures and diagrams really are worth a thousand words each.

The disadvantages are

- The documents may not reflect actual practices. Documents often deal with what should happen rather than what really happens.
- Documentation is often out of date.

Conceptual Design

The conceptual design phase involves designing the externals of the application(s) and database(s). In fact, many methodologies use the term *external design* for this project phase. The layout of reports, screens, forms, web pages, and other data entry and presentation vehicles are finalized during this phase. In addition, the flow of the external application is documented in the form of a flow chart, storyboard, or screen flow diagram. This helps the project team understand the logical flow of the system. Process diagramming techniques are discussed further in Chapter 7.

During this phase, the database specialist (DBA or data modeler) assigned to the project updates the enterprise conceptual data model, which is usually maintained in the form of an entity-relationship diagram (ERD). New or changed entities discovered are added to the ERD, and any additional or changed business rules are also noted. The user views, entities, and business rules are essential for the successful logical database design that follows in the next phase.

Logical Design

During logical design, the bulk of the technical design of the application(s) and database(s) included in the project is carried out. Many methodologies call this phase *internal design* because it involves the design of the internals of the project that the business users will never see.

The work to be accomplished by the application(s) is segmented into *modules* (individual units of application programming that will be written and tested together) and a detailed specification is written for each unit. The specification should be complete enough that any programmer with the proper programming skills can write the module and test it with little or no additional information. Diagrams such as data flow diagrams or flow charts (an older technique) are often used to document the logic flow between modules. Process modeling is covered in more detail in Chapter 7.

From the database perspective, the major effort in this phase is *normalization,* a technique developed by Dr. E.F. Codd for designing relational database tables that are best for transaction-based systems (that is, those that insert, update, and delete data in the relational database tables). Normalization is covered in great detail in Chapter 6. Normalization is the single most important topic in this entire book. Once normalization is completed, the overall logical data model for the enterprise (assuming one exists) is updated to reflect any newly discovered entities.

Physical Design

During the physical design phase, the logical design is mapped or converted to the actual hardware and systems software that will be used to implement the application(s) and database(s). From the process side, there may be little or nothing to do if the application specifications were written in a manner that can be directly implemented. However, there is much work to be done in specifying the hardware on which the application(s) and database(s) will be installed, including capacity estimates for the processors, disk devices, and network bandwidth on which the system will run.

On the database side, the normalized relations that were designed in the prior logical design phase are implemented in the relational DBMS(s) to be used. In particular, DDL is coded or generated to define the database objects, including the SQL clauses that define the physical storage of the tables and indexes. Preliminary analysis of required database queries is conducted to identify any additional indexes that may be necessary to achieve acceptable database performance. An essential outcome of this phase is the DDL for creation of the development database objects that the developers will need for testing the application programs during the construction phase that follows. Physical database design is covered in more detail in Chapter 8.

Construction

During the construction phase, the application developers code and test the individual programming units. Tested program units are promoted to a system test environment where the entire application and database system is assembled and tested from end to end. Figure 5-2 shows the environments that are typically used as an application system is developed, tested, and implemented. Each environment is a complete hardware and software environment that includes all the components necessary to run the application system. Once system testing is completed, the system is promoted to a quality assurance (QA) environment. Most medium and large size organizations have a separate QA department that tests the application system to ensure that it conforms to the stated requirements. Some organizations also have business users test the system to make sure it also meets their needs. The sooner errors are found in a computer system, the less expensive they are to repair. After QA has passed the application system, it is promoted to a staging environment. It is important that the staging environment be as near a duplicate of the production environment as possible. In this environment, stress testing is conducted to ensure that the application and database will perform reasonably when deployed into live production use. Often final user training is conducted here as well because it will be most like the live environment they will soon use.

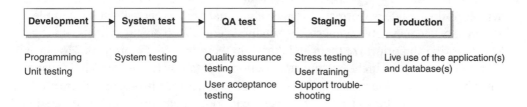

Development	System test	QA test	Staging	Production

Programming
Unit testing

System testing

Quality assurance testing

User acceptance testing

Stress testing

User training

Support trouble-shooting

Live use of the application(s) and database(s)

Figure 5-2   Development hardware/software environments

The major work of the DBA is already complete by the time construction begins. However, as each part of the application system is migrated from one environment to the next, the database components needed by the application must also be migrated. Hopefully, a script is written that deploys the database components to the development environment, and that script is re-used in each subsequent environment. However, it is more complicated when an existing database is being enhanced or an older data storage system is being replaced, because data must be converted from the old storage structures to the new. Data transcends systems. Therefore, data conversion between old and new versions of systems is quite commonplace, ranging from simply adding new tables and columns to complex conversions that require extensive programming efforts in and of themselves.

Implementation and Rollout

Implementation is the process of installing the new application system's components (application programs, forms or web pages, reports, database objects, and so on) into the live system and carrying out any required data conversions. *Rollout* is the process of placing groups of business users on the new application. Sometimes a new project is implemented *cold turkey*, meaning everyone is placed on the new version at the same time. However, with more complicated applications or those involving large numbers of users, a phased implementation is often used to reduce risk. The old and new versions of the application must run in parallel for a time while groups of users—often partitioned by physical work location or by department—are trained and migrated over to the new application. This method is often humorously referred to as the *chicken method* (in contrast to the cold turkey method).

Ongoing Support

Once a new application system and database have been implemented in a production environment, support of the application is often turned over to a production support team. This team must be prepared to isolate and respond to any issues that may arise, which could include performance issues, abnormal or unexpected results, complete failures, or the inevitable requests for enhancements. With enhancements, it is best to categorize and prioritize them and then fold them into future projects. However, genuine errors found in the existing application or database (called *bugs* in IT slang) must be fixed more immediately. Each bug fix becomes a mini-project, where all the SDLC phases must be revisited. At the very least, documentation must be updated as changes are made. As noted in Figure 5-2, the staging environment provides an ideal place for the validation of errors and the fixes for them, and makes it possible to fix errors in parallel with the next major enhancement to the application system, which may have already been started in the development environment.

Assuming no gross errors were made during database design, the database support required during this phase is usually minor. Here are some of the tasks that may be required:

- Patches must be applied when the problems turn out to be bugs in the vendor's RDBMS software.
- Performance tuning, such as moving data files or adding indexes, may be necessary to circumvent performance problems.
- Space must be monitored and storage added as the database grows.
- Some application bug fixes may require new table columns or alterations to existing columns. If testing was done well, gross errors that require extensive database changes simply do not occur. Some application changes are required by statutory or regulatory changes beyond the control of the organization, and those changes can lead to extensive modifications to application(s) and database(s).

Nontraditional Methods

In response to the belief that SDLC projects take too much time and too many resources, some nontraditional methods have come into routine use in some organizations. The two most prevalent of these are prototyping and Rapid Application Development (RAD).

Prototyping

Prototyping involves rapid development of the application using iterative sets of design, development, and implementation steps as a method of determining user requirements. Extensive business user involvement is required throughout the development process. In its extreme form, a meeting is held during the business day to review the latest iteration of the application, followed by a development team working through the evening and often late into night. The next iteration is then reviewed during the following workday.

Some prototyping techniques carry all the way through to a production version of the application and database. In this variation, iterations have increasing levels of detail added to them until they become completely functional applications. If this path is chosen, prototyping never ends, and even after implementation and rollout, any future enhancements fall right back into more prototyping. The most common downside to this implementation technique is development team burnout.

Another variation of prototyping restricts the effort to only the definition of requirements. Once requirements and the user-facing parts of the conceptual design (that is, user views) are determined, a traditional SDLC methodology is used to complete the project. IBM introduced a version of this methodology called *Joint Application Design (JAD)*, which was highly successful in situations where user requirements could not be determined using more traditional techniques. The biggest exposure for this variant of prototyping is in not setting and maintaining expectations with the business sponsors of the project. The prototype is more or less a façade, much like a movie set where the buildings look real from the front, but have no substance beyond that. Nontechnical audiences have no understanding of what it takes to develop the logic and data storage structures that form the inner workings of the application, and they become most disappointed when they realize that what looked like a complete, functional application system was really just an empty shell. However, when done correctly, this technique can be remarkably successful in determining user requirements that describe precisely the application system the business users want and need.

Rapid Application Development (RAD)

Rapid Application Development (RAD) is a software development process that allows functioning application systems to be built in as little as 60–90 days. Compromises are often made using the 80/20 rule, which assumes that 80 percent of the required work can be completed in 20 percent of the time. Complicated exception handling, for example, can be omitted in the interest of delivering a working system sooner. If the process is repeated on the same set of requirements, the system is ultimately built out to meet 100 percent of the requirements in a manner similar to prototyping.

RAD is not useful in controlling project schedules or budgets, and in fact requires a project manager who is highly skilled at managing schedules and controlling costs. It is most useful in situations where a rapid schedule is more important than product quality (measured in terms of conforming to all known requirements).

Quiz

Choose the correct responses to each of the multiple-choice questions. Note that there may be more than one correct response to each question.

1. The phases of a systems development life cycle (SDLC) methodology include
   a. Physical design
   b. Logical design
   c. Prototyping
   d. Requirements gathering
   e. Ongoing support

2. During the planning phase of an SDLC project:
   a. The database design is normalized.
   b. A feasibility study is often conducted.
   c. A database specialist may be assigned to the project.
   d. Prototyping takes place.
   e. Interviews are conducted.

3. During the requirements phase of an SDLC project:
   a. User views are discovered.
   b. The quality assurance (QA) environment is used.
   c. Surveys may be conducted.
   d. Interviews are often conducted.
   e. Observation may be used.

4. The advantages of conducting interviews are
   a. Interviews take less time than other methods.
   b. Answers may be obtained for unasked questions.
   c. A lot can be learned from nonverbal responses.
   d. Questions are presented more objectively compared to survey techniques.
   e. Entities are more easily discovered.

5. The advantages of conducting surveys include
   a. A lot of ground can be covered quickly.
   b. Nonverbal responses are not included.
   c. Most survey recipients respond.
   d. Surveys are simple to develop.
   e. Prototyping of requirements is unnecessary.

6. The advantages of observation are
   a. You always see people acting normally.
   b. You are likely to see lots of situations where exceptions are handled.
   c. You may see the way things really are instead of the way management and/or documentation presents them.
   d. The Hawthorne effect enhances your results.
   e. You may observe events that would not be described to you by anyone.

7. The advantages of document reviews are
   a. Pictures and diagrams are valuable tools for understanding systems.
   b. Document reviews can be done relatively quickly.
   c. Documents will always be up to date.
   d. Documents will always reflect current practices.
   e. Documents often present overviews better than other techniques can.

8. During the conceptual design phase:
   a. Normalization takes place.
   b. New entities may be discovered.
   c. The conceptual data model is updated.
   d. Web pages may be designed.
   e. Application program modules are specified.

9. During the logical design phase:
   a. The internal components of the application are designed.
   b. Normalization takes place.
   c. System testing takes place.
   d. Program modules are written.
   e. Program specifications are written.

10. During the physical design phase:
    a. Hardware capacity planning takes place.
    b. Additional hardware is added as the database grows.
    c. Additional database indexes may be added.
    d. DDL is written to define database objects.
    e. Application programs are written.

11. During the construction phase:
    a. Application programs are tested.
    b. Quality assurance testing takes place.
    c. DBA work may be limited to merely running deployment scripts.
    d. Data conversion for production deployment takes place.
    e. New entities are discovered.

12. During implementation and rollout:
    a. Users are placed on the live system.
    b. Enhancements are designed.
    c. The old and new applications may be run in parallel.
    d. Quality assurance testing takes place.
    e. User training takes place.

13. During ongoing support:
    a. Enhancements are immediately implemented.
    b. Storage for the database may require expansion.
    c. The staging environment is no longer required.
    d. Bug fixes may take place.
    e. Patches may be applied if needed.

14. Prototyping:
    a. May be used to create complete systems
    b. May be used only for gathering requirements
    c. Is an integral part of most SDLC methodologies
    d. Works well when requirements are sketchy
    e. Helps in setting user expectations

15. Rapid Application Development:
    a. Focuses on developing complete systems
    b. Is useful for controlling costs and schedules
    c. Incorporates complex error handling
    d. Develops systems rapidly by skipping 20 percent of the requirements
    e. Incorporates quality assurance testing

16. Normalization takes place during:
    a. Logical design
    b. Physical design
    c. Construction
    d. Implementation and rollout
    e. Ongoing support

17. The database is initially constructed in the:
    a. Production environment
    b. Quality assurance environment
    c. Staging environment
    d. System test environment
    e. Development environment

18. Database conversion is tested during:
    a. Logical design
    b. Physical design
    c. Construction
    d. Implementation and rollout
    e. Ongoing support

19. Dr. E.F. Codd invented:
    a. The SDLC methodology
    b. The relational database
    c. Quality assurance testing
    d. Normalization
    e. Rapid Application Development (RAD)

20. User views are analyzed during:
    a. Requirements gathering
    b. Logical design
    c. Physical design
    d. Construction
    e. Quality assurance testing

Logical Database Design Using Normalization

In this chapter, you will learn how to perform logical database design using a process called *normalization*. In terms of understanding relational database technology, this is the most important topic in this book, because it is normalization that teaches you how to best organize your data into tables.

Normalization is a technique for producing a set of relations that possesses a certain set of properties. Dr. E.F. Codd, the father of the relational database, developed the process in 1972, using three normal forms. The name was a bit of a political gag at the time. President Nixon was "normalizing" relations with China, so Dr. Codd figured if you could normalize relations with a country, you should be able to "normalize" data relations as well. Additional normal forms were added later, as discussed toward the end of this chapter.

The normalization process is shown in Figure 6-1. On the surface, it is quite simple and straightforward to understand, but it takes considerable practice to execute the process consistently and correctly. Briefly, we take any *relation* (data represented logically in a two-dimensional format using rows and columns) and choose a unique identifier for the entity that the relation represents. Then, through a series of steps that apply various rules, we reorganize the relation into continuously more progressive normal forms. The definitions of each of these normal forms and the process required to arrive at each one are covered in the sections that follow.

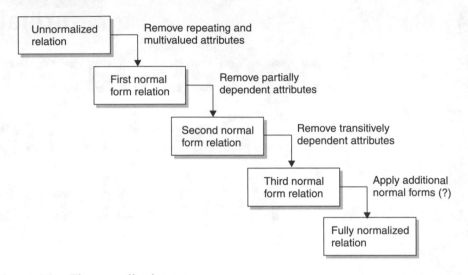

Figure 6-1   The normalization process

Throughout the normalization process, we will use the *logical* terms for everything. For beginners, it is often easier to think in terms of the physical objects that will eventually be created from our logical design. This is because learning to think of databases at the conceptual and logical levels of abstraction instead of the physical level is, in fact, a very difficult discipline for your mind to master. If you find yourself thinking of tables instead of relations, and primary keys instead of unique identifiers, you need to break the habit as soon as possible. Those who think only physically while attempting to normalize tables run into difficulties later because there is not necessarily a one-to-one correspondence between normalized relations and tables. In fact, it is physical database design that transforms the normalized relations into relational tables, and there is some latitude in mapping normalized relations to physical tables. The following table may help you remember the correspondence between the logical and physical terms:

Logical Term	Physical Term
Relation	Table
Unique identifier	Primary key
Attribute	Column
Tuple	Row

The Need for Normalization

In his early work with relational database theory, Dr. Codd discovered that unnormalized relations presented certain problems when attempts were made to update the data in them. He used the term *anomalies* for these problems. The reason we normalize the relations is to *remove* these anomalies from the data. These anomalies are essential to understand because they also tell us when it is acceptable to bend the rules during physical design by "denormalizing" the relations. Denormalization is covered in a section near the end of this chapter. It only makes sense that in order to bend the rules, you have to understand why the rules exist in the first place.

Figure 6-2 shows an invoice from Acme Industries, a fictitious company. The invoice contains attributes that are typical for a printed invoice from a supply company. Conceptually, the invoice is a user view. We will use this invoice example throughout our exploration of the normalization process.

```
                        Acme Industries
                           INVOICE

Customer Number:  1454837              Terms:  Net 30
Customer:  W. Coyote                   Ship Via: USPS
           General Delivery
           Falling Rocks, AZ 84211     Order Date: 11/05/06
           (599) 555-9345

Product No.   Description            Quantity  Unit Price  Extended Amount
===========   ========================  ========  ==========  ===============
SPR-2290      Super strength springs       2        24.00       $  48.00
STR-67        Foot straps, leather         2         2.50       $   5.00
HLM-45        Deluxe Crash Helmet          1        67.88       $  67.88
SFR-1         Rocket, solid fuel           1    128,200.40      $ 128,200.40
ELT-7         Emergency Location Transmitter 1      79.88   ** FREE GIFT **

TOTAL ORDER AMOUNT:                                            $ 128,321.28
```

Figure 6-2   Invoice from Acme Industries

Insert Anomaly

The *insert anomaly* refers to a situation wherein one cannot insert a new tuple into a relation because of an artificial dependency on another relation. The error that has caused the anomaly is that attributes of two different entities are mixed into the same relation. Referring to Figure 6-2, we see that the ID, name, and address of the customer are included in the invoice view. Were we to merely make a relation from this view as it is, and eventually a table from the relation, we would soon discover that we could not insert a new customer into the database unless they had bought something. This is because all the customer data is embedded in the invoice.

Delete Anomaly

The *delete anomaly* is just the opposite of the insert anomaly. It refers to a situation wherein a deletion of data about one particular entity causes unintended loss of data that characterizes another entity. In the case of the Acme Industries invoice, if we delete the last invoice that belongs to a particular customer, we lose all the data related to that customer. Again, this is because data from two entities (customers and invoices) would be incorrectly mixed into a single relation if we merely implemented the invoice as a table without applying the normalization process to the relation.

Update Anomaly

The *update anomaly* refers to a situation where an update of a single data value requires multiple tuples (rows) of data to be updated. In our invoice example, if we wanted to change the customer's address, we would have to change it on every single invoice for the customer. This is because the customer address would be redundantly stored in every invoice for the customer. To make matters worse, redundant data provides the golden opportunity to update many copies of the data, but miss a few of them, which results in inconsistent data. The mantra of the skilled database designer is, For each attribute, capture it once, store it once, and use that one copy everywhere.

Applying the Normalization Process

The normalization process is applied to each user view collected during earlier design stages. Some people find it easier to apply the first step (choosing a primary key) to each user view, then the next step (converting to first normal form), and so forth. Other people prefer to take the first user view and apply all the normalization steps to it, then the next user view, and so forth. With practice, you'll know which one works best for you, but whichever you do, you must be *very* systematic in your approach, lest you miss something. Our example has only one user view (the Acme Industries invoice), so this may seem a moot point, but there are two practice problems toward the end of the chapter containing several user views each, so you will be able to try this out soon enough. Using dry-erase markers or chalk on a wall-mounted board is most helpful because you can easily erase and rewrite relations as you go.

We start with each user view being a relation, which means we represent it as if it is a two-dimensional table. As you work through the normalization process, you will be rewriting existing relations and creating new ones. Some find it useful to draw the relations with sample tuples (rows) of data in them to assist in visualizing the work. If you take this approach, be certain that your data represents real-world situations. For example, you might not think of two customers having exactly the same name in our invoice example, so then your normalization results might be incorrect. Therefore, *always* think of as many possibilities as you can when using this approach. Figure 6-3 shows the information from our invoice example (Figure 6-2) represented in tabular form. Only one invoice is shown here, but many more could be filled in to show examples of multiple invoices per customer, multiple customers, the same product on multiple invoices, and so on.

You probably noticed that each invoice has many line items. This will be essential information when we get to first normal form. In Figure 6-3, multiple values are placed in the cells for the columns that hold data from the line items. We call these

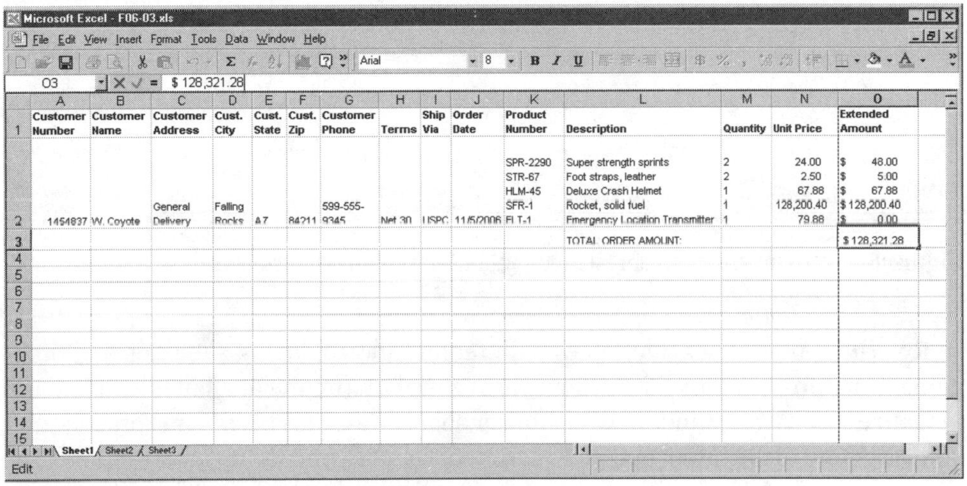

Figure 6-3   Acme Industries invoice represented in tabular form

multivalued attributes because they have multiple values for at least some tuples (rows) in the relation. If we were to construct an actual database table in this manner, our ability to use a language such as SQL to query those columns would be very limited. For example, finding all orders that contained a particular product would require us to parse the column data with a LIKE operator. Updates would be equally awkward because SQL was not designed to handle multivalued columns. Worst of all, a delete of one product from an invoice would require an SQL UPDATE instead of a DELETE because we would not want to delete the entire invoice. As we look at first normal form later in this chapter, you will see how to work around this problem.

Figure 6-4 shows another way we could organize a relation using the invoice shown in Figure 6-2. Here, the multivalued column data has been placed in separate rows and the other columns' data has been repeated to match. The obvious problem here is all the repeated data. For example, the customer's name and address are repeated for each line item on the invoice, which is not only wasteful of resources, but also exposes us to inconsistencies whenever the data is not maintained in the same way (for example, we update the city for one line item but not all the others).

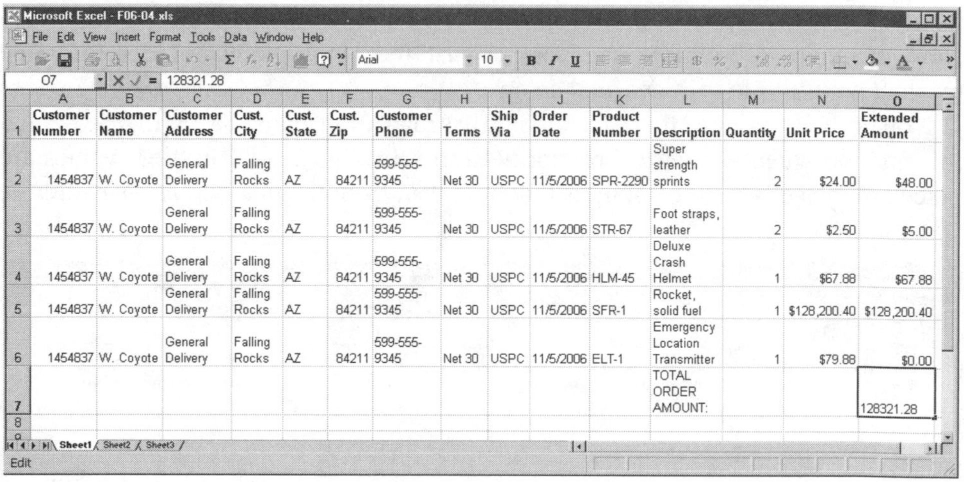
Microsoft Excel - F06-04.xls

O7 = 128321.28

	A	B	C	D	E	F	G	H	I	J	K	L	M	N	O
1	Customer Number	Customer Name	Customer Address	Cust. City	Cust. State	Cust. Zip	Customer Phone	Terms	Ship Via	Order Date	Product Number	Description	Quantity	Unit Price	Extended Amount
2	1454837	W. Coyote	General Delivery	Falling Rocks	AZ	84211	599-555-9345	Net 30	USPC	11/5/2006	SPR-2290	Super strength sprints	2	$24.00	$48.00
3	1454837	W. Coyote	General Delivery	Falling Rocks	AZ	84211	599-555-9345	Net 30	USPC	11/5/2006	STR-67	Foot straps, leather	2	$2.50	$5.00
4	1454837	W. Coyote	General Delivery	Falling Rocks	AZ	84211	599-555-9345	Net 30	USPC	11/5/2006	HLM-45	Deluxe Crash Helmet	1	$67.88	$67.88
5	1454837	W. Coyote	General Delivery	Falling Rocks	AZ	84211	599-555-9345	Net 30	USPC	11/5/2006	SFR-1	Rocket, solid fuel	1	$128,200.40	$128,200.40
6	1454837	W. Coyote	General Delivery	Falling Rocks	AZ	84211	599-555-9345	Net 30	USPC	11/5/2006	ELT-1	Emergency Location Transmitter	1	$79.88	$0.00
7												TOTAL ORDER AMOUNT:			128321.28

Figure 6-4 Acme Invoice represented without multivalued attributes

Rewriting user views into tables with representative data is a tedious and time-consuming process. For this reason, we'll simply write the attributes as a list and visualize them in our minds as two-dimensional tables. This takes some practice and some training of the mind, but once mastered, speeds your ability to normalize relations several fold over writing out exhaustive examples. Here is the list for the invoice example from Figure 6-2:

```
INVOICE: Customer Number, Customer Name, Customer Address,
         Customer City, Customer State, Customer Zip Code,
         Customer Phone, Terms, Ship Via, Order Date,
         Product Number, Product Description, Quantity,
         Unit Price, Extended Amount, Total Order Amount
```

For clarity, a name for the relation has been added, with the relation name in all capital letters and separated from the attributes with a colon. This is the convention we will use for the remainder of this chapter. However, if another technique works better for you, by all means use it. The best news of all is that no matter which representation we use (Figure 6-3, Figure 6-4, or the preceding list), if we properly apply the normalization process and its rules, we will arrive at the same database design.

Choosing a Primary Key

As we normalize, we consider each user view as a relation. In other words, we conceptualize each view as if it is already implemented in a two-dimensional table. The first step in normalization is to choose a primary key from among the unique identifiers we find in the relation.

Recall that a *unique identifier* is a collection of one or more attributes that uniquely identifies each occurrence of a relation. In many cases, a single attribute can be found. In our example, the customer number on the invoice uniquely identifies the customer data within the invoice, but because a customer may have multiple invoices, it is inadequate as an identifier for the entire invoice.

When no single attribute can be found to use for a unique identifier, we can concatenate several attributes to form the unique identifier. You will see this happen with our invoice example when we split the line items from the invoice as we normalize it. It is very important to understand that when a unique identifier is composed of multiple attributes, the attributes themselves are not combined—they still exist as independent attributes and will become individual columns in the table(s) created from our normalized relations.

In a few cases, there is no reasonable set of attributes in a relation that can be used as the unique identifier. When this occurs, we must invent a unique identifier, often with values assigned sequentially or randomly as we add entity occurrences to the database. This technique (some might say "act of desperation") is the source of such unique identifiers as social security numbers, employee IDs, and vehicle identification numbers. We call unique identifiers that have real-world meaning *natural* identifiers, and those that do not (which of course includes the ones we must invent) *surrogate* or *artificial* identifiers. In our invoice example, there appears to be no natural unique identifier for the relation. We could try using customer number combined with order date, but if a customer has two invoices on the same date, this would not be unique. Therefore, it would be much better to invent one, such as an invoice number.

Whenever we choose a unique identifier for a relation, we must be *certain* that the identifier will *always* be unique. If there is only *one* case where it is not unique, we cannot use it. People's names, for example, make lousy unique identifiers. You may have never met someone with exactly your name, but there are people out there with completely identical names. As an example of the harm poorly chosen unique identifiers cause, consider the case of the Brazilian government when it started registering voters in 1994 to reduce election fraud. Father's name, mother's name, and date of birth were chosen as the unique identifier. Unfortunately, this combination is only unique for siblings born on *different* dates, so as a result, when siblings born on the same date (twins, triplets, and so on) tried to register to vote, the first one that showed up was allowed to register, and the rest were turned away. Sound impossible? It's not—this really happened. And to make matters worse, citizens are *required* to vote in Brazil and sometimes have to prove they voted in order to get a job. Someone should have spent more time thinking about the uniqueness of the chosen "unique" identifier.

Sometimes a relation will have more than one possible unique identifier. When this occurs, we call each possibility a *candidate*. Once we have identified all the possible candidates for a relation, we must choose one of them to be the primary key for the relation. Choosing a primary key is *essential* to the normalization process because all the normalization rules reference the primary key. The criteria for choosing the primary key from among the candidates is as follows (in order of precedence, most important first):

- *If there is only one candidate, choose it.*
- *Choose the candidate least likely to have its value change.* Changing primary key values once we store the data in tables is a complicated matter because the primary key can appear as a foreign key in many other tables. Incidentally, surrogate keys are almost always less likely to change compared with natural keys.
- *Choose the simplest candidate.* The one that is composed of the fewest number of attributes is considered the simplest.
- *Choose the shortest candidate.* This is purely an efficiency consideration. However, when a primary key can appear in many tables as a foreign key, it is often worth it to save some space with each one.

For our invoice example, we have elected to add a surrogate primary identifier called Invoice Number. This gives us a simple primary key for the Acme Industries invoices that is guaranteed unique because we can have the database automatically assign sequential numbers to new invoices as they are generated. This will likely make Acme's accountants happy at the same time, because it gives them a simple tracking number for the invoices. There are many conventions for signifying the primary key as we write the contents of relations. Using capital letters causes confusion because we tend to write acronyms such as DOB (date of birth) that way, and those attributes are not always the primary key. Likewise, underlining and bolding the attribute names can be troublesome because these may not always display in the same way. Therefore, we'll settle on the use of a hash mark (#) preceding the attribute name(s) of the primary key. Rewriting our invoice relation in list form with the primary key added, we get the following:

```
INVOICE: # Invoice Number, Customer Number, Customer Name,
         Customer Address, Customer City, Customer State,
         Customer Zip Code, Customer Phone, Terms,
         Ship Via, Order Date, Product Number,
         Product Description, Quantity, Unit Price,
         Extended Amount, Total Order Amount
```

First Normal Form: Eliminating Repeating Data

A relation is said to be in *first normal form* when it contains no multivalued attributes. That is, every intersection of a row and column in the relation must contain *at most* one data value (saying "at most" allows for missing or null values). Sometimes, we will find a group of attributes that repeat together, as with the line items on the invoice. Each attribute in the group is multivalued, but several attributes are so closely related that their values repeat together. This is called a *repeating group,* but in reality, it is just a special case of the multivalued attribute problem.

By convention, we enclose repeating groups and multivalued attributes in pairs of parentheses. Rewriting our invoice in this way to show the line item data as a repeating group, we get this:

```
INVOICE: # Invoice Number, Customer Number, Customer Name,
         Customer Address, Customer City, Customer State,
         Customer Zip Code, Customer Phone, Terms,
         Ship Via, Order Date, (Product Number,
         Product Description, Quantity, Unit Price,
         Extended Amount), Total Order Amount
```

It is essential to understand that although we know there are many customers of Acme Industries, there is only one customer for any given invoice, so the customer data on the invoice is *not* a repeating group. You may have noticed that the customer data for a given customer is repeated on every invoice for that customer, but this is a problem that we will address when we get to third normal form. Because there is only one customer per invoice, the problem is not addressed when we transform the relation to first normal form.

To transform unnormalized relations into first normal form, we must move multivalued attributes and repeating groups to new relations. Because a repeating group is a set of attributes that repeat *together,* all attributes in a repeating group should be moved to the same new relation. However, a multivalued attribute (individual attributes that have multiple values) should be moved to its own new relation rather than combined with other multivalued attributes in the new relation. As you will see later, this technique avoids fourth normal form problems. The procedure for moving a multivalued attribute or repeating group to a new relation is as follows:

1. Create a new relation with a meaningful name. Often, it makes sense to include all or part of the original relation's name in the new relation's name.

2. Copy the primary key from the original relation to the new one. The data depended on this primary key in the original relation, so it must still depend on this key in the new relation. This copied primary key now becomes a *foreign key* to the original relation. As you apply normalization to a database design, always keep in mind that eventually you will have to write SQL to reproduce the original user view from which you started. So, foreign keys to join things back together are nothing less than essential.

3. Move the repeating group or multivalued attribute to the new relation. (The word *move* is used because these attributes are *removed* from the original relation.)

4. Make the primary key (as copied from the original relation) unique by adding attributes from the repeating group to it. If you move a multivalued attribute, which is basically a repeating group of only one attribute, it is that attribute that is added to the primary key. This will seem odd at first, but the primary key attribute(s) that you copied from the original table is a *foreign key* in the new relation. It is quite normal for part of a primary key to also be a foreign key. One additional point: It is perfectly acceptable to have a relation where all the attributes are part of the primary key (that is, there are no "non-key" attributes). This is relatively common in intersection tables.

5. Optionally, you may choose to replace the primary key with a single surrogate key attribute. If you do so, you must keep the attributes that make up the natural primary key formed in steps 2 and 4.

For our Acme Industries invoice example, here is the result of converting the original relation to first normal form:

```
INVOICE: # Invoice Number, Customer Number, Customer Name,
         Customer Address, Customer City, Customer State,
         Customer Zip Code, Customer Phone, Terms,
         Ship Via, Order Date, Total Order Amount
INVOICE LINE ITEM: # Invoice Number, # Product Number,
         Product Description, Quantity, Unit Price,
         Extended Amount
```

Note the following:

- The Invoice Number attribute was copied from INVOICE to INVOICE LINE ITEM and Product Number was added to it to form the primary key of the INVOICE LINE ITEM relation.
- The entire repeating group (Product Number, Product Description, Quantity, Unit Price, and Extended Amount) was removed from the INVOICE relation.
- Invoice Number is still the primary key in INVOICE, and it now also serves as a foreign key in INVOICE LINE ITEM as well as being *part* of the primary key of INVOICE LINE ITEM.
- There are no repeating groups or multivalued attributes in the relations, so they are therefore in first normal form.

There is an interesting consequence of composing a natural primary key for the INVOICE LINE ITEM relation: We cannot put the same product on a given invoice more than one time. This might be desirable, but it could also restrict Acme Industries. We have to understand their business rules to know. If Acme Industries wants the option of putting multiple line items on the same invoice for the same product (perhaps with different prices), we should make up a surrogate key instead. Moreover, there are those who believe that primary keys composed of multiple attributes are undesirable, along with software products that simply do not support them. The alternative is to make up a surrogate primary key for the INVOICE LINE ITEM relation. If we choose to do so, the relation may be rewritten this way:

```
INVOICE LINE ITEM: # Invoice Line Item Number,
                   Invoice Number, Product Number,
                   Product Description, Quantity,
                   Unit Price, Extended Amount
```

We are going to use the previous form (the one with the compound primary key made up of Invoice Number and Product Number, often called the *natural key*) as we continue with normalization.

Second Normal Form: Eliminating Partial Dependencies

Before we explore second normal form, you must understand the concept of *functional dependence.* For this definition, we'll use two arbitrary attributes, cleverly named "A" and "B." Attribute B is *functionally dependent* on attribute A if at any moment in time, there is no more than one value of attribute B associated with a given value of attribute A. Lest you wonder what planet the author lived on before this one, let's try to make the definition more understandable. First, if we say that attribute B is functionally dependent on attribute A, what we are also saying is that attribute A *determines* attribute B, or that A is a *determinant* (unique identifier) of attribute B. Second, let's look again at the first normal form relations in our Acme Industries example:

```
INVOICE: # Invoice Number, Customer Number, Customer Name,
         Customer Address, Customer City, Customer State,
         Customer Zip Code, Customer Phone, Terms,
         Ship Via, Order Date, Total Order Amount
INVOICE LINE ITEM: # Invoice Number, # Product Number,
         Product Description, Quantity, Unit Price,
         Extended Amount
```

In the INVOICE relation, we can easily see that Customer Number is functionally dependent on Invoice Number because at any point in time, there can be only one value of Customer Number associated with a given value of Invoice Number. The very fact that the Invoice Number uniquely identifies the Customer Number in this relation means that, in return, the Customer Number is *functionally dependent* on the Invoice Number.

In the INVOICE LINE ITEM relation, we can also say that Product Description is functionally dependent on Product Number because, at any point in time, there is only one value of Product Description associated with the Product Number. However, the fact that the Product Number is only part of the key of the INVOICE LINE ITEM is the very issue addressed by second normal form.

A relation is said to be in *second normal form* if it meets both the following criteria:

- The relation is in first normal form.
- All non-key attributes are functionally dependent on the *entire* primary key.

If we look again at Product Description, it should be easy to see that Product Number *alone* determines the value. Said another way, if the same product appears as a line item on many different invoices, the Product Description is the same *regardless* of the Invoice Number. Or we can say that Product Description is functionally dependent on only *part of* the primary key, meaning it depends only on Product Number and not on the *combination* of Invoice Number *and* Product Number.

It should also be clear by now that second normal form only applies to relations where we have concatenated primary keys (that is, those made up of multiple attributes). If we have a primary key composed of only a single attribute, as we do with the first normal form version of the Invoice relation, and the primary key is atomic (that is, has no subparts that make sense by themselves), as all attributes should be, then it is simply not possible for anything to depend on *part* of the primary key. It follows, then, that any first normal form relation that has only a single attribute for its primary key is *automatically* in second normal form.

Looking at the INVOICE LINE ITEM relation, however, second normal form violations should be readily apparent: Product Description and Unit Price depend only on the Product Number instead of the *combination* of Invoice Number and Product Number. But not so fast! What about price changes? If Acme decides to change their prices, how could we possibly want that change to be retroactive for every invoice we have ever created? After all, an invoice is an official record that we must maintain for seven years, per current tax laws. This is a common dilemma with fast-changing attributes such as prices. Either we must be able to recall the price at any point in time or we must store the price with the invoice so we can reproduce the invoice as needed (that is, when the friendly tax auditors come calling). For simplicity, we have elected to store the price in two places, one being the current selling price and the other being the price at the time the sale was made. Because the later is a snapshot at a point in time that is not expected to change, there are no anomalies to this seemingly redundant storage. An alternative would be to store a date-sensitive price history somewhere that we could use to reconstruct the correct price for any invoice. That is a practical alternative here, but you would never be able to do that with stock or commodities market transactions, for example. The point is that while the sales price *looks* redundant, there are no *anomalies* to the additional attribute, so it does no harm. Notice that we adjusted the attribute names so their meaning is abundantly clear.

Once we find a second normal form violation, the solution is to move the attribute(s) that is (are) partially dependent to a new relation where it depends on the *entire* key instead of *part* of the key. Here is our invoice example rewritten into second normal form:

```
INVOICE: # Invoice Number, Customer Number, Customer Name,
         Customer Address, Customer City, Customer State,
         Customer Zip Code, Customer Phone, Terms,
         Ship Via, Order Date, Total Order Amount
INVOICE LINE ITEM: # Invoice Number, # Product Number,
         Quantity, Sale Unit Price, Extended Amount
PRODUCT: # Product Number, Product Description,
         List Unit Price
```

The improvement from our first normal form solution is that maintenance of the Product Description now has no anomalies. We can set up a new product independent of there being an invoice for the product. If we wish to change the Product Description, we may do so by merely changing one value in one row of data. Also, should the last invoice for a particular product be deleted from the database for whatever reason, we won't lose its description (it will still be in the row in the Product relation). *Always* remember that the reason we are normalizing is to eliminate these anomalies.

Third Normal Form: Eliminating Transitive Dependencies

To understand third normal form, you must first understand transitive dependency. An attribute that depends on another attribute that is not the primary key of the relation is said to be *transitively dependent*. Looking at our INVOICE relation in second normal form, one can clearly see that Customer Name is dependent on Invoice Number (each Invoice Number has only one Customer Name value associated with it), but at the same time, Customer Name is also dependent on Customer Number. The same can be said of the rest of the customer attributes as well. The problem here is that attributes of another entity (Customer) have been included in our INVOICE relation.

A relation is said to be in *third normal form* if it meets both the following criteria:

- The relation is in second normal form.
- There is no transitive dependence (that is, all the non-key attributes depend *only* on the primary key).

To transform a second normal form relation into third normal form, simply move any transitively dependent attributes to relations where they depend only on the primary key. Be careful to leave the attribute on which they depend in the original relation as a foreign key. You will need it to reconstruct the original user view via a join.

If you have been wondering about easily calculated attributes such as Extended Amount in the INVOICE LINE ITEM relation, it is actually third normal form that forbids them, but it takes a subtle interpretation of the rule. Because the Extended Amount is calculated by multiplying Sale Unit Price by Quantity, it follows that Extended Amount is *determined by* the combination of Sale Unit Price and Quantity and therefore is *transitively dependent* on those two attributes. Thus, it is third normal form that tells us to remove easily calculated attributes. And in this case, they are simply removed. Using similar logic, we also removed the Total Order Amount from the INVOICE relation because we can simply sum the INVOICE LINE ITEM relation to reproduce the value. A good designer will make a note in the documentation specifying the formula for the calculated attribute so that its value can be reproduced when needed. Another effective alternative is to always write the SQL that reproduces the original views when you complete a normalization process. It's an excellent way to *test* your normalization because you can use the SQL to *prove* that the original user views can be easily reproduced.

Here is the Acme Industries invoice data rewritten into third normal form:

```
INVOICE: # Invoice Number, Customer Number, Terms,
         Ship Via, Order Date
INVOICE LINE ITEM: # Invoice Number, # Product Number,
         Quantity, Sale Unit Price
PRODUCT: # Product Number, Product Description,
         List Unit Price
CUSTOMER: # Customer Number, Customer Name,
         Customer Address, Customer City, Customer State,
         Customer Zip Code, Customer Phone
```

Did you notice one more possible third normal form violation? If we have the complete nine-digit ZIP code for the customer, doesn't that determine the Customer City and State? Yes, but it must be the *complete* nine-digit ZIP code (called "zip plus 4" by the U.S. Postal Service). In the past there have been five-digit ZIP codes in the United States that actually cross state lines. Moreover, there are thousands of examples of different cities and towns sharing the same five-digit ZIP codes. So be careful when you assume things. The U.S. Postal Service will be the first to tell you that they are not responsible for aligning their zoning system with political boundaries. By the way, ZIP is actually an acronym for Zoning Improvement Program, introduced in 1963. But we digress....

Should we then make a Zip Code relation and normalize the City and State out of all our addresses? Or would that be considered overdesign? The question can be answered by going back to the anomalies, because removal of the insert, update, and delete anomalies is the entire reason we normalize data in the first place:

- If a new city is formed, do we need to add it to our database even if we have no customers located there? (This is an insert anomaly.)
- If a city is dissolved, do we have a need to delete its information without losing other data? (This is a delete anomaly.)
- If a city changes its name (this rarely occurs, but it has happened), is it a burden to us to find all the customers in that city and change their address accordingly?

If you answered yes to any of the above, then you should normalize the City and State attributes into a table with a primary key of Zip Code. In fact, you can purchase that data on a regular basis from the U.S. Postal Service or other sources. Furthermore, if you maintain other data by ZIP code, such as shipping rates, you have all the more reason to normalize it. But if not, the Zip Code example is a valuable lesson in why we normalize and when it may not be as important. Common sense must prevail at all times.

Here is an easy way to remember the rules of first, second, and third normal form: In a third normal form relation, every non-key attribute must depend on the key, the whole key, and nothing but the key, so help me Codd.

Beyond Third Normal Form

Since the original introduction of normalization, various authors have offered advanced versions. Third normal form will cover well over 90 percent of the cases you will see in business information systems, and it's considered the "gold standard" in business systems. Once you have mastered third normal form, additional normal forms are worth knowing.

Boyce-Codd Normal Form

Boyce-Codd normal form (BCNF) is a stronger version of third normal form. It addresses anomalies that occur when a non-key attribute is a *determinant* of an attribute that is part of the primary key (that is, when an attribute that is part of the primary key is functionally dependent on a non-key attribute).

As an example, let's assume that Acme Industries assigns multiple product support specialists to each customer, and each support specialist handles only one particular product line. Following is a relation that assigns specialists to customers. In reality, we would use Customer ID and Support Specialist (Employee) ID instead of the customer and support specialist names, but their names are used here for better illustration of the issue.

Customer	Product Line	Support Specialist
W. Coyote	Springs	R. E. Coil
W. Coyote	Straps	B. Brown
W. Coyote	Helmets	C. Bandecoot
W. Coyote	Rockets	R. Goddard
USAF	Rockets	R. Goddard
S. Gonzalez	Springs	R. E. Coil
S. Gonzalez	Straps	B. Brown
S. Gonzalez	Rockets	E. John
L. Armstrong	Helmets	S. D. Osborne

In this example, we must concatenate the Customer and Product Line attributes to form a primary key. However, because a given support specialist only supports one product line, it is also true that the Support Specialist attribute determines the Product Line attribute. If we had chosen a surrogate primary key instead of combining Customer and Product Line for the primary key, the third normal form violation—a non-key attribute determining another non-key attribute (Support Specialist determining Product Line in this case)—would be obvious. However, we masked the normalization error by making Product Line part of the primary key. This is why BCNF is considered a *stronger* version of third normal form.

The Boyce-Codd normal form has two requirements:

- The relation must be in third normal form.
- No determinants exist that are not either the primary key or a candidate key for the table. That is, a non-key attribute may not uniquely identify (determine) any other attribute, including one that participates in the primary key.

The solution is to split the unwanted determinant to a different table, just as you would with a third normal form violation. The BCNF version of this relation is shown here:

```
SUPPORT SPECIALIST ASSIGNMENT: # CUSTOMER ID,
                                 SUPPORT SPECIALIST ID
SUPPORT SPECIALIST SPECIALTY: # SUPPORT SPECIALIST ID,
                                PRODUCT LINE
```

In tabular form, the relations and data look like this (again, names have been substituted for the IDs to make the data easier to visualize):

Customer	Support Specialist
W. Coyote	R. E. Coil
W. Coyote	B. Brown
W. Coyote	C. Bandecoot
W. Coyote	R. Goddard
USAF	R. Goddard
S. Gonzalez	R. E. Coil
S. Gonzalez	B. Brown
S. Gonzalez	E. John
L. Armstrong	S. D. Osborne

Support Specialist	Product Line
B. Brown	Straps
C. Bandecoot	Helmets
E. John	Rockets
R. E. Coil	Springs
R. Goddard	Rockets
S. D. Osborne	Helmets

Fourth Normal Form

An additional anomaly surfaces when two or more multivalued attributes are included in the same relation. Suppose, for example, that we wish to track both office skills and language skills for our employees. We might come up with a relation such as this one:

Employee ID	Office Skill	Language Skill
1001	Typing, 40 wpm	Spanish
1001	10 key	French
1002	Spreadsheets	Spanish
1002	10 key	German

We can form a primary key for this relation by choosing the combination of either Employee ID and Office Skill, or Employee ID and Language Skill. That leaves us with either of these two alternatives for third normal form relations:

```
EMPLOYEE SKILL: # EMPLOYEE ID, # OFFICE SKILL,
                LANGUAGE SKILL
EMPLOYEE SKILL: # EMPLOYEE ID, # LANGUAGE SKILL,
                OFFICE SKILL
```

Both the alternatives shown are in third normal form, and in fact, both pass Boyce-Codd normal form as well. The problem, of course, is that there is an implied relationship between office skills and language skills. Does the first tuple for employee 1001 imply that he or she can only type in Spanish? And does the second tuple imply he or she can only work a French 10 Key pad?

Relations such as these are rare in real life because when experienced designers resolve multivalued attribute problems to satisfy first normal form, they move each multivalued attribute to its own relation rather than combining them as shown here.

So, with some strict interpretation of first normal form procedures, this can be avoided altogether. However, should you encounter a fourth normal form violation, the remedy is simply to put each multivalued attribute in a separate relation, such as these:

```
EMPLOYEE OFFICE SKILL: # EMPLOYEE ID, # OFFICE SKILL
EMPLOYEE LANGUAGE SKILL: # EMPLOYEE ID, # LANGUAGE SKILL
```

Fifth Normal Form

Some authors and researchers have suggested the need for fifth normal form, which deals with a special type of constraint known as a *join dependency* that requires knowledge of relational calculus to understand. Others have described fifth normal form exactly the way fourth normal form is described here. In short, there is no clear standard definition of fifth normal form in the industry, and while join dependencies may be of theoretical interest, there is no clear evidence that they have practical value in business applications.

Domain-Key Normal Form (DKNF)

R. Fagin introduced domain-key normal form (DKNF) in a research paper published in 1981. The theory is that a relation is in DKNF if and only if every constraint on the relation is a result of the definitions of domains and keys. Although Fagin was able to prove that relations in DKNF have no modification anomalies, he provided no procedure or step-by-step rules to achieve it. The dilemma then is that designers have no solid indication of when DKNF has been achieved for a relation. This is likely why DKNF is not in widespread use and is not generally expected in the design of databases for business applications.

Denormalization

As you have seen, normalization leads to more relations, which translates to more tables and more joins. When database users suffer performance problems that cannot be resolved by other means, such as tuning the database or upgrading the hardware on which the RDBMS runs, then denormalization may be required. Most database experts consider denormalization a last resort, if not an act of desperation. With continuous improvements in hardware and RDBMS efficiencies, denormalization has become far less necessary than in the earlier days of relational databases. The most essential point is that denormalization is not the same as not bothering to normalize in the first place. Once a normalized database design has been achieved, adjustments can be made with the potential consequences (anomalies) in mind. Possible denormalization steps include the following:

- Recombining relations that were split to satisfy normalization rules
- Storing redundant data in tables
- Storing summarized data in tables

Note also that normalization is intended to remove anomalies from databases that are used for online transaction-processing systems. Databases that store historical data used solely for analytical purposes are not as subject to insert, update, and delete anomalies. Chapter 12 contains more information on databases that hold historical information.

Practice Problems

This section contains two practice problems with solutions so you can try normalization for yourself. These are very narrow, scaled-down case problems that most readers should be able to solve in about an hour each. As you work them, you will be more successful if you focus just on the views presented and not worry about other business processes and data that might be needed. For each case problem, the intent is for you to produce third normal form relations that support the views presented and then draw an ERD for the normalized relations. As you draw the ERDs, keep in mind that they are quite easy to do once normalization is complete—you simply create a rectangle for each normalized relation and then draw relationships everywhere a primary key in one relation is used as a foreign key in another (or the same) relation. These should all be one-to-many relationships, and the foreign key must always be on the *many* side of the relationship. Each problem concludes with the author's solution.

TLA University Academic Tracking

The University of Three Letter Acronyms (UTLA) is a small academic facility offering undergraduate and continuing adult education. Most of the recordkeeping is either manual or done by individuals using personal tools such as spreadsheets. A modernization effort is underway, which includes building integrated application and database systems to perform basic business functions.

The User Views

UTLA wishes to construct a system to track their academic activities, including course offerings, instructor qualifications for the courses, course enrollment, and student grades. The following illustrations show the desired output reports with sample data (these are the user views that should be normalized).

Student report:

ID	Name	Mailing Address		Home Phone
4567	Helen Wheels	127 Essex Drive	Hayward CA 94545	510-555-2859
4973	Barry Bookworm	P.O. Box 45	Oakland CA 94601	510-555-9403
6758	Carla Coed	South Hall #23	Berkeley CA 94623	510-555-DORM

Course report:

ID	Title	No. Credits	Prerequisite Courses	Description
X100	Concepts of Data Proc.	4	none	This course.....
X301	COBOL I	4	X100	blah, blah....
X302	COBOL II	6	X301	Continuation of...
X422	Systems Analysis	6	X301	Introduction to...
X408	Concepts of DBMS	6	X301, X422	more blah, blah,

Instructor report:

ID	Name	Home Address	Home Phone	Office Phone	Courses
756	Werdna Leppo	12 Main St. Alameda CA 94501	510-976-CLAS	x-7463	X408, X422
795	Cura Cuder	32767 Binary Way Abend CA 21304	510-555-1010	x-5382	X301, X302
801	Tillie Talker	123 Forms Rd. Paperwork CA 95684	510-555-BLAB	x-3547	X100

Section report:

Year: 1994   Semester: Spr   Building: Evans   Room: 70   Day(s): Tu   Time(s): 7-10

Instructor: 756, Werdna Leppo   Course: X408   Credits: 6

Student ID	Student Name	Grade
4567	Helen Wheels	A
6758	Carla Coed	B+

Year: 1994   Semester: Spr   Building: SFO   Room: 70   Day(s): We   Time(s): 7-10

Instructor: 756, Werdna Leppo   Course: X408   Credits: 6

Student ID	Student Name	Grade
4973	Barry Bookworm	B+

One cannot design a database without some knowledge of the business rules and processes of an organization. Here are a few such items to keep in mind:

- Only one mailing address and one contact phone number are kept for each student.
- Each course has a fixed number of credits (that is, there are no variable credit courses).
- Each course may have one or more prerequisite courses. The list of all prerequisite courses for each course is shown in the Course report.
- Only one mailing address, one home phone number, and one office phone number are kept for each instructor.
- A qualifications committee must approve instructors before they are permitted to teach a particular course. The qualifications (that is, the courses that the committee has determined the instructor is qualified to teach) are then added to the instructor's records, as shown in the Instructor report. The list of qualified courses does not imply that the instructor has ever actually taught the course but only that he or she is qualified to do so.
- Based on demand, any course may be offered multiple times, even in the same year and semester. Each offering is called a "section," as shown in the Section report.
- Students enroll in a particular section of a course and receive a grade for their participation in that course offering. Should they take the course again at a later time, they receive another grade, and both grades are part of their permanent academic record.

- Although the day, time, building, and room for each section is noted in the Section report, this is done merely to facilitate registering students. The scheduling of classrooms is out of scope for this project.
- The day(s) and time(s) attributes on the Section report are merely text descriptions of the meeting schedule. The building of a meeting calendar for sections is out of scope for this project.

As a convenience, here are the attributes rewritten using our relation listing method, with repeating groups and multivalued attributes enclosed in parentheses:

```
STUDENT REPORT: # ID, NAME, STREET ADDRESS, CITY, STATE,
                ZIP CODE, HOME PHONE
COURSE REPORT: # ID, TITLE, NUMBER OF CREDITS,
                (PREREQUISITE COURSES), DESCRIPTION
INSTRUCTOR REPORT: # ID, NAME, STREET ADDRESS, CITY, STATE,
                ZIP CODE,
                HOME PHONE, OFFICE PHONE, (QUALIFIED COURSES)
SECTION REPORT: YEAR, SEMESTER, BUILDING, ROOM, DAYS,
                TIMES, INSTRUCTOR ID, INSTRUCTOR NAME,
                COURSE ID, NUMBER OF CREDITS,
                (STUDENT ID, STUDENT NAME, GRADE)
```

Author's Solution

Database design is not an exact science, so there is some latitude for alternative solutions. However, all must meet the criteria for third normal form. Here are the normalized relations, with the hash mark (#) denoting primary key attributes:

```
COURSE: # COURSE ID, TITLE, DESCRIPTION, NUMBER OF CREDITS
INSTRUCTOR: # INSTRUCTOR ID, NAME, HOME ADDRESS STREET,
            HOME ADDRESS CITY, HOME ADDRESS STATE,
            HOME ADDRESS ZIP CODE, HOME PHONE, OFFICE PHONE
COURSE SECTION: # SECTION ID, YEAR, SEMESTER, COURSE ID,
            BUILDING, ROOM, MEETING DAY, MEETING TIME,
            INSTRUCTOR ID
STUDENT: # STUDENT ID, NAME, HOME ADDRESS, CITY, STATE,
            ZIP CODE, PHONE
STUDENT SECTION: # STUDENT ID, # SECTION ID, GRADE
COURSE PREREQUISITE: COURSE ID, PREREQUISITE COURSE ID
COURSE INSTRUCTOR QUALIFIED: INSTRUCTOR ID, COURSE ID
```

A few notes on this particular solution are in order:

- There was no simple natural key for the Course Section relation, so a surrogate key was added.

- The Course Prerequisite relation can be quite confusing. This is the intersection relation for a many-to-many recursive relationship. A course can have many prerequisites, which may be found by joining COURSE ID in the COURSE relation with COURSE ID in the COURSE PREREQUISITE relation. At the same time, any course may be a prerequisite for many other courses. These may be found by joining COURSE ID in the COURSE relation with PREREQUISITE COURSE ID in the COURSE PREREQUISITE relation. This means that there are *two* relationships between the COURSE and COURSE PREREQUISITE: one where COURSE ID is the foreign key and another where PREREQUISITE COURSE ID is the foreign key. Comparing the upcoming illustrations for the COURSE and COURSE_PREREQUISITE tables should help make this point clear.

To assist you in visualizing how all this works, the following illustrations show each of the tables as implemented in a Microsoft Access database, each loaded with the data from the original user view (report) examples. Figure 6-5 shows the ERD for the solution, using the Microsoft Relationships panel as the presentation media.

COURSE table:

Microsoft Access - [COURSE : Table]
File Edit View Insert Format Records Tools Window Help

COURSE_ID	TITLE	DESCRIPTION	NUMBER_CREDITS
X100	Concepts of Data Processing	This course....	4
X301	COBOL I	blah, blah	4
X302	COBOL II	Continuation of CBOOL 1	6
X408	Concepts of DBMS	more blah, blah...	6
X422	Systems Analysis	Introduction to...	6
			0

Record: 1 of 5
Datasheet View

INSTRUCTOR table:

Microsoft Access - [INSTRUCTOR : Table]
File Edit View Insert Format Records Tools Window Help

INSTRU	NAME	HOME_ADDRESS	HOME_ADDRESS_CITY	HOME_ADDRESS_STATE	HOME_ADDRESS_ZIP	HOME_PHONE	OFFICE_PHON
756	Werdna Leppo	12 Main St.	Alameda	CA	94501	510-976-CLAS	x-7463
795	Carla Coder	32767 Binary Way	Abend	CA	21304	510-101-1010	x-5382
801	Tillie Talker	123 Forms Rd.	Paperwork City	CA	95684	510-888-BLAB	x-3547
0							

Record: 4 of 4
Datasheet View

COURSE_SECTION table:

	EDP_NUMBER	YEAR	SEMESTER	COURSE_ID	BUILDING	ROOM	MEETING_DAY	MEETING_TIME	INSTRUCTOR_
+	1	1994	Spr	X408	Evans	70	Tu	7-10	756
+	2	1994	Spr	X408	SFO	70	We	7-10	756
+	3	1994	Spr	X100	Evans	70	M, Fr	7-9	801
▶	(AutoNumber)	0							0

Record: 14 ◄ | 4 ► ►I ►* of 4

Datasheet View

STUDENT table:

	ID	NAME	ADDRESS	CITY	STATE	ZIP_CODE	PHONE_NUMBER
+	4567	Helen Wheels	127 Essex Drive	Hayward	CA	94545	510-555-2859
+	4973	Barry Bookworm	P.O. Box 45	Oakland	CA	94601	510-555-9403
+	6758	Carla Coed	South Hall #23	Berkeley	CA	94623	510-976-DORM
▶	0						

Record: 14 ◄ | 4 ► ►I ►* of 4

Datasheet View

STUDENT_SECTION table:

STUDENT_ID	EDP_NUMBER	GRADE
4567	1	A
4567	2	C
4973	2	B+
6758	1	B+
▶ 0	0	

Record: 14 ◄ | 5 ► ►I ►* of 5

Datasheet View

COURSE_PREREQUISITE table:

COURSE_ID	PREREQUISITE_COURSE_ID
▶ X301	X100
X302	X301
X408	X301
X408	X422
X422	X301
*	

Record: 14 ◄ | 1 ► ►I ►* of 5

Datasheet View

COURSE_INSTRUCTOR_QUALIFIED table:

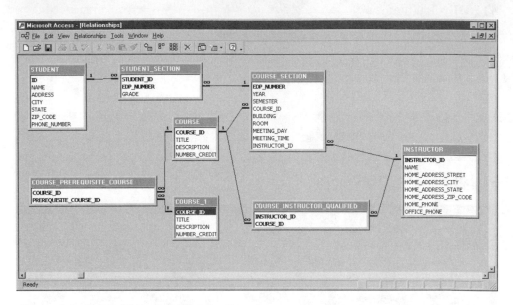

Figure 6-5 ERD (Relationships panel)

Computer Books Company

The Computer Books Company (CBC) buys books from publishers and sells them to individuals via mail and telephone orders. They are looking to expand their services by offering online ordering via the Internet, and in doing so, have a compelling need to build a database to hold their business information.

The User Views

Throughout these user views, "sale" and "price" are references to the retail sale of a book to a CBC customer, whereas "purchase" and "cost" are references to the purchase of books from a publisher (CBC supplier). Each user view is described briefly with a list of the attributes in the view following each description. Per our convention, multivalued attributes and repeating groups are enclosed in parentheses.

The Book Catalog lists all the books that CBC has for sale. Each book is uniquely identified by the International Standard Book Number (ISBN). Although an ISBN uniquely identifies a book, it is essentially a surrogate key, so there is no way to tell what edition a particular book is simply by looking at the ISBN. When new editions come out, CBC typically has leftover stock of prior editions and offers them at a reduced price. The previous edition code in the Book Catalog is intended to help the buyer find the prior edition, if there is one. Books are organized by subject, with each book having only one subject. Any book may have multiple authors. (Although the catalog shows only author names, keep in mind that people's names are seldom unique, and nothing would stop two people with the same name from both writing books). Here is the information in the Book Catalog:

```
BOOK CATALOG: SUBJECT CODE, SUBJECT DESCRIPTION, BOOK TITLE,
              BOOK ISBN, BOOK PRICE, PREVIOUS EDITION ISBN,
              PREVIOUS EDITION PRICE, (BOOK AUTHORS),
              PUBLISHER NAME
```

The Book Inventory Report helps the warehouse manager control the inventory in the warehouse. The Recommended Quantity is the reorder point, meaning when on-hand inventory falls below the recommended quantity, it is time to order more books of that title.

```
INVENTORY REPORT: BOOK ISBN, BOOK EDITION CODE, COST,
                  SELLING PRICE, QUANTITY ON HAND,
                  QUANTITY ON ORDER, RECOMMENDED QUANTITY
```

The Customer Book Orders view shows orders placed by CBC customers for purchases of books:

```
CUSTOMER BOOK ORDERS: CUSTOMER ID, CUSTOMER NAME,
                      STREET ADDRESS, CITY, STATE,
                      ZIP CODE (ISBN, BOOK EDITION CODE,
                      QUANTITY, PRICE), ORDER DATE,
                      TOTAL PRICE
```

CBC bills customers as books are shipped. An invoice is created for each shipment. (An order can have zero, one, or more invoices, but each invoice belongs to only one order.) The Book Sales Invoice looks like this:

```
BOOK SALES INVOICE: SALES INVOICE NUMBER, CUSTOMER ID,
                    CUSTOMER NAME, CUSTOMER STREET ADDRESS,
                    CUSTOMER CITY, CUSTOMER STATE,
                    CUSTOMER ZIP CODE, (BOOK ISBN, TITLE,
                    EDITION CODE, (BOOK AUTHORS), QUANTITY,
                    PRICE, PUBLISHER NAME),
                    SHIPPING CHARGES, SALES TAX
```

The Master Billing Report helps the Collections and Customer Service Departments manage customer accounts. A system for recording customer payments against invoices is out of scope for the current project, but the CBC project sponsors do want to keep a running balance showing what each customer owes CBC. As invoices are generated, a database trigger will be used to add invoice totals to the Balance Due. As payments are received, the CBC staff will manually adjust the Balance Due. The Master Billing Report attributes are as follows:

```
MASTER BILLING REPORT: CUSTOMER ID, NAME, STREET ADDRESS,
                       CITY, STATE, ZIP CODE, PHONE,
                       BALANCE DUE
```

Each time CBC buys books from a publisher, the publisher sends an invoice to CBC. To assist in managing inventory cost, CBC wishes to store the Purchase Invoice information and report it using this view:

```
PURCHASE INVOICE: PUBLISHER ID, PUBLISHER NAME,
                  STREET ADDRESS, CITY, STATE, ZIP CODE,
                  PURCHASE INVOICE NUMBER, INVOICE DATE,
                  (BOOK ISBN, EDITION CODE, TITLE,
                  QUANTITY, COST EACH, EXTENDED COST),
                  TOTAL COST
```

Note that Extended Cost is calculated as Cost Each times Quantity.

Author's Solution

As before, there is some room for alternative solutions, provided all relations are in third normal form. The normalized relations in this solution follow, with primary keys noted with a hash mark (#):

```
BOOK: # ISBN, BOOK TITLE, SUBJECT CODE, PUBLISHER ID,
      EDITION CODE, COST, SELLING PRICE, QUANTITY ON HAND,
      QUANTITY ON ORDER, RECOMMENDED QUANTITY,
```

```
      PREVIOUS EDITION ISBN
CUSTOMER ORDER: # CUSTOMER ORDER NUMBER, CUSTOMER ID,
      ORDER DATE, CANCEL DATE
CUSTOMER ORDER BOOK: # CUSTOMER ORDER NUMBER, # ISBN,
      QUANTITY, BOOK PRICE
SUBJECT: # SUBJECT CODE, DESCRIPTION
AUTHOR: # AUTHOR ID, AUTHOR NAME
BOOK-AUTHOR: # AUTHOR ID, # ISBN
CUSTOMER: # CUSTOMER ID, NAME, STREET ADDRESS, CITY, STATE,
      ZIP CODE, PHONE, BALANCE DUE
PUBLISHER: # PUBLISHER ID, NAME, STREET ADDRESS, CITY,
      STATE, ZIP CODE, AMOUNT PAYABLE
RECEIVABLE (SHIPPED) ORDER: # SALES INVOICE NUMBER,
      CUSTOMER ORDER NUMBER, SALES TAX, SHIPPING CHARGES
RECEIVABLE ORDER BOOK: # SALES INVOICE NUMBER, # ISBN,
      QUANTITY
PAYABLE (PURCHASES): # PURCHASE INVOICE NUMBER,
      PUBLISHER ID, INVOICE DATE, INVOICE AMOUNT
PAYABLE BOOK: # PURCHASE INVOICE NUMBER, # ISBN, QUANTITY,
      COST EACH
```

Figure 6-6 shows the complete design, implemented in Microsoft Access.

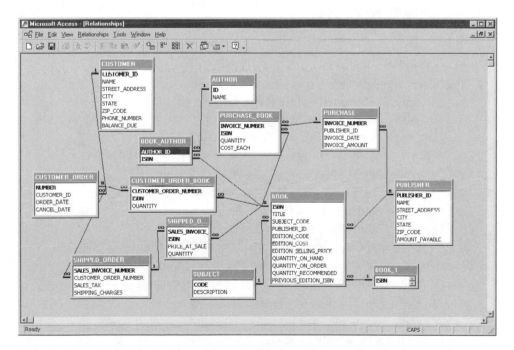

Figure 6-6   CBC ERD (Microsoft Access Relationships panel)

Quiz

Choose the correct responses to each of the multiple-choice questions. Note that there may be more than one correct response to each question.

1. Normalization:
   a. Was developed by Dr. Codd
   b. Was first introduced with five normal forms
   c. First appeared in 1972
   d. Provides a set of rules for each normal form
   e. Provides a procedure for converting relations to each normal form

2. The purpose of normalization is
   a. To eliminate redundant data
   b. To remove certain anomalies from the relations
   c. To provide a reason to denormalize the database
   d. To optimize data-retrieval performance
   e. To optimize data for inserts, updates, and deletes

3. When implemented, a third normal form relation becomes
   a. An index
   b. A referential constraint
   c. A table
   d. A view
   e. A database

4. The insert anomaly refers to a situation where:
   a. Data must be inserted before it can be deleted.
   b. Too many inserts cause the table to fill up.
   c. Data must be deleted before it can be inserted.
   d. A required insert cannot be done due to an artificial dependency.
   e. A required insert cannot be done due to duplicate data.

5. The delete anomaly refers to a situation where:
   a. Data must be deleted before it can be inserted.
   b. Data must be inserted before it can be deleted.
   c. Data deletion causes unintentional loss of another entity's data.
   d. A required delete cannot be done due to referential constraints.
   e. A required delete cannot be done due to lack of privileges.

6. The update anomaly refers to a situation where:
   a. A simple update requires updates to multiple rows of data.
   b. Data cannot be updated because it does not exist in the database.

    c. Data cannot be updated due to lack of privileges.
    d. Data cannot be updated due to an existing unique constraint.
    e. Data cannot be updated due to an existing referential constraint.

7. The roles of unique identifiers in normalization are
    a. They are unnecessary.
    b. They are required once you reach third normal form.
    c. All normalized forms require designation of a primary key.
    d. You cannot normalize relations without first choosing a primary key.
    e. You cannot choose a primary key until relations are normalized.

8. Writing sample user views with representative data in them is
    a. The only way to successfully normalize the user views
    b. A tedious and time-consuming process
    c. An effective way to understand the data being normalized
    d. Only as good as the examples shown in the sample data
    e. A widely used normalization technique

9. Criteria useful in selecting a primary key from among several candidate keys are
    a. Choose the simplest candidate.
    b. Choose the shortest candidate.
    c. Choose the candidate most likely to have its value change.
    d. Choose concatenated keys over single attribute keys.
    e. Invent a surrogate key if that is the best possible key.

10. First normal form resolves anomalies caused by:
    a. Transitive dependencies
    b. Multivalued attributes
    c. Partial dependency on the primary key
    d. Repeating groups
    e. Join dependencies

11. Second normal form resolves anomalies caused by:
    a. Transitive dependencies
    b. Multivalued attributes
    c. Partial dependency on the primary key
    d. Repeating groups
    e. Join dependencies

12. Third normal form resolves anomalies caused by:
    a. Transitive dependencies
    b. Multivalued attributes
    c. Partial dependency on the primary key

      d. Repeating groups

      e. Join dependencies

13. In general, violations of a normalization rule are resolved by:

      a. Combining relations

      b. Moving attributes or groups of attributes to a new relation

      c. Combining attributes

      d. Creating summary tables

      e. Denormalization

14. A foreign key in a normalized relation may be

      a. The entire primary key of the relation

      b. Part of the primary key of the relation

      c. A repeating group

      d. A non-key attribute in the relation

      e. A multivalued attribute

15. Boyce-Codd normal form deals with anomalies caused by:

      a. Multivalued attributes

      b. Transitive dependencies

      c. Join dependencies

      d. Determinants that are not primary or candidate keys

      e. Constraints that are not the result of the definitions of domains and keys

16. Fourth normal form deals with anomalies caused by:

      a. Multivalued attributes

      b. Transitive dependencies

      c. Join dependencies

      d. Determinants that are not primary or candidate keys

      e. Constraints that are not the result of the definitions of domains and keys

17. Fifth normal form deals with anomalies caused by:

      a. Multivalued attributes

      b. Transitive dependencies

      c. Join dependencies

      d. Determinants that are not primary or candidate keys

      e. Constraints that are not the result of the definitions of domains and keys

18. Domain key normal form deals with anomalies caused by:

      a. Multivalued attributes

      b. Transitive dependencies

      c. Join dependencies

      d. Determinants that are not primary or candidate keys

      e. Constraints that are not the result of the definitions of domains and keys

19. Most business systems require that you normalize only as far as:
    a. First normal form
    b. Second normal form
    c. Third normal form
    d. Boyce-Codd normal form
    e. Fourth normal form

20. Proper handling of multivalued attributes when converting relations to first normal form usually prevents subsequent problems with:
    a. First normal form
    b. Second normal form
    c. Third normal form
    d. Boyce-Codd normal form
    e. Fourth normal form

Data and Process Modeling

As you saw in Chapter 5, data and process modeling are major undertakings that are part of the logical design stage of an application system development project. You have already seen the rudiments of data modeling when we used entity relationship diagrams (ERDs) in prior chapters. In this chapter, we will look at ERDs and data modeling in more detail. Process modeling, on the other hand, is less important to a database designer because application processes are designed by application designers and seldom directly involve the database designer. However, because the database designer must work closely with the application designer in gathering data requirements and in supplying a database design that will support the processes being designed, the database designer should be at least familiar with the basic concepts. It is for this reason that the second part of this chapter includes a high-level survey of process design concepts and diagramming techniques.

Entity Relationship Modeling

Entity relationship modeling is the process of visually representing entities, attributes, and relationships, producing a diagram called an *entity relationship diagram (ERD)*. The process is iterative in nature because entities are discovered throughout the design process. The chief advantage of ERDs is that they can be understood by nontechnical people while still providing great value to technical people. Done correctly, ERDs are platform independent and can even be used for nonrelational databases if desired.

ERD Formats

Peter Chen developed the original ERD format in 1976. Since then, vendors, computer scientists, and academics have developed many variations, all of them conceptually the same. It is important to understand the most commonly used variations because you are likely to encounter them in active use in IT organizations. Here are the elements common to all ERD formats:

- Entities are represented as rectangles or boxes.
- Relationships are represented as lines.
- Line ends indicate the maximum cardinality of the relationship (that is, one or many).
- Symbols near the line ends indicate the minimum cardinality of the relationship (that is, whether participation in the relationship is mandatory or optional).
- Attributes may be optionally included (the format for displaying attributes varies quite a bit).

Chen's Format

For simplicity, we'll use the normalized solution for the Acme Industries invoice application from Chapter 6 for the examples in this chapter. Figure 7-1 shows the ERD using Chen's format.

Here are the particulars of the Chen format:

- Relationship lines contain a diamond in which is written a word or short phrase that describes the relationship. For example, the relationship between Invoice and Product may be read as "An invoice *contains* many products."

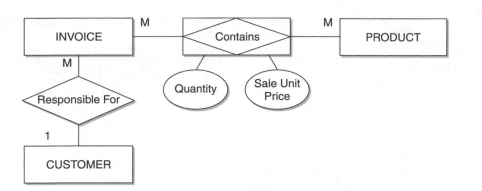

Figure 7-1   Acme Industries logical ERD in Chen's format

- For many-to-many relationships that require an intersection table in an RDBMS, such as the one between Invoice and Product, a rectangle is often drawn around the diamond.
- Maximum cardinality of each relationship is shown using the symbol "1" for "one" or "M" for "many."
- Minimum cardinality is not shown.
- Attributes, when shown, appear in ellipses, connected to the entity or relationship to which they belong with a line.

In practice, Chen ERDs proved to be cumbersome for complicated data models. The diamonds take a lot of space for the added value they provide. Also, any ERD that includes many attributes becomes very difficult to read. Notwithstanding, we owe Chen a lot for his pioneering work, which laid the foundation for the techniques that followed.

The Relational Format

Over time, an ERD format known generically as the *relational format* evolved. It is in use (or available as an option) by several of the better-known data modeling software tools, including PowerDesigner from Sybase and ER/Studio from Embarcadero Technologies, and in popular general drawing tools such as Visio from Microsoft. Figure 7-2 shows the ERD from Figure 7-1, converted to the relational format. In this example, the ERD is represented at a physical level, meaning that physical table names are shown instead of logical entity names, and physical column names are shown instead of logical attribute names. Also, intersection tables are shown to resolve many-to-many relationships. As the logical data model is transformed into a physical database design, it is essential to have a physical ERD that the

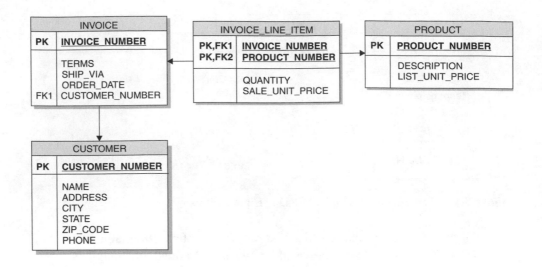

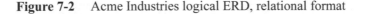

Figure 7-2   Acme Industries logical ERD, relational format

project team can use in developing the application system. The beginnings of the physical model are shown here to help make that point.

Here are the particulars of the relational ERD format:

- Relationship cardinality is shown with an arrowhead on the line end to signify "one" and nothing on the line end to signify "many." This will seem odd at first, but it aligns nicely with object diagrams, so this format is favored by object-oriented designers and developers.
- Attributes are shown inside the rectangle that represents each entity.
- Unique identifier attributes are shown above a horizontal line within the rectangle and are usually also shown in bold with "PK" (signifying "primary key") in the margin to the left of the attribute name.
- Attributes that are foreign keys are shown with "FK" and a number in the margin to the left of the attribute name.

The IDEF1X Format

The Computer Systems Laboratory of the National Institute of Standards and Technology released the IDEF1X standard for data modeling in FIPS Publication 184, which was released in December 1993. The standard covers both a method for data modeling as well as the format for the ERDs produced during the modeling effort. It is widely used and understood across the information technology industry and is a U.S. Federal Government standard. Thanks to its underlying standard, it has few variants. Figure 7-3 shows our sample ERD converted to the IDEF1X standard format. You will note that it is strikingly similar to the relational format shown in Figure 7-2, except for the relationship lines.

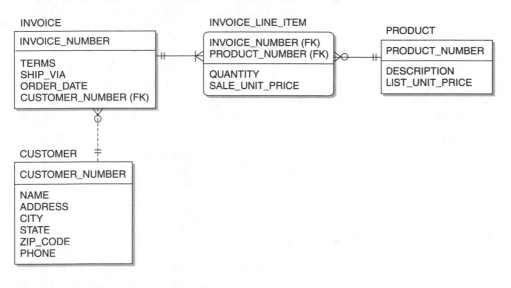

Figure 7-3   Acme Industries logical ERD, IDEF1X standard

Because IDEF1X is so similar to the relational format already presented, let's focus on the differences between the two. In IDEF1X:

- *Identifying relationships,* which are those where the foreign key is part of the child entity's primary key, are shown with a solid line. *Non-identifying relationships,* which are those where the foreign key is a non-key attribute in the child entity, are shown with a dotted line. In Figure 7-3, the relationship between Product and Invoice Line Item is identifying, but the one between Customer and Invoice is non-identifying.
- Maximum relationship cardinality is shown with a short perpendicular line across the relationship near its line end to signify "one," and a "crow's foot" on the line end to signify "many." This is best understood in combination with minimum cardinality, described next.
- Minimum relationship cardinality is shown with a small circle near the end of the line to signify "zero" (participation in the relationship is optional) or a short perpendicular line across the relationship line to signify "one" (participation in the relationship is mandatory). Figure 7-3 notes a few combinations of minimum and maximum cardinality.

- A Product may have zero to many associated Invoice Line Items (shown as a circle and a crow's foot); an Invoice Line Item must have one and only one associated Product (shown as two vertical bars).
- An Invoice must have one or more associated Invoice Line Items (shown as a vertical bar and a crow's foot); an Invoice Line Item must have one and only one associated Invoice (shown as two vertical bars).

- *Dependent entities,* which are those that have an existence dependency on one or more other entities (that is, ones that cannot exist without the existence of another), are shown with the corners of the rectangle rounded. For example, the Invoice Line Item entity depends on both the Product and Invoice entities. Therefore, we cannot delete either an invoice or a product unless we somehow deal with any related invoice line items. This is valuable information during physical database design because we must consider the options for handling situations when the application attempts to delete table rows when dependent entities exist.

Super Types and Subtypes

Some entities can be broken down into more specific categories or types. When this occurs, we call the more detailed entities *subtypes* and the more general entity to which they belong a *super type*. In object terminology, the super type is called a *super class* and the subtypes are called *subclasses* of the super class. It is essential to understand that subtypes break down entities by type rather than by *state,* meaning their mode or condition. An easy way to distinguish the two is that existing entities can change state, but they seldom, if ever, change type. For example, a motor vehicle entity can logically be broken down by type into automobile, bus, truck, motorcycle, and so on. However, the distinction between vehicles that are new or used, or between those that are operable or inoperable, is one of *state* rather than *type* because new vehicles become used once they are sold, and vehicles change between operable and inoperable states as they break down and are subsequently repaired.

The decisions involved in which entities should be broken down into subtypes and how detailed the subtypes should be revolve around the tradeoff between specialization and generalization. Unfortunately, there are no firm rules for resolving the tradeoff. Therefore, generalization versus specialization becomes one of the topics that prevents database design from becoming an exact science. The general guideline to follow (in addition to common sense) is that the more the various subtypes share common attributes, the more the designer should be inclined to combine the subtypes into the super type. The physical design tradeoffs involved are addressed in Chapter 8. Here we will focus on the logical design tradeoffs.

Let's look at an example. Assume for a moment that the database design shown in Figure 7-3 has been implemented, and now the Customer Service Department at Acme Industries has requested database and application enhancements that will allow it to record and track more information about customers. In particular, there is interest in knowing the type of customer (individual person, sole proprietorship, partnership, corporation, and so on) so that correspondence can be addressed appropriately for each type. Figure 7-4 shows the logical data model that was developed based on the new requirements.

In IDEF1X notation, the type or category is shown using a symbol that looks like a circle with a line under it. Therefore, we know that Individual Customer and Commercial Customer are subtypes of Customer because of the symbol that appears in the line that connects them. Also note that they share the exact same primary key and

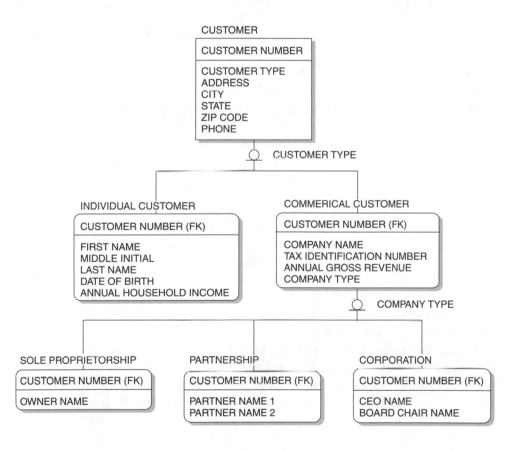

Figure 7-4   Customer subclasses

that in the subtypes, the primary key of the entity is also a foreign key to the super type entity. This makes perfect sense when one considers the fact that an Individual Customer entity *is* a Customer, meaning that any occurrence of the Individual Customer entity would have a tuple in the Customer relation as well as a matching tuple in the Individual Customer entity. Usually there is an attribute in the super type entity that indicates which type is assigned to each entity occurrence (tuple). Once this is implemented in tables, database users can use the type attribute to know where to look for (that is, which subtype table contains) the remainder of the information about each entity occurrence (each row). Such an attribute is called the *type discriminator* and is named next to the type symbol on the ERD. Therefore, Customer Type is the type discriminator that indicates whether a given Customer is an Individual Customer or a Commercial Customer. Similarly, Company Type is the type discriminator that indicates whether a given Commercial Customer is a Sole Proprietorship, Partnership, or Corporation.

As you might imagine, this IDEF1X notation is not the only format used in ERDs for super types and subtypes. However, it is the most commonly used. Another popular format is to draw the subtype entities within the super type entity (that is, subtype entity rectangles drawn inside the corresponding super type entity's rectangle). Although this format makes it visually clear that the subtypes really are just a part of the super type, it has practical limitations when the entities are broken down into many levels.

As mentioned earlier, finding the right level of specialization is a significant database design challenge. In reviewing the logical design as proposed in Figure 7-4, the database design team noticed something: The only difference among the Sole Proprietorship, Partnership, and Corporation subtypes is in the way that the names of key people in those types of companies appear as attributes. Moreover, the use of two nearly identical attributes for the names of the co-owners in the Partnership subtype could be considered a repeating attribute, and therefore a first normal form violation. The design team elected to generalize these names into the Commercial Customer entity, but in doing so, recognized the first normal form problems and decided to place them into a separate relation called Commercial Customer Principal. This led to the ERD shown in Figure 7-5.

Clearly this is a simpler design that will result in fewer tables when it is physically implemented. There is a very big win here because not only is there no loss of function when we consolidate the subtypes into the super type, but we actually have *more* function available because we can add as many names as we wish to any type of commercial customer.

Further study by the design team caused them to notice the striking similarity between the name attributes now contained in the Commercial Customer Principal entity and those contained in the Individual Customer entity. In discussing options

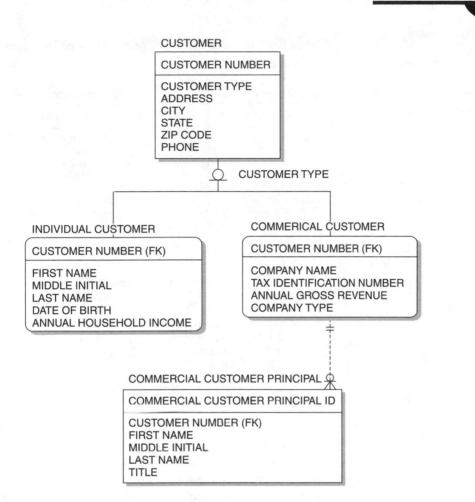

Figure 7-5   Customer subtypes, version 2

further with the Customer Service Department, they uncovered a few cases where it would be desirable for multiple contact names to be recorded for individual customers as well as for commercial customers. For example, customers who have legal disputes often request that all contact go through their attorney. With that information, the design team decided to generalize these names and move Commercial Customer Principal up to be a child of Customer and name it Customer Contact so that it could be used to hold the information about either a principal (owner, co-owner, partner, officer) of the customer or any other contact person for the customer that the Customer Service Department might find useful. The design team further realized that contact names would be more useful if a phone number was included. The Phone attribute was left in the Customer entity because it is intended to hold the general phone number for the customer. The phone number in the Customer Contact entity is intended to hold the phone for an individual contact person. The resultant logical design is shown in Figure 7-6.

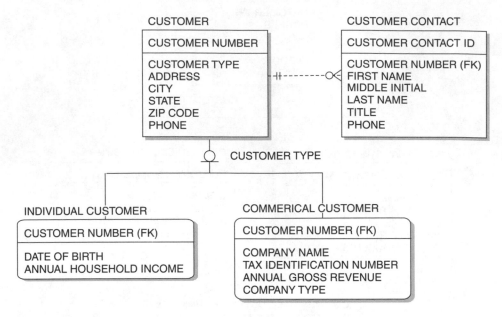

Figure 7-6 Customer subtypes, version 3

The fact that all three of the designs presented (Figures 7-4, 7-5, and 7-6) are workable should underscore the generalization versus specialization dilemma: There is no one "right" answer. The art to database design then, is to arrive at the design that best fits what is known about the expected uses of the database. This is best done by comparing the relative strengths and weaknesses of each alternative design. And there is no better vehicle for communicating the alternatives than the ERD.

Guidelines for Drawing ERDs

Here are some general guidelines to follow when constructing ERDs:

- Do not try to relate every entity to every other entity. Entities should only be related when the *entire* primary key in one entity appears as a foreign key in another.
- Except for subtypes, avoid relationships involving more than two entities. Although drawing fewer lines may seem simpler, it is far too easy to misread relationships drawn from one parent entity to multiple child entities using a single line.

- Be consistent with entity and attribute names. Develop a naming convention and stick with it.
- Use abbreviations in names only when absolutely necessary, and in those cases, use a standard list of abbreviations.
- Name primary keys and foreign keys consistently. Most experts prefer the foreign key to have exactly the same name as the primary key.
- When relationships are named, strive for action words, avoiding nondescriptive terms such as "has," "belongs to," "is associated with," and so on.

Process Models

As already mentioned, process design is seldom the responsibility of the database designer or DBA, but understanding the basics helps the DBA communicate with the process designers and ensure that the database design supports the process design. Therefore, this section presents a brief survey of common process model diagram techniques. If you want more detail about these or other process model techniques, a good book on systems analysis and design is the recommended source.

Throughout this section, the Acme Industries order-fulfillment process, a very simple business process, will be used as an example. This process has the following steps:

1. Find all unshipped orders in the database.

2. For each order:
    - Check for available inventory. If sufficient inventory for the order is not available, skip to the next order.
    - Check the customer's credit to make sure they are not over their credit limit or have some other credit problem, such as overdue payments. This would typically be done at the time the order is entered, but it needs to be done again here because a customer's credit status with Acme Industries can change at any time. If there is a credit problem, skip to the next order.
    - Generate the documents required to pack and ship the order (packing slip, shipping labels, and so on) and route them to the shipping department.
    - When the shipping department has finished with the order, create the invoice for the order and bill the customer accordingly.

Obviously, this process could be a lot more complicated in a large company, but here it has been reduced to the basics so that it is easier to use for illustration of process models.

The Flowchart

The flowchart (or structure chart) is probably the oldest form of computer systems documentation. Some believe that flowcharts existed when dinosaurs still roamed our planet, or that anyone who still uses flowcharts is a dinosaur. Levity aside, flowcharts are often considered outmoded, but they still have much to offer in certain circumstances and are still widely used. Figure 7-7 shows the flowchart for our sample order-fulfillment process.

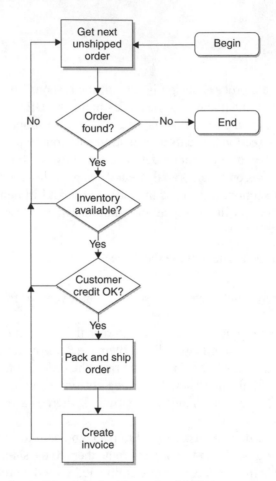

Figure 7-7   Flowchart of Acme Industries order-fulfillment process

Here are the basic components of the flowchart:

• Process steps are shown with rectangles.

- Decision points are shown with diamonds. At each decision point, the logic branches are based on the outcome of the decision. For example, a decision might be "Is today Friday?", with a "Yes" outcome going in one direction and a "No" outcome going in another.
- Lines with arrows show the flow of control through the diagram. When one process completes, it hands over control to the next process or decision point.
- Start and end points are shown with ellipses (elongated circles). Flowcharts can be used to show perpetual processes that have no start and no end, but more often they are used to show finite processes where there is a specific beginning and ending point.
- Connector symbols that look like home plate on a baseball diamond can be used to connect lines to processes or decision points, on the same or another page. Usually these are given a reference letter with a control flow line assumed between any two connectors that have the same reference letter.

Figure 7-7 is a very straightforward loop process flow. We begin with a process step that gets the next unshipped order from the database. We add a decision after it to stop the loop (end the flow) if we don't find an unshipped order. If we do find the order, we continue with decision points that check for available inventory and acceptable customer credit, with a "No" outcome of either going back to the top of the loop (the Get Next Unshipped Order process), which essentially skips the order and moves on to find the next one. If we get a "Yes" outcome from all the decision points, the process Pack and Ship Order is invoked next, followed by Create Invoice. After the Create Invoice process completes, control goes back to Get Next Unshipped Order, at the top of the loop. The loop continues until we find no more unshipped orders.

Flowcharts have the following strengths:

- Procedural language programmers find them naturally easy to learn and use. A *procedural language* is a programming language where the programmer must describe the process steps required to do something, as opposed to a *nonprocedural language*, such as SQL, where the programmer merely describes the desired results. The most commonly used procedural language today is probably C and its variants (C++, C#, and so on), but others, such as FORTRAN and COBOL, still see some use. Also, specialized procedural languages for relational databases, including PL/SQL for Oracle and Transact SQL for Sybase and Microsoft SQL Server, are heavily used.
- Flowcharts are applicable to procedures outside of a programming context. For example, flowcharts are often used to walk repair technicians through troubleshooting procedures for the equipment they service.

- Flowcharts are useful for spotting reusable (common) components. The designer can easily find any process that appears multiple times in the flowcharts for a particular application system.
- Flowcharts may be easily modified and can evolve as requirements change.

On the other hand, flowcharts present these weaknesses:

- They are not applicable to nonprocedural or object-oriented languages.
- They cannot easily model some situations, such as recursive processes (processes that invoke themselves).

The Function Hierarchy Diagram

The function hierarchy diagram, as the name suggests, shows all the functions of a particular application system or business process, organized into a hierarchical tree. Figure 7-8 shows this type of process model diagram from our sample order-fulfillment process.

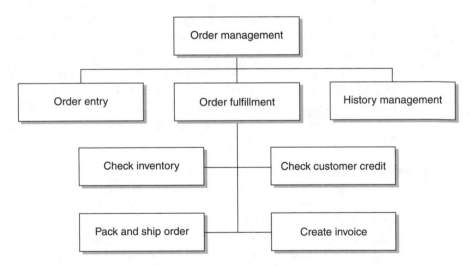

Figure 7-8   Function hierarchy of the Acme order-fulfillment process

Because the function hierarchy for a single process makes little sense out of context, two other processes have been added to the hierarchy: Order Entry and History Management. To be effective, a function hierarchy must contain *all* the processes required to carry out the function it describes. Figure 7-8 attempts to show all the processes required for the Order Management function at Acme Industries. Order Entry is intended to cover all the process steps involved in a customer placing an order and having it recorded in Acme's database. History Management is intended to cover all the steps required to archive and purge old (historical) orders and any required reporting on order history. Both of these processes need to be expanded by adding process steps below them (as was done with Order Fulfillment) to make this a complete diagram. Under Order Fulfillment, the four main process steps involved in fulfilling orders have been added.

The strengths of function hierarchy diagrams are as follows:

- They are quick and easy to learn and use.
- They can quickly document the bulk of the function (they get to 80 percent of the processes quickly).
- They provide a good overview at high and medium levels of detail.

And here are the weaknesses of function hierarchy diagrams:

- Checking quality is difficult and subjective.
- They cannot handle complex interactions between functions.
- They do not clearly show the sequence of process steps or dependencies between steps.
- They are not an effective presentation tool for large hierarchies or at very detailed levels.

The Swim Lane Diagram

The swim lane diagram gets it name from the vertical lanes in the diagram, which resemble the lanes in a swimming pool. Each lane represents an organizational unit such as a department, with process steps placed in the lane for the unit that is responsible for the step. Lines with arrows show the sequence or control flow of the process steps. Figure 7-9 shows the swim lane diagram for our sample order-fulfillment process.

Strengths of the swim lane diagram include

- It has the unmatched ability to show who does what in the organization.
- It's excellent for identifying inefficiencies of existing processes and lends itself well to business process reengineering efforts.

Its weaknesses include

- It does not represent complicated processes (those with many steps or with complex step dependencies) well.
- It does not show error and exception handling.

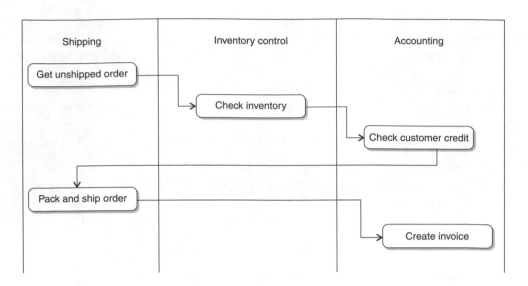

Figure 7-9   Swim lane diagram for the Acme Industries order-fulfillment process

The Data Flow Diagram

The data flow diagram (DFD) is the most data centric of all the process diagrams. Instead of showing a control flow through a series of process steps, it focuses instead on the data that flows through the process steps. By combining diagrams hierarchically, the DFD combines the best of the flowchart and the function diagram. DFDs became immensely popular in the late 1970s and early 1980s, largely due to the work of Chris Gane and Trish Sarson. Each process on a DFD may be broken down using another complete page until the desired level of detail is reached. Figure 7-10 shows one page of the DFD for the Acme Industries order-fulfillment process.

The components of a DFD are simple:

- Processes are represented with rounded rectangles. Processes are typically numbered hierarchically. The first page of a DFD might have processes number 1, 2, 3, and 4. The next page might break down process number 1, and would have processes numbered 1.1, 1.2, and so forth. If process 1.2 were broken down on yet another page, the processes on that page would be numbered 1.2.1, 1.2.2, and so forth.
- Data stores are represented with an open-ended rectangle. A *data store* is a generic representation of data that is made persistent through being stored somewhere, such as a file, database, or even a printed page. The term was

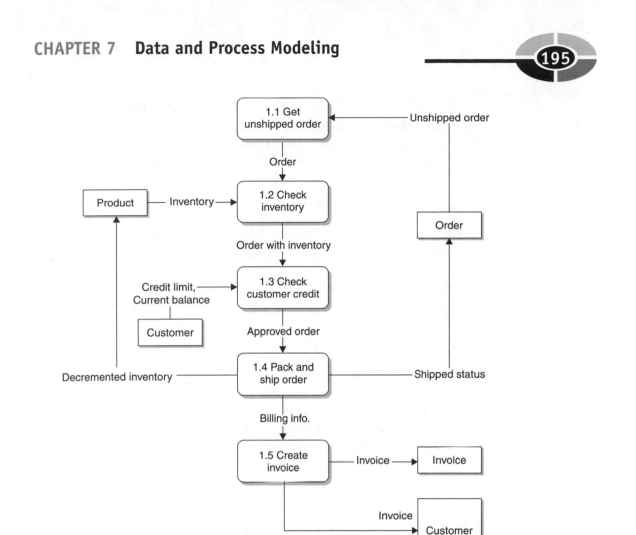

Figure 7-10   Data flow diagram page for the Acme Industries order-fulfillment process

chosen so that no particular type of storage is implied. Because we already
have an ERD for our example, the data stores should closely align with the
entities we have already identified.

- Sources and destinations of data (external entities in relational terminology)
  are shown using squares. Figure 7-10 shows the customer as the destination
  of the invoice data flow (in addition to a local data store that will hold the
  invoice data). Try not to confuse data flows with material flows. Yes, the
  invoice is printed and mailed to the customer, but the data flow is attempting
  to show that the *data* is sent to the customer with no regard for the medium
  used to send it.

- Flows of data are shown using lines with arrowheads indicating the direction of flow. Above each flow, words are used to describe the content of the data being sent. Bidirectional flows are permissible but are usually shown as separate flows because the data is seldom exactly the same in both directions.

The strengths of the data flow diagram are as follows:

- It easily shows the overall structure of the system without sacrificing detail (details are shown on subsequent pages that expand on the higher level processes).
- It's good for top-down design work.
- It's good for presentation of systems designs to management and business users.

And here are the weaknesses of the data flow diagram:

- It's time consuming and labor intensive to develop for complex systems.
- Top-down design has proved to be ineffective in situations where requirements are sketchy and continuously evolving during the life of the project.
- It's poor at showing complex logic, but the lowest-level diagrams may easily be supplemented with other documents, such as narratives or decision tables.

Relating Entities and Processes

Once the database designer has completed logical database design and an ERD for the proposed database, and, in parallel, the process designers have completed their process model, how can we have any confidence that the two will be able to work together in solving the business problem the new project is supposed to address? Part of the answer lies in a charting technique intended to show how the entities and processes interact, known as the CRUD matrix.

Fortunately, CRUD is not slang for a lousy design but rather an acronym formed from the first letters for the words Create, Read, Update, and Delete, which are the letters used in the body of the diagram. The concept of the CRUD matrix is very simple:

- One axis of the matrix represents the major processes of the application system.

- The other axis represents the major entities used by the application system.
- In each cell of the matrix, the appropriate combination of letters is written:
  - *C,* if the process creates new occurrences of the entity
  - *R,* if the process reads information about the entity from a data source
  - *U,* if the process updates one or more attributes for the entity
  - *D,* if the process deletes occurrences of the entity

Here is a sample CRUD matrix for the order management function at Acme Industries, following the major processes shown in the function hierarchy diagram (refer to Figure 7-8). To be effective, only high-level processes and super-type entities should be shown in the matrix. Too much detail clouds the effect of the diagram.

	ENTITY: Product	Order	Customer	Invoice
PROCESS: Order Entry	R	CRU	RU	
Order Fulfillment	RU	RU	R	C
History Management		RD	R	

The CRUD matrix is valuable for verifying the consistency of the process and data (entity) designs. At a glance, one can find the following potential problems:

- Entities that have no Create process
- Entities that have no Delete process
- Entities that are never updated
- Entities that are never read
- Processes that delete or update entities without reading them
- Processes that only read (no Create, Delete, or Update processes)

Our example has multiple problems, which only proves that our process design is incomplete (that is, we are probably missing some key processes for the application system). At the conclusion of the logical design phase of a project, the CRUD matrix is an excellent vehicle for a final review of the work completed. The next step in the database life cycle is to complete the physical database design, which is discussed in Chapter 8.

Quiz

Choose the correct responses to each of the multiple-choice questions. Note that there may be more than one correct response to each question.

1. It is important for a database designer to understand process modeling because:
   a. Process design is a primary responsibility of the DBA.
   b. The process model must be completed before the data model.
   c. The data model must be completed before the process model.
   d. The database designer must work closely with the process designer.
   e. The database design must support the intend process model.

2. Peter Chen's ERD format:
   a. Was developed in 1976
   b. Represents entities as rectangles or boxes
   c. Uses a crow's foot to represent "many"
   d. May optionally include attributes
   e. Shows minimum cardinality with vertical lines

3. The diamond in Chen's ERD format:
   a. Represents an entity
   b. Represents an attribute
   c. Contains a word or phrase that describes the relationship
   d. Shows the cardinality of the relationship
   e. Contains the name of an entity

4. In the relational ERD format:
   a. Unique identifier attributes are marked with "PK" in the margin.
   b. Foreign key attributes are marked with "FK" in the margin.
   c. Attributes are shown in ellipses connected to the entity with a line.
   d. Relationship lines have an arrowhead that points at the "child" entity.
   e. A crow's foot is used to signify "many."

5. The IDEF1X ERD format:
   a. Was first released in 1983
   b. Follows a standard developed by the National Institute of Standards and Technology
   c. Has many variants
   d. Has been adopted as a U.S. Federal Government standard
   e. Covers both data and process models

6. The IDEF1X ERD format shows
   a. Identifying relationships with a solid line
   b. Minimal cardinality using a combination of small circles and vertical lines shown on the relationship line
   c. Maximum cardinality using a combination of small vertical lines and crow's feet drawn on the relationship line
   d. Dependent entities with squared corners on the rectangle
   e. Independent entities with rounded corners on the rectangle

7. A subtype:
   a. Is a subset of the super type
   b. Has a one-to-many relationship with the super type
   c. Has a conditional one-to-one relationship with the super type
   d. Shows various states of the super type
   e. Is a superset of the super type

8. Examples of possible subtypes for an Order entity super type include
   a. Order line items
   b. Shipped order, unshipped order, invoiced order
   c. Office supplies order, professional services order
   d. Approved order, pending order, canceled order
   e. Auto parts order, aircraft parts order, truck parts order

9. In IDEF1X notation, subtypes:
   a. May be shown with a type discriminator attribute name
   b. May be connected to the super type via a symbol composed of a circle with a line under it
   c. Have the primary key of the subtype shown as a foreign key in the super type
   d. Usually have the same primary key as the super type
   e. May be shown using a crow's foot

10. When subtypes are being considered in a database design:
    a. The more subtypes that can be found, the better.
    b. They should be avoided as much as possible because they complicate the design.
    c. There is a tradeoff between generalization and specialization.
    d. There is one correct design—the challenge is to find it.
    e. There are multiple correct designs—the challenge is to find the one that best fits the organization's intended use of the database.

11. The basic components of a flowchart are
    a. Process steps shown as diamonds
    b. Lines with arrows showing the flow of control
    c. Decision points shown as rectangles
    d. Ellipses showing starting and ending points
    e. Connector symbols for connecting lines on the same page or
       across pages

12. The strengths of flowcharts are
    a. They are natural and easy to use for procedural language programmers.
    b. They are useful for spotting reusable components.
    c. They are specific to application programming only.
    d. They are equally useful for nonprocedural and object-oriented
       languages.
    e. They can be easily modified as requirements change.

13. The basic components of a function hierarchy diagram are
    a. Ellipses to show attributes
    b. Rectangles to show process functions
    c. Lines connecting the processes in order of execution
    d. A hierarchy to show which functions are subordinate to others
    e. Diamonds to show decision points

14. The strengths of the function hierarchy diagram are
    a. Checking quality is easy and straightforward.
    b. Complex interactions between functions are easily modeled.
    c. It is quick and easy to learn and use.
    d. It clearly shows the sequence of process steps.
    e. It provides a good overview at high and medium levels of detail.

15. The basic components of a swim lane diagram are
    a. Lines with arrows to show the sequence of process steps
    b. Diamonds to show decision points
    c. Vertical lanes to show the organization units that carry out process steps
    d. Ellipses to show process steps
    e. Open-ended rectangles to show data stores

16. The data flow diagram (DFD):
    a. Is the most data centric of all process models
    b. Was first developed in the 1980s
    c. Combines diagram pages together hierarchically
    d. Was first developed by Dr. E.F. Codd
    e. Combines the best of the flowchart and the function diagram

17. The components of the DFD are
    a. Squares to show data stores
    b. Rounded rectangles to show processes
    c. Diamonds to show sources and destinations of data
    d. Lines with arrowheads to show flows of data
    e. Dotted lines to show the flow of control

18. The strengths of the DFD are
    a. It's good for top-down design work.
    b. It's quick and easy to develop, even for complex systems.
    c. It shows overall structure without sacrificing detail.
    d. It shows complex logic easily.
    e. It's great for presentation to management.

19. The components of the CRUD matrix are
    a. Ellipses to show attributes
    b. Major processes shown on one axis
    c. Major entities shown on the other axis
    d. Reference numbers to show the hierarchy of processes
    e. Letters to show the operations that processes carry out on entities

20. The CRUD matrix helps find the following problems:
    a. Entities that are never read
    b. Processes that are never deleted
    c. Processes that only read
    d. Entities that are never updated
    e. Processes that have no create entity

Physical Database Design

As introduced in Chapter 5 in Figure 5-1, once the logical design phase of a project is complete, it is time to move on to physical design. Other members of a typical project team will define the hardware and system software required for the application system. We will focus on the database designer's physical design work, which is transforming the logical database design into one or more physical database designs. In situations where an application system is being developed for internal use, it is normal to have only one physical database design for each logical design. However, if the organization is a software vendor, for example, the application system must run on all the various platform and RDBMS versions that the vendor's customers use, and that requires multiple physical designs. The sections that follow cover each of the major steps involved in physical database design.

Designing Tables

The first step in physical database design is to map the normalized relations shown in the logical design to tables. The importance of this step should be obvious because tables are the primary unit of storage in relational databases. However, if adequate work was put into the logical design, then translation to a physical design is that much easier. As you work through this chapter, keep in mind that Chapter 2 contains an introduction to each component in the physical database model, and Chapter 4 contains the SQL syntax for the DML commands required to create the various physical database components (tables, constraints, indexes, views, and so on). Briefly, the process goes as follows:

1. Each normalized relation becomes a table. A common exception to this is when super types and subtypes are involved, a situation we will look at in more detail in the next section.

2. Each attribute within the normalized relation becomes a column in the corresponding table. Keep in mind that the column is the smallest division of meaningful data in the database, so columns should not have subcomponents that make sense by themselves. For each column, the following must be specified:

   - *A unique column name within the table.* Generally, the attribute name from the logical design should be adapted as closely as possible. However, adjustments may be necessary to work around database reserved words and to conform to naming conventions for the particular RDBMS being used. You may notice some column name differences between the Customer relation and the CUSTOMER table in the example that follows. The reason for this change is discussed in the "Naming Conventions" section later in this chapter.

   - *A data type, and for some data types, a length.* Data types vary from one RDBMS to another, so this is why different physical designs are needed for each RDBMS to be used.

   - *Whether column values are required or not.* This takes the form of a NULL or NOT NULL clause for each column. Be careful with defaults—they can fool you. For example, when this clause is not specified, Oracle assumes NULL, but Sybase and Microsoft SQL Server assume NOT NULL. It's always better to specify such things and be certain of what you are getting.

   - *Check constraints.* These may be added to columns to enforce simple business rules. For example, a business rule requiring that the unit price on an invoice must always be greater than or equal to zero can be implemented with a check constraint, but a business rule requiring the unit price to be lower in certain states cannot be. Generally, a check constraint is limited to a comparison of a column value with a single value, with a range or list of values, or with other column values in the same row of table data.

3. The unique identifier of the relation is defined as the primary key of the table. Columns participating in the primary key must be specified as NOT NULL, and in most RDBMSs, the definition of a primary key constraint causes automatic definition of a unique index on the primary key column(s). Foreign key columns should have a NOT NULL clause if the relationship is mandatory; otherwise, they may have a NULL clause.

4. Any other sets of columns that must be unique within the table may have a unique constraint defined. As with primary key constraints, unique constraints in most RDBMSs cause automatic definition of a unique index on the unique column(s). However, unlike primary key constraints, a table may have *multiple* unique constraints, and the columns in a unique constraint may contain null values (that is, they may be specified with the NULL clause).

5. Relationships among the normalized relations become referential constraints in the physical design. For those rare situations where the logical model contains a one-to-one relationship, you can implement it by placing the primary key of one of the tables as a foreign key in the other (do this for only *one* of the two tables) *and* placing a unique constraint on the foreign key to prevent duplicate values. For example, Figure 2-2 in Chapter 2 shows a one-to-one relationship between Employee and Automobile, and we chose to place EMPLOYEE_ID as a foreign key in the AUTOMOBILE table. We should also place a unique constraint on EMPLOYEE_ID in the AUTOMOBILE table so that an employee may be assigned to only one automobile at any point in time.

6. Large tables (that is, those that exceed several gigabytes in total size) should be partitioned if the RDBMS being used supports it. *Partitioning* is a database feature that permits a table to be broken into multiple physical components, each stored in separate data files, in a manner that is transparent to the database user. Typical methods of breaking tables into partitions use a range or list of values for a particular table column (called the *partitioning column*) or use a randomizing method known as *hashing* that evenly distributes table rows across available partitions. The benefits of breaking large tables into partitions are easier administration (particularly for backup and recovery operations) and improved performance, achieved when the RDBMS can run an SQL query in parallel against all (or some of the) partitions and then

combine the results. Partitioning is solely a physical design issue that is never addressed in logical designs. After all, a partitioned table really is still *one* table. There is wide variation in the way database vendors have implemented partitioning in their products, so you need to consult your RDBMS documentation for more details.

7. The logical model may be for a complete database system, whereas the current project may be an implementation of a subset of that entire system. When this occurs, the physical database designer will select and implement only the subset of tables required to fulfill current needs.

Here is the logical design for Acme Industries from Chapter 6:

```
PRODUCT: # Product Number, Product Description,
          List Unit Price
CUSTOMER: # Customer Number, Customer Name,
           Customer Address, Customer City, Customer State,
           Customer Zip Code, Customer Phone
INVOICE: # Invoice Number, Customer Number, Terms,
          Ship Via, Order Date
INVOICE LINE ITEM: # Invoice Number, # Product Number,
                    Quantity, Sale Unit Price
```

And here is the physical table design we created from the logical design, shown in the form of SQL DDL statements. These statements are written for Oracle and require some modification, mostly of data types, to work on other RDBMSs:

```
CREATE TABLE PRODUCT
  (PRODUCT_NUMBER         VARCHAR(10)    NOT NULL,
   PRODUCT_DESCRIPTION    VARCHAR(100)   NOT NULL,
   LIST_UNIT_PRICE        NUMBER(7,2)    NOT NULL);

ALTER TABLE PRODUCT
  ADD CONSTRAINT PRODUCT_PK_PRODUCT_NUMBER
      PRIMARY KEY (PRODUCT_NUMBER);

CREATE TABLE CUSTOMER
  (CUSTOMER_NUMBER        NUMBER(5)      NOT NULL,
   NAME                   VARCHAR(25)    NOT NULL,
   ADDRESS                VARCHAR(255)   NOT NULL,
   CITY                   VARCHAR(50)    NOT NULL,
   STATE                  CHAR(2)        NOT NULL,
   ZIP_CODE               VARCHAR(10));
```

```
ALTER TABLE CUSTOMER
   ADD CONSTRAINT CUSTOMER_PK_CUST_NUMBER
      PRIMARY KEY (CUSTOMER_NUMBER);

CREATE TABLE INVOICE
  (INVOICE_NUMBER        NUMBER(7)     NOT NULL,
   CUSTOMER_NUMBER       NUMBER(5)     NOT NULL,
   TERMS                 VARCHAR(20)   NULL,
   SHIP_VIA              VARCHAR(30)   NULL,
   ORDER_DATE            DATE          NOT NULL);

ALTER TABLE INVOICE
   ADD CONSTRAINT INVOICE_PK_INVOICE_NUMBER
      PRIMARY KEY (INVOICE_NUMBER);

ALTER TABLE INVOICE
   ADD CONSTRAINT INVOICE_FK_CUSTOMER_NUMBER
      FOREIGN KEY (CUSTOMER_NUMBER)
      REFERENCES CUSTOMER (CUSTOMER_NUMBER);

CREATE TABLE INVOICE_LINE_ITEM
  (INVOICE_NUMBER    NUMBER(7)      NOT NULL,
   PRODUCT_NUMBER    VARCHAR(10)    NOT NULL,
   QUANTITY          NUMBER(5)      NOT NULL,
   SALE_UNIT_PRICE   NUMBER(7,2)    NOT NULL);

ALTER TABLE INVOICE_LINE_ITEM
   ADD CONSTRAINT INVOICE_LI_PK_INV_PROD_NOS
      PRIMARY KEY (INVOICE_NUMBER, PRODUCT_NUMBER);

ALTER TABLE INVOICE_LINE_ITEM
   ADD CONSTRAINT INVOICE_CK_SALE_UNIT_PRICE
      CHECK (SALE_UNIT_PRICE >= 0);

ALTER TABLE INVOICE_LINE_ITEM
   ADD CONSTRAINT INVOICE_LI_FK_INVOICE_NUMBER
      FOREIGN KEY (INVOICE_NUMBER)
      REFERENCES INVOICE (INVOICE_NUMBER);

ALTER TABLE INVOICE_LINE_ITEM
   ADD CONSTRAINT INVOICE_LI_FK_PRODUCT_NUMBER
      FOREIGN KEY (PRODUCT_NUMBER)
      REFERENCES PRODUCT (PRODUCT_NUMBER);
```

Implementing Super Types and Subtypes

Most data modelers tend to specify every conceivable subtype in the logical data model. This is not really a problem because the logical design is supposed to encompass not only where things currently stand, but also where things are likely to end up in the future. The designer of the physical database therefore has some decisions to make in choosing to implement or not implement the super types and subtypes depicted in the logical model. The driving motivators here should be reasonableness and common sense. These, along with input from the application designers about their intended uses of the database, will lead to the best decisions.

Looking back at Figure 7-6 in Chapter 7, you will recall that we ended up with two subtypes for our Customer entity: Individual Customer and Commercial Customer. There are basically three choices for physically implementing such a logical design, and we will explore each in the subsections that follow.

Implementing Subtypes As Is

This is called the "three table" solution because it involves creating one table for the super type and one table for each of the subtypes (two in this example). This design is most appropriate when there are many attributes that are particular to individual subtypes. In our example, only two attributes are particular to the Individual Customer subtype (Date of Birth and Annual Household Income), and four are particular to the Commercial Customer subtype. Figure 8-1 shows the physical design for this alternative.

This design alternative is favored when there are many common attributes (located in the super type table) as well as many attributes particular to one subtype or another (located in the subtype tables). In one sense, this design is simpler than the other alternatives because no one has to remember which attributes apply to which subtype. On the other hand, it is also more complicated to use because the database user must join the CUSTOMER table to either the INDIVIDUAL_CUSTOMER table or the COMMERCIAL_CUSTOMER table, depending on the value of CUSTOMER_TYPE. The data-modeling purists on your project team are guaranteed to favor this approach, but the application programmers who must write the SQL to access the tables may likely take a counter position.

Implementing Each Subtype as a Discrete Table

This is called the "two-table" solution because it involves creating one table for each subtype and including all the columns from the super type table in each subtype. At first, this may appear to involve redundant data, but in fact there is no redundant

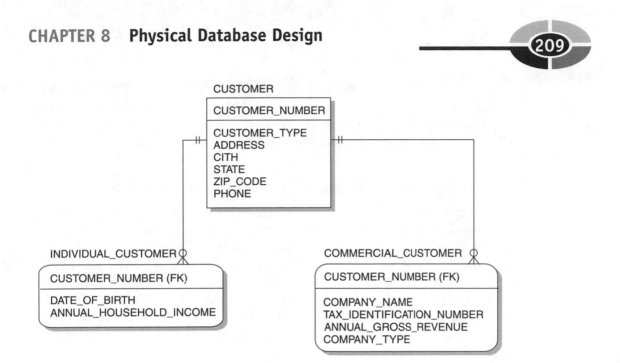

Figure 8-1   Customer subclasses: three-table physical design

storage because a given customer can be only one of the two subtypes. However, some columns are redundantly defined. Figure 8-2 shows the physical design for this alternative.

This alternative is favored when very few attributes are common between the subtypes (that is, when the super type table contains very few attributes). In our example, the situation is further complicated because of the CUSTOMER_CONTACT table, which is a child of the super type table (CUSTOMER). You cannot (or at least *should* not) make a table the child of two different parents based on the same foreign key. Therefore, if we eliminate the CUSTOMER table, we must create two versions

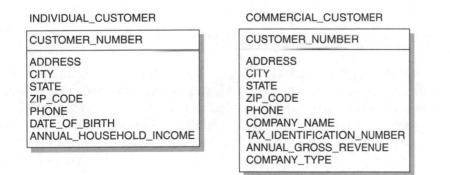

Figure 8-2   Customer subclasses: two-table physical design

of the CUSTOMER_CONTACT table—one as a child of INDIVIDUAL_ CUSTOMER and the other as a child of COMMERCIAL_CUSTOMER. Although this alternative may be a viable solution in some situations, the complication of the CUSTOMER_CONTACT table makes it a poor choice in this case.

Collapsing Subtypes into the Super type Table

This is called the "one-table" solution because it involves creating a single table that encompasses the super type and both subtypes. Figure 8-3 shows the physical design for this alternative. Check constraints are required to enforce the optional columns. For the CUSTOMER_TYPE value that signifies "Individual," DATE_OF_BIRTH and ANNUAL_HOUSEHOLD_INCOME would be allowed to (or required to) contain values, and COMPANY_NAME, TAX_IDENTIFICATION_NUMBER, ANNUAL_GROSS_INCOME, and COMPANY_TYPE would be required to be null. For the CUSTOMER_TYPE value that signifies "Commercial," the behavior required would be just the opposite.

```
CUSTOMER
┌─────────────────────────────────┐
│ CUSTOMER_NUMBER                  │
├─────────────────────────────────┤
│ CUSTOMER_TYPE                    │
│ ADDRESS                          │
│ CITY                             │
│ STATE                            │
│ ZIP_CODE                         │
│ PHONE                            │
│ COMPANY_NAME                     │
│ TAX_IDENTIFICATION_NUMBER        │
│ ANNUAL_GROSS_REVENUE             │
│ COMPANY_TYPE                     │
│ DATE_OF_BIRTH                    │
│ ANNUAL_HOUSEHOLD_INCOME          │
└─────────────────────────────────┘
```

Figure 8-3   Customer subclasses: one-table physical design

This alternative is favored when relatively few attributes are particular to any given subtype. In terms of data access, it is clearly the simplest alternative because no joins are required. However, it is perhaps more complicated in terms of logic because one must always keep in mind which attributes apply to which subtype (that is, which value of CUSTOMER_TYPE in this example). With only two subtypes, and a total of six subtype-determined attributes between them, this seems a very attractive alternative for this example.

Naming Conventions

Naming conventions are important because they help promote consistency in the names of tables, columns, constraints, indexes, and other database objects. Every organization should develop a standard set of naming conventions (with variations as needed when multiple RDBMSs are in use), publish it, and enforce its use. The conventions offered here are only suggestions based on current industry best practices.

Table Naming Conventions

Here are some suggested naming conventions for database tables:

- Table names should be based on the name of the entity they represent. They should be descriptive, yet concise.
- Table names should be unique across the entire organization (that is, across all databases), except where the table really is an exact duplicate of another (that is, a replicated copy).
- Some designers prefer singular words for table names whereas others prefer plural names (for example, CUSTOMER versus CUSTOMERS). Oracle Corporation recommends singular names for entities and plural names for tables (a convention this author has never understood). It doesn't matter which convention you adopt as long as you are *consistent* across *all* your tables, so do set one or the other as your standard.
- Do not include words such as "table" or "file" in table names.
- Use only uppercase letters, and use an underscore to separate words. Not all RDBMSs have case-sensitive object names, so mixed-case names limit applicability across multiple vendors.
- Use abbreviations when necessary to shorten names that are longer than the RDBMS maximum (typically 30 characters or so). Actually, it is a good idea to stay a few characters short of the RDBMS maximum to allow for suffixes when necessary. All abbreviations should be placed on a standard list and the use of nonstandard abbreviations discouraged.
- Avoid limiting names such as WEST_SALES. Some organizations add a two- or three-character prefix to table names to denote the part of the organization that owns the data in the table. However, this is not considered a best practice because it can lead to a lack of data sharing. Moreover, placing geographic or organizational unit names in table names plays havoc every time the organization changes.

Column Naming Conventions

Here are some suggested naming conventions for table columns:

- Column names should be based on the attribute name as shown in the logical data model. They should be descriptive, yet concise.
- Column names must be unique within the table, but where possible, it is best if they are unique across the entire organization. Some conventions make exceptions for common attributes such as City, which might describe several entities such as Customer, Employee, and Company Location.
- Use only uppercase letters, and use an underscore to separate words. Not all RDBMSs have case-sensitive object names, so mixed-case names limit applicability across multiple vendors.
- Prefixing column names with entity names is a controversial issue. Some prefer prefixing names. For example, in the CUSTOMER table, they would use column names such as CUSTOMER_NUMBER, CUSTOMER_NAME, CUSTOMER_ADDRESS, CUSTOMER_CITY, and so forth. Others (this author included) prefer to prefix *only* the primary key column name (for example, CUSTOMER_NUMBER), which leads easily to primary key and matching foreign key columns having exactly the same names. Still others prefer no prefixes at all, and end up with a column name such as ID for the primary key of every single table.
- Use abbreviations when necessary to shorten names that are longer than the RDBMS maximum (typically 30 characters or so). All abbreviations should be placed on a standard list and the use of nonstandard abbreviations discouraged.
- Regardless of any other convention, most experts prefer that foreign key columns always have exactly the same name as their matching primary key column. This helps other database users understand which columns to use when coding joins in SQL.

Constraint Naming Conventions

In most RDBMSs, the error message generated when a constraint is violated contains the constraint name. Unless you want to field questions from database users every time one of these messages shows up, you should name the constraints in a standard way that is easily understood by the database users. Most database designers prefer a convention similar to the one presented here.

Constraint names should be in the format TNAME_TYPE_CNAME, where:

- TNAME is the name of the table on which the constraint is defined, abbreviated if necessary.

- TYPE is the type of constraint:
  - "PK" for primary key constraints.
  - "FK" for foreign key constraints.
  - "UQ" for unique constraints.
  - "CK" for check constraints.
- CNAME is the name of the column on which the constraint is defined, abbreviated if necessary. For constraints defined across multiple columns, another descriptive word or phrase may be substituted if the column names are too long (even when abbreviated) to make sense.

Index Naming Conventions

Indexes that are automatically defined by the RDBMS to support primary key or unique constraints are typically given the same name as the constraint name, so you seldom have to worry about them. For other types of indexes, it is wise to have a naming convention so that you know the table and column(s) on which they are defined without having to look up anything. The following is a suggested convention.

Index names should be in the format TNAME_TYPE_CNAME, where:

- TNAME is the name of the table on which the index is defined, abbreviated if necessary.
- TYPE is the type of index:
  - "UX" for unique indexes.
  - "IX" for nonunique indexes.
- CNAME is the name of the column on which the index is defined, abbreviated if necessary. For indexes defined across multiple columns, another descriptive word or phrase may be substituted if the column names are too long (even when abbreviated) to make sense.

Also, any abbreviations used should be documented in the standard abbreviations list.

View Naming Conventions

View names present an interesting dilemma. The object names used in the FROM clause of SQL statements can be for tables, views, or synonyms. A *synonym* is an alias (nickname) for a table or view. So how does the DBMS know whether an object name in the FROM clause is a table or view or synonym? Well, it doesn't until it looks up the name in a metadata table that catalogs all the objects in the database. This means, of course, that the names of tables, views, and synonyms must come from the same *namespace*, or list of possible names. Therefore, a view name must be unique among all table, view, and synonym names.

Because it is useful for at least some database users to know if they are referencing a table or a view, and as an easy way to ensure that names are unique, it is common practice to give views distinctive names by employing a standard that appends "VW" to the beginning or end of each name, with a separating underscore. Again, the exact convention chosen matters a lot less than picking *one* standard convention and sticking to it for all your view names. Here is a suggested convention:

- All view names should end with "_VW" so they are easily distinguishable from table names.
- View names should contain the name of the most significant base table included in the view, abbreviated if necessary.
- View names should describe the purpose of the views or the kind of data included in them. For example, CALIFORNIA_CUSTOMERS_VW and CUSTOMERS_BY_ZIP_CODE_VW are both reasonably descriptive view names, whereas CUSTOMER_LIST_VW and CUSTOMER_JOIN_VW are much less meaningful.
- Any abbreviations used should be documented in the standard abbreviations list.

Integrating Business Rules and Data Integrity

Business rules determine how an organization operates and utilizes its data. Business rules exist as a reflection of an organization's policies and operational procedures and because they provide control. *Data integrity* is the process of ensuring that data is protected and stays intact through defined constraints placed on the data. We call these database *constraints* because they prevent changes to the data that would violate one or more business rules. The principal benefit of enforcing business rules using data integrity constraints in the database is that database constraints cannot be circumvented. Unlike business rules enforced by application programs, database constraints are enforced no matter *how* someone connects to the database. The only way around database constraints is for the DBA to remove or disable them.

Business rules are implemented in the database as follows:

- NOT NULL constraints
- Primary key constraints
- Referential (foreign key) constraints
- Unique constraints

- Check constraints
- Data types, precision and scale
- Triggers

The subsections that follow discuss each of these implementation techniques and the effect the constraints have on database processing. Throughout this topic, we will use the following table definition as an example. A remark (REM statement) has been placed above each component to help you identify it. Note that the INVOICE table used here has a column difference—TERMS is replaced with CUSTOMER_ PO_NUMBER, which is needed to illustrate some key concepts. A DROP statement is included to drop the INVOICE table in case you created it when following previous examples.

```
REM  Drop Invoice Table (in case there already is one)
DROP TABLE INVOICE CASCADE CONSTRAINTS;
REM  Create Invoice Table
CREATE TABLE INVOICE
  (INVOICE_NUMBER        NUMBER(7)      NOT NULL,
   CUSTOMER_NUMBER       NUMBER(5)      NOT NULL,
   CUSTOMER_PO_NUMBER    VARCHAR(10)    NULL,
   SHIP_VIA              VARCHAR(30)    NULL,
   ORDER_DATE            DATE           NOT NULL);

REM Create Primary Key Constraint
ALTER TABLE INVOICE
  ADD CONSTRAINT INVOICE_PK_INVOICE_NUMBER
      PRIMARY KEY (INVOICE_NUMBER);

REM Create Referential Constraint
ALTER TABLE INVOICE
  ADD CONSTRAINT INVOICE_FK_CUSTOMER_NUMBER
      FOREIGN KEY (CUSTOMER_NUMBER)
      REFERENCES CUSTOMER (CUSTOMER_NUMBER);

REM Create Unique Constraint
ALTER TABLE INVOICE
  ADD CONSTRAINT INVOICE_UNQ_CUST_NUMB_PO
      UNIQUE (CUSTOMER_NUMBER, CUSTOMER_PO_NUMBER);

REM Create CHECK Constraint
ALTER TABLE INVOICE
  ADD CONSTRAINT INVOICE_CK_ORDER_DATE
      CHECK (ORDER_DATE <= SYSDATE);
```

NOT NULL Constraints

As you have already seen, business rules that state which attributes are required translate into NOT NULL clauses on the corresponding columns in the table design. In fact, the NOT NULL clause is how we define a NOT NULL constraint on table columns. Primary keys must always be specified as NOT NULL (Oracle will automatically do this for you, but most other RDBMSs will not). And, as already mentioned, any foreign keys that participate in a mandatory relationship should also be specified as NOT NULL.

In our example, if we attempt to insert a row in the INVOICE table and fail to provide a value for any of the columns that have NOT NULL constraints (that is, the INVOICE_NUMBER, CUSTOMER_NUMBER, and ORDER_DATE columns), the insert will fail with an error message indicating the constraint violation. Also, if we attempt to update any existing row and set one of those columns to a NULL value, the update statement will fail.

Primary Key Constraints

Primary key constraints require that the column(s) that make up the primary key contain unique values for every row in the table. In addition, primary key columns must be defined with NOT NULL constraints. A table may have only one primary key constraint. The RDBMS will automatically create an index to assist in enforcing the primary key constraint.

In our sample INVOICE table, if we attempt to insert a row without specifying a value for the INVOICE_NUMBER column, the insert will fail because of the NOT NULL constraint on the column. If we instead try to insert a row with a value for the INVOICE_NUMBER column that already exists in the INVOICE table, the insert will fail with an error message that indicates a violation of the primary key constraint. This message usually contains the constraint name, which is why it is such a good idea to give constraints meaningful names. Finally, assuming the RDBMS in use permits updates to primary key values (some do not), if we attempt to update the INVOICE_NUMBER column for an existing row and we provide a value that is already used by another row in the table, the update will fail.

Referential (Foreign Key) Constraints

The referential constraint on the INVOICE table defines CUSTOMER_NUMBER as a foreign key to the CUSTOMER table. It takes some getting used to, but referential constraints are always defined on the child table (that is, the table on the "many" side of the relationship). The purpose of the referential constraint is to make sure that foreign key values in the rows in the child table *always* have matching primary key values in the parent table.

In our INVOICE table example, if we try to insert a row without providing a value for CUSTOMER_NUMBER, the insert will fail due to the NOT NULL constraint on the column. However, if we try to insert a row and provide a value for CUSTOMER_NUMBER that does not match the primary key of a row in the CUSTOMER table, the insert will fail due to the referential constraint. Also, if we attempt to update the value of CUSTOMER_NUMBER for an existing row in the INVOICE table and the new value does not have a matching row in the CUSTOMER table, the update will fail, again due to the referential constraint.

Always keep in mind that referential constraints work in both directions, so they can prevent a child table row from becoming an "orphan," meaning it has a value that does not match a primary key value in the parent table. Therefore, if we attempt to delete a row in the CUSTOMER table that has INVOICE rows referring to it (or if we attempt to update the primary key value of such a row), the statement will fail because it would cause child table rows to violate the constraint. However, many RDBMSs provide a feature with referential constraints written as ON DELETE CASCADE, which causes referencing child table rows to be *automatically* deleted when the parent row is deleted. Of course, this option is not appropriate in all situations, but it is nice to have when you need it.

Unique Constraints

Like primary key constraints, unique constraints ensure that no two rows in the table have duplicate values for the column(s) named in the constraint. However, there are two important differences:

- Although a table may have only one primary key constraint, it may have as many unique constraints as necessary
- Columns participating in a unique constraint do not have to have NOT NULL constraints on them.

As with a primary key constraint, an index is automatically created to assist the DBMS in efficiently enforcing the constraint.

In our example, a unique constraint is defined on the CUSTOMER_NUMBER and CUSTOMER_PO_NUMBER columns, to enforce a business rule that states that customers may only use a PO (purchase order) number once. It is important to understand that it is the *combination* of the values in the two columns that must be unique. There can be many invoices for any given CUSTOMER_NUMBER, and there can be multiple rows in the INVOICE table with the same PO_NUMBER (we cannot prevent two customers from using the same PO number, nor do we wish to). However, no two rows for the same customer number may have the same PO number.

As with the primary key constraint, if we attempt to insert a row with values for the CUSTOMER_NUMBER and PO_NUMBER columns that are already in use by another row, the insert will fail. Similarly, we cannot update a row in the INVOICE table if the update would result in the row having a duplicate combination of CUSTOMER_NUMBER and PO_NUMBER.

Check Constraints

Check constraints are used to enforce business rules that restrict a column to a list or range of values or to some condition that can be verified using a simple comparison to a constant, calculation, or a value of another column in the same row. Check constraints may *not* be used to compare column values between different rows, whether in the same table or not. Check constraints are written as conditional statements that must always be true. The term comes from the fact that the database must always "check" the condition to make sure it evaluates to true before allowing an insert or update to a row in the table.

In our example, we have a check constraint that requires the ORDER_DATE to be less than or equal to the current date. The expression used for the current date, SYSDATE, is Oracle syntax; for Microsoft SQL Server and Sybase, we would use TODAY() instead. This enforces a business rule that forbids putting dates in the future on invoices. Keep in mind that the condition is only checked when we insert or update a row in the INVOICE table, so it will not be applied to existing rows as the system date changes. Therefore, the business rule could be circumvented by setting the system clock forward, updating an invoice, and then setting the date back again (assuming someone had the privileges to do all that). With the constraint in force, if we attempt to insert or update a row with an INVOICE_DATE set to a future date, the statement will fail.

Data Types, Precision, and Scale

The data type assigned to the table columns automatically constrains the data to values that match the data type. For example, anything placed in a column with a date format must be a valid date. You cannot put nonnumeric characters in numeric columns. However, you can put just about anything in a character column.

For data types that support the specification of the precision (maximum size) and scale (positions to the right of the decimal point), these specifications also constrain the data. You simply cannot put a character string or number larger than the maximum size for the column into the database. Nor can you specify decimal positions beyond those allowed for in the scale of a number.

In our example, CUSTOMER_NUMBER must contain only numeric digits and cannot be larger than 99,999 (five digits) or smaller than –99,999 (again, five digits). Also, because the scale is 0, it cannot have decimal digits (that is, it must be an integer). It may seem silly to allow negative values for CUSTOMER_NUMBER, but there is no SQL data type that restricts a column to only positive integers. However, if it is easy enough to restrict a column to only positive numbers using a check constraint if such a constraint is required.

Triggers

As you may recall, a *trigger* is a unit of program code that executes automatically based on some event that takes place in the database, such as inserting, updating, or deleting data in a particular table. Triggers must be written in a language supported by the RDBMS. For Oracle, this is either a proprietary extension to SQL called PL/SQL (Procedural Language/SQL) or Java (available in Oracle8*i* or later). For Sybase and Microsoft SQL Server, the supported language is Transact-SQL. Some RDBMSs have no support for triggers, whereas others support a more general programming language such as C. Trigger code must either end normally, which allows the SQL statement that caused the trigger to fire to end normally, or must raise a database error, which in turn causes the SQL statement that caused the trigger to fire to fail as well.

Triggers can enforce business rules that cannot be enforced via database constraints. Because they are written using a full-fledged programming language, they can do just about anything that can be done with a database and a program (some RDBMSs do place some restrictions on triggers). Whether a business rule should be enforced in normal application code or through the use of a trigger is not always an easy decision. The application developers typically want control of such things, but on the other hand, the main benefit of triggers is that they run automatically and cannot be circumvented (unless the DBA removes or disables them), even if someone connects directly to the database, bypassing the application.

A common use of triggers in RDBMSs that do not support ON DELETE CASCADE in referential constraints is to carry out the cascading delete. For example, if we want invoice line items to be automatically removed from the INVOICE_LINE_ITEM table when the corresponding invoice in the INVOICE table is deleted, we could write a trigger that carries that out. The trigger would be set to fire when a delete from the INVOICE table takes place. It would then issue a delete for all the child rows related to the parent invoice (those matching the primary key value of the invoice being deleted) and then end normally, which would permit the original invoice delete to complete (because the referencing child rows will be done by this time, the delete will not violate the referential constraint).

Designing Views

As covered in Chapter 2, views can be thought of as virtual tables. They are, however, merely stored SQL statements that do not themselves contain any data. Data can be selected from views just as it can from tables, and with some restrictions, data can be inserted into, updated in, and deleted from views. Here are the restrictions:

- For views containing joins, any DML (that is, insert, update, or delete) statement issued against the view must reference only one table.
- Inserts are not possible using views where any required (NOT NULL) column has been omitted.
- Any update against a view may only reference columns that directly map to base table columns. Calculated and derived columns may not be updated.
- Appropriate privileges are required (just as with base tables).
- There are various other product specific restrictions to view usage, so the RDBMSs documentation should always be consulted.

Views can be designed to provide the following advantages:

- In some RDBMSs, views provide a performance advantage over ordinary SQL statements. Views are precompiled, so the resources required to parse and bind the statement are saved when views are repeatedly referenced. However, there is no such advantage with RDBMSs that provide an automatic SQL statement cache, as Oracle does. Moreover, poorly written SQL can be included in a view, so putting SQL in a view is not a magic answer to performance issues.
- Views may be tailored to individual department needs, providing only the rows and columns needed, and perhaps renaming columns using terms more readily understood by the particular audience.
- Because views hide the real table and column names from their users, they insulate users from changes to those names in the base tables.
- Data usage can be greatly simplified by hiding complicated joins and calculations from the database users. For example, views can easily calculate ages based on birth dates, and they can summarize data in nearly any way imaginable.

- Security needs can be met by filtering rows and columns that users are not supposed to see. Some RDBMS products permit column-level security, where users are granted privileges by column as well as by table, but using views is far easier to implement and maintain. Moreover, a WHERE clause in the view can filter rows easily.

Once created, views must be managed like any other database object. If many members of a database project are creating and updating views, it is very easy to lose control. Moreover, views can become invalid as maintenance is carried out on the database, so their status must be reviewed periodically.

Adding Indexes for Performance

Indexes provide a fast and efficient means of finding data rows in tables, much like the index at the back of a book helps you in quickly finding specific references. Although the implementation in the database is more complicated than this, it's easiest to visualize an index as a table with one column containing the key value and another containing a pointer to where the row with that key value physically resides in the table, in the form of a row ID or a relative block address (RBA). For nonunique indexes, the second column contains a list of matching pointers.

Indexes provide faster searches than scanning tables for two reasons. First, index entries are considerably shorter than typical table rows, so many more index entries fit per physical file block than the corresponding table rows. Therefore, when the database must scan the index sequentially looking for matching rows, it can get a lot more index entries with a single read to the file on disk than a corresponding read to the file holding the table. Second, index entries are always maintained in key sequence, which is not at all true of tables. The RDBMS software can take advantage of this by using binary search techniques that remarkably reduce search times and the resources required for searching.

There are no free lunches, however, and so there is a price—indexes take up space and must be maintained. Storage space seems less of an issue with every passing day because storage devices keep getting cheaper. However, they still cost something, and they require maintenance and must be backed up. Most RDBMS vendors provide tools to help calculate the storage space required for indexes. These will assist you in estimating storage requirements. The more important consideration is maintenance of the index. Whenever a row is inserted into a table, every index defined on that table must have a new entry inserted as well. As rows are deleted, index entries must also be removed. And when columns that have an index defined on them are updated, the index must be updated as well. It's easy to forget this point because the

RDBMS does this work automatically, but every index has a detrimental effect on the performance of inserts, updates, and deletes to table data. In essence, this is a typical tradeoff, sacrificing a bit of DML statement performance for considerable gains in SELECT statement performance.

Here are some general guidelines regarding the use of indexes:

- Keep in mind that primary key constraints and unique constraints automatically create indexes on the key columns.
- Indexes on foreign keys can markedly improve the performance of joins.
- Consider using indexes on columns that are frequently referenced in WHERE clauses.
- The larger the table, the less you want any database query to have to scan the entire table (in other words, the more you want *every* query to use an index).
- The more a table is updated, the fewer the number of indexes you should have on the table, particularly on the columns that are updated most often.
- For relatively small tables (less than 1,000 rows or so), sequential table scans are probably more efficient than indexes. Most RDBMSs have optimizers that decide when an index should be used, and typically they will choose a table scan over an index until there are at least a few hundred rows in the table.
- For tables with relatively short rows that are most often accessed using the primary key, consider the use of an *index organized table* (on RDBMSs that support such a table), where all the table data is stored in the index. This can be a highly efficient structure for lookup tables (tables containing little more than code and description columns).
- Consider the performance consequences carefully before you define more than two or three indexes on a single table.

Quiz

Choose the correct responses to each of the multiple-choice questions. Note that there may be more than one correct response to each question.

1. Physical database design:
   a. Includes the design of application programs
   b. Immediately follows the requirements gathering stage
   c. Immediately follows the logical design stage
   d. Is done in parallel with the definition of the hardware and system software required for the application system
   e. Can be done without a corresponding logical design

2. When you're designing tables:
   a. Each normalized relation becomes a table.
   b. Each attribute in the relation becomes a table column.
   c. Relationships become check constraints.
   d. Unique identifiers become triggers.
   e. Primary key columns must be defined as NOT NULL.

3. Relationships in the logical model:
   a. Become check constraints in the physical model
   b. Become referential constraints in the physical model
   c. Require a NOT NULL constraint in the physical model
   d. Become a primary key in the parent table and a foreign key in the child table
   e. Are enforced with triggers in the physical design

4. Super types and subtypes:
   a. Must be implemented exactly as specified in the logical design
   b. May be collapsed in the physical database design
   c. May have the super-type columns folded into each subtype in the physical design
   d. Usually have the same primary key in the physical tables
   e. Only apply to the logical design

5. Table names:
   a. Should be based on the attribute names in the logical design
   b. Should always include the word "table"
   c. Should only use uppercase letters
   d. Should include organization or location names
   e. May contain abbreviations when necessary

6. Column names:
   a. Must be unique within the database
   b. Should be based on the corresponding attribute names in the logical design
   c. Must be prefixed with the table name
   d. Must be unique within the table
   e. Should use abbreviations whenever possible

7. Constraint names:
   a. Are not important because no one except the DBA ever sees them
   b. Should include the name of the table
   c. Should include the name of the column
   d. Should include the name of the parent table
   e. Should include the type of constraint

8. View names:
   a. May be identical to one of the table names
   b. Should contain something to denote that the name is for a view
   c. Should communicate the purpose of the view
   d. Should never contain abbreviations
   e. Should contain the name of the corresponding parent table

9. Business rules are implemented in the database using:
   a. Unique constraints
   b. Primary key constraints
   c. Abbreviations
   d. Check constraints
   e. Referential constraints

10. NOT NULL constraints:
    a. Are required on primary key columns
    b. Are required on unique identifier columns
    c. Are required on foreign key columns
    d. Prevent inserts from omitting mandatory columns
    e. Allow columns to be set to null values

11. Primary key constraints:
    a. Are required on foreign key columns
    b. Require columns that have NOT NULL constraints
    c. Require columns that have check constraints
    d. Require column values to be unique within the table
    e. Require column values to be unique within the database

12. Referential constraints:
    a. Define relationships identified in the logical model
    b. Are always defined on the parent table
    c. Require that foreign keys be defined as NOT NULL
    d. Should have descriptive names
    e. Name the parent and child tables and the foreign key column

13. Unique constraints:
    a. Require columns that have NOT NULL constraints
    b. Force column values to be unique within the table
    c. May only be defined once per table
    d. Are identical to primary key constraints
    e. Are usually implemented using an index

14. Check constraints:
    a. May be used to force a column to match a list of values
    b. May be used to force a column to match a range of values

     c. May be used to force a column to match another column in the same row
     d. May be used to force a column to match a column in another table
     e. May be used to enforce a foreign key constraint

15. Data types:
     a. Prevent incorrect data from being inserted into a table
     b. Can be used to prevent alphabetic characters from being stored in numeric columns
     c. Can be used to prevent numeric characters from being stored in character format columns
     d. Require that precision and scale be specified also
     e. Can be used to prevent invalid dates from being stored in date columns

16. Precision and scale:
     a. Can be used to prevent decimal digits in columns that should contain only integers
     b. Can be used to prevent negative numbers in numeric columns
     c. Can be used to prevent numbers that are too large from being stored in a column
     d. Can be used to prevent numbers that are too small from being stored in a column
     e. Apply to all data types

17. View restrictions include
     a. Views containing joins can never be updated.
     b. Updates to calculated columns in views are prohibited.
     c. Privileges are required in order to update data using views.
     d. If a view omits a mandatory column, inserts to the view are not possible.
     e. Any update involving a view may only reference columns from one table.

18. Some advantages of views are
     a. Views may provide performance advantages.
     b. Views may insulate database users from table and column name changes.
     c. Views may be used to hide joins and complex calculations.
     d. Views may filter columns or rows that users should not see.
     e. Views may be tailored to the needs of individual departments.

19. Indexes:
     a. May be used to assist with primary key constraints
     b. May be used to improve query performance
     c. May be used to improve insert, update, and delete performance
     d. Are usually smaller than the tables they reference
     e. Are slower to sequentially scan than corresponding tables

20. General rules to follow regarding indexes include
    a. The larger the table, the more important indexes become.
    b. Indexing foreign key columns often helps join performance.
    c. Columns that are frequently updated should always be indexed.
    d. The more a table is updated, the more indexes will help performance.
    e. Indexes on very small tables tend not to be very useful.

Connecting Databases to the Outside World

In this chapter, we begin with a look at the evolution of database deployment models, meaning the ways that databases have been connected with the database users and the other computer systems within the enterprise computing *infrastructure* (that is, the internal structure that organizes all the computing resources of an enterprise, including databases, applications, computer hardware, and the network). We then explore the methods used to connect databases to applications that use a web browser as the primary user interface, which is the way many modern application systems are constructed. Finally, we look at current methods for connecting databases to applications, namely using ODBC connections (for most programming languages) and various methods for connecting databases to applications written in Java (the most commonly used object-oriented language).

Deployment Models

The history of the information technology (IT) industry is a very interesting study because it clearly proves the old adage that history repeats itself. Nowhere is this truer than in the ways that we have deployed databases, and computer systems in general, on enterprise networks. The subsections that follow outline the major deployment models that have been used. Most of these models are still in active use.

Centralized Model

The centralized model, shown in Figure 9-1, was the original method used to connect databases to the enterprise computing infrastructure. Database users were equipped with what are now called "dumb" terminals, meaning that there was very little processing power or intelligent programming in the device. The only functions the terminals had were to present screens of data that came across the network, move the cursor about the screen, and capture user keystrokes, sending those back across the network. On the other end of the network was a mainframe or other large centralized server that housed all the other functions, including the business logic (in application programs), the database, and any advanced presentation features, such as composing graphs and charts and selecting colors to display (if color terminals were connected).

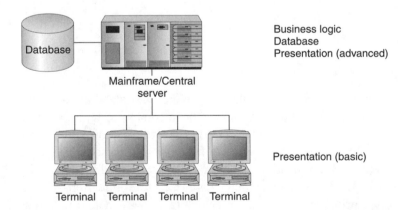

Figure 9-1 The centralized deployment model

Today people often scoff at this seemingly primitive arrangement. Keep in mind, however, that personal computers had not been invented yet, and when they came on the scene, some of their first uses were to replace the dumb terminals, thereby giving computer users a desktop device that they could at least use for other purposes, such as word processing (or perhaps playing those early computer games, which sure beat working for a living). Programs on the early personal computers called *terminal emulators* took care of the network connection in such a way that the mainframe still thought it was connected to the original dumb terminal.

The benefits of the centralized model are as follows:

- Very easy administration. Upgrades and maintenance were straightforward because all the application logic and the database were centralized.
- Lower development labor costs. Fewer specialists were required because everything ran on one platform.
- Potentially higher data input productivity. Studies have shown that the fancy GUI screens that appeared later actually slowed down experienced users who were performing repetitive tasks. Many an experienced Windows user can perform some tasks much more quickly using the command prompt (DOS window) instead of the available GUI tools. Much of this is due to the time required to move one hand between keys used for typing and the pointing device (mouse, trackball, and so on). If we all had a third hand, or if we could somehow use something else to control the pointing device (for example, our feet or eye movements), perhaps this could be overcome.

Here are the drawbacks:

- The mainframe or centralized server is a single point of failure.
- Graphical displays were quite primitive, limiting the user interface.
- Until the advent of the personal computer, the dumb terminal took a lot of desktop space for the purpose it served.

Distributed Model

As computer networks became more readily available in the late 1970s and early 1980s, the IT industry became enamored with the concept of distributed databases and distributed applications. In this case, *distributed* means the partitioning (dividing up) of the application and/or database into parts and the placement of different parts on different computing devices, all connected by a network. Done correctly, the distribution is *transparent* to the users, meaning that the system hides the distribution details from the users, making everything appear to be from a single source. Figure 9-2 shows a simple distributed model, using two centralized servers.

Unfortunately, the marketing hype attached to the initial appearance of the distributed model never played out due to high costs, along with performance and reliability issues. Among other things, network technology was not mature enough to

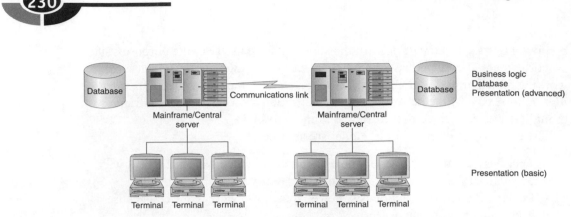

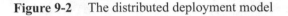

Figure 9-2   The distributed deployment model

handle the load. In many ways, the early versions were solutions in need of problems to solve. Much like the Ford Edsel, the implementation of the new ideas was simply ahead of its time. This architecture has reappeared since the advent of more advanced networks, including the Internet, and is now successfully used for backup data centers, data warehouses, departmental computer systems, and much more. In some object-oriented architectures, an agent known as an *object request broker* manages objects distributed across a network so applications can access objects without regard to their location. Moreover, the current trends in grid computing can be easily seen as extensions to the original distributed model. History really does repeat itself.

The benefits of the distributed deployment model are as follows:

- Improved fault tolerance, because any component deployed on more than one device is no longer a single point of failure
- Potential performance improvement by placing data and application logic closer to the users that need them (that is, departmental computer systems)

Here are the drawbacks:

- Much more complicated
- Potential performance issues related to synchronizing data updates for any redundantly stored data
- More expensive than the centralized model
- Lack of guidelines and best practices for how to partition data and applications across the available computing devices

Client/Server Model

The client/server model involves one or more shared computers, called *servers*, that are connected by a network to the individual users' workstations, called *clients*. Client/server computing arrived in the 1980s, riding a wave of marketing hype from hardware and software vendors the likes of which had never before been seen in the IT industry. The original model used is now called the *two-tier client/sever model*, and later evolved into what we call the *three-tier client/server model*, and finally into the N-tier client/server model, which is also known as the *Internet computing model*. Each of these is discussed in the following subsections.

Two-Tier Client/Server Model

The two-tier client/server model, shown in Figure 9-3, is almost the opposite of the centralized model in that all the business and presentation logic is placed on the client workstation, which typically is a high-powered personal computer system. The only thing remaining on a centralized server is the database.

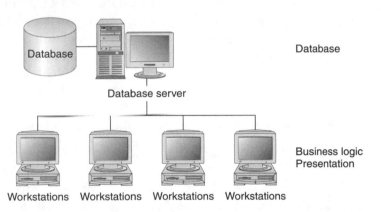

Figure 9-3   The two-tier client/server deployment model

The notion was to take advantage of the superior presentation and user interface capabilities of the modern workstation. However, the marketing hype of the day promised *faster* development of *better* application systems at a *lower* cost. It didn't pan out this way, nor is it ever possible to do so. Among the variables of delivery time, number of defects, and cost, you can, in fact, only minimize *two* of the three. If you think of the three as the legs of a triangle and the area inside the triangle as the amount of work required to complete the system, it becomes clear that you cannot shrink all three legs of the triangle and hold the area inside the triangle the same.

However, the vendors were offering a "silver bullet" solution, and business managers of the day were far too willing to believe them.

The white lie of the day was in cost comparisons between mainframes and central servers and workstations. The vendors typically showed cost comparisons in dollars per millions of instructions per second (MIPS). The problem was that a given instruction on the personal computers of the day did far less than a given instruction on a mainframe or high-powered server. So it really was comparing apples and oranges. Cynics of the day defined MIPS as "meaningless indicator of processor speed," and they were not far wrong. The other factor that was largely ignored was that personal computers of the day did not read from and write to their disks at anywhere near the rates achieved by mainframes and high-powered servers. So although moving all the application programs (business logic) to the client workstations appeared to be a much less expensive solution, it was in fact, a false economy.

Nearly every two-tier client/server project finished late and well over budget. Moreover, there were sobering failures. For example, the California Department of Motor Vehicles spent $44 million on a vehicle-registration system that ended up being far slower and less functional than the centralized model system that it was supposed to replace. It was eventually scrapped at a total loss—even the hardware was so specialized that it could not be used for any other purpose, so it went on the junk pile. There were some successes, however. For example, Peoplesoft built a two-tier client/server human resources system that was successfully deployed by many large enterprises. Today, incidentally, Peoplesoft has migrated to the N-tier client/server model with no code running on the client workstations aside from a standard web browser.

The benefits of the two-tier client/server model include the following:

- It greatly improved the user interface compared with systems using dumb terminals.
- It offered the potential for improved performance because the workstation processor did all the work and did not have to be shared with anyone else.

Here are the drawbacks:

- Very expensive client workstations were required because all the application logic ran on the client. Client workstation costs in the $10,000–$20,000 range were not unusual.
- Administrative nightmares mounted because the application was installed on every client workstation, and all had to be updated with a new software release at the same time.

- Much more complicated (and often more expensive) development resulted because the database server and the client workstation were almost always completely different platforms that required a different set of skills.

Three-Tier Client/Server Model

The many failures of the two-tier client/server model led to some serious rethinking. The result was the three-tier client/server model, which essentially moved the application logic from the client workstation back to a centralized server, now dubbed the *application server*. Figure 9-4 shows this architecture, which proved very workable.

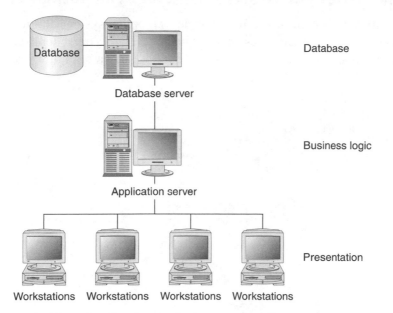

Figure 9-4   The three-tier client/server deployment model

The benefits of the three-tier client/server model include the following:

- It solved the administrative issues of the two-tier model by centralizing application logic on the application server.
- It improved scalability because multiple application servers can be added as needed. (The same can be done with database servers, but that requires distributed database technology to synchronize any data updates across all copies of the data.)

- It retained the user interface advantages of the two-tier model.
- The client workstations were far less expensive (standard personal computers could easily do the job).

Here are the drawbacks:

- It was still more complicated compared with the centralized model.
- Custom presentation methods and logic added to expense and limited portability across client platforms.

The N-Tier Client/Server (Internet Computing) Model

As web browsers became ubiquitous, business computer systems migrated to using web pages as the primary presentation method. The N-tier client/server model (which some call the *Internet computing model*) is shown in Figure 9-5.

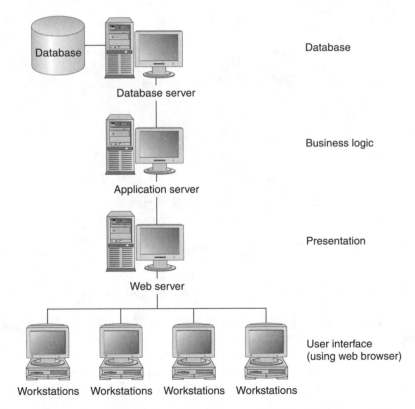

Figure 9-5   The N-tier client/server (Internet computing) deployment model

The evolution from three-tier to N-tier involved adding a web server to handle responding to client requests and the rendering (composing) of web pages, as well as swapping proprietary display logic on the workstation to a standard web browser. The interaction between the client and the web server goes something like this:

1. Using the web browser, the client submits a request in the form of a URL (Uniform Resource Locator).

2. The web server processes the request, renders the requested web page, and sends it to the client.

3. The user at the client workstation works with the web page, and eventually submits a new request to the web server, and the cycle repeats.

This architecture has been wildly successful in deployment of modern business systems. The benefits of the N-tier client/server model are as follows:

- It offers an industry-standard presentation method using web pages.
- The same architecture can be used for internal (intranet) and external (Internet) applications.
- It retains all the benefits of the two-tier client/server model.

Client workstations can be even be scaled all the way down to so-called *network computing devices* that do not even have a disk drive—a "smart" version of the original "dumb" terminals, if you will. Is this evolution or history repeating itself?
Here are the drawbacks of the N-tier client/server model:

- Security challenges exist because the Internet and World Wide Web were not designed with security in mind.
- Potentially necessitates larger development project teams because each layer requires a specialist.
- Potentially requires more hardware. It is possible to combine some of the servers onto common devices, but this is seldom a recommended approach because separation by function improves security.

Connecting Databases to the Web

The "technology stack" required to deploy an application system and corresponding database on the Internet is extensive. The basic components are shown in Figure 9-6. For completeness, we'll review each component. However, our focus is on the database, so you may wish to consult other publications for more detail on other components.

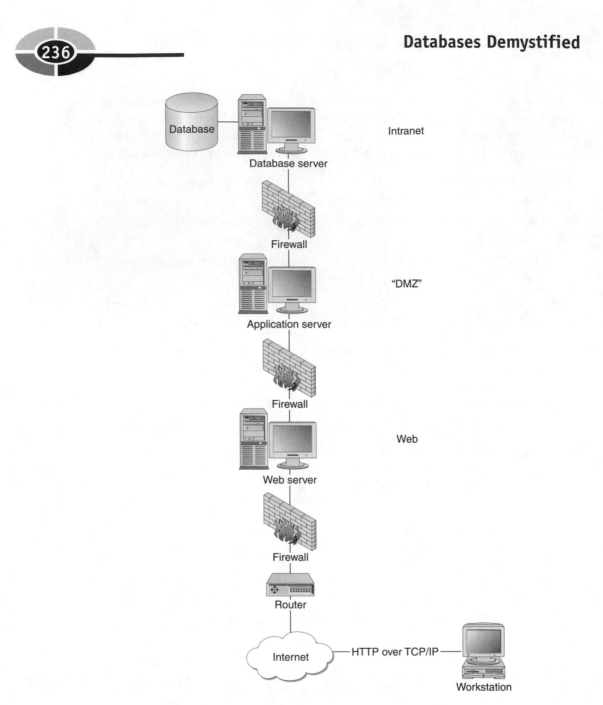

Figure 9-6   Web-connected databases

Introduction to the Internet and the Web

The *Internet* is a worldwide collection of interconnected computer networks. It began in the late 1960s and early 1970s as the U.S. Department of Defense (DoD)

ARPANET, intended as a way of connecting DoD facilities with the colleges and universities that had DoD research grants. TCP/IP (Transmission Control Protocol/Internet Protocol) was adopted as a standard in 1982. Other protocols include FTP (File Transfer Protocol), SMTP (Simple Mail Transfer Protocol), Telnet (remote login protocol), DNS (Domain Name System), and POP (Post Office Protocol).

An *intranet* is a segment of a network, including a web site or group of web sites, that is accessible only to members of an organization. An *extranet* is an intranet that is accessible to authorized outsiders. Both are typically protected by a *firewall*, which is a dedicated gateway that applies security precautions such that only network traffic that meets certain criteria is allowed to pass through.

The *World Wide Web* is a hypermedia-based system that provides a simple "point and click" means of browsing information on the Internet using hyperlinks. Hyperlinks allow users to navigate pages in a nonsequential manner. Clients use a web browser to present pages. The web server hosts (stores and renders) pages and responds to client requests. Web pages may be static (always the same) or dynamic (custom built for a particular request). Dynamic pages are of a special interest in the database world because they are the vehicles for sending requested data from the database to the business user. Typically, a dynamic page has a static portion (title, help text, data field labels) and a dynamic portion in the form of placeholders where current and applicable data content (customer number, customer name) will be placed when serving a specific request from the client.

A *URL (Uniform Resource Locator)* is a string of alphanumeric characters that represents the location or address of a resource on the Internet and how the resource should be accessed. It ultimately must translate to an IP address, port, and a protocol (for example, HTTP). The general format of a URL is

```
<protocol>://<host>[:<port>]/<absolute path> [?arguments]
```

In most browsers, the protocol is understood to be HTTP if omitted. The host can be an IP address, but is more commonly a host name (for example, www.Microsoft.com) that is resolved by looking up the corresponding IP address for the host using the domain name system (DNS). The port generally defaults to 80 (the standard port for HTTP) if omitted. The absolute path identifies the specific page (or other resource) requested, and the web server selects a default if it is omitted. Arguments are variables passed to the web server and are considered optional.

HTTP (Hypertext Transfer Protocol) is the protocol used to transfer web pages through the Internet. It uses a request-based paradigm that is "stateless," meaning that each request is treated as an independent transaction. Statelessness makes it difficult to support the concept of a session, which is essential to basic DBMS transactions. Typically, data must be hidden in the web page or in arguments in the URL for the page to assist the web and application servers in distinguishing between pages from one user session versus another.

HTML (Hypertext Markup Language) is the document formatting language used to design most web pages. The HTML system for marking up or tagging a document for publication on the Web was derived from the Standardized General Markup Language (SGML), a 1986 ISO standard.

XML (Extensible Markup Language) is an extended version of HTML that not only supports all the standard HTML tabs, but also allows developers to create their own tags. Some refer to it as "HTML on steroids." Among the features of XML is the ability to define an XML schema, which allows data to be stored in a hierarchical tree of XML tags within the XML document. Various RDBMS vendors now directly support XML as a data type, and there are also several proprietary XML databases on the market. However, businesses have been reluctant to abandon relational databases and undergo a major paradigm shift in the way they organize and store data. So, thus far, XML is most widely used for exchanging data between organizations in industry-standard XML formats. There are standards committees working on standard XML vocabularies (that is, data tags, schema structures, and conventions for using them) for specific data areas, such as HR-XML Consortium, Inc., which works solely on human resources (HR) data.

Components of the Web "Technology Stack"

Here's a list of the components shown in Figure 9-6 and what they do:

- The client workstation runs a web browser and communicates on the Internet using HTTP over TCP/IP.
- The web site sits behind a *router,* which forwards packets between networks, and a firewall. The router makes decisions on which packets are transferred between the Internet and the subnetwork on which the web server resides. Although some routers do rudimentary filtering, the additional firewall protection is considered the best way to protect the web server from intruders.
- The web server is responsible for hosting and rendering web pages.
- URLs handled by the web server may cause transactions to be run on the application server. There is more on this in the next topic. The application server typically resides between a pair of firewalls to isolate it from both the web server and the intranet, where the database server typically resides. This area is commonly called the "DMZ," a term borrowed from buffer zones between two countries in dispute.
- The application server submits SQL (or similar language) requests to the database server when data from the database is required.

Invoking Transactions from Web Pages

There are several ways in which information in a web request received by the web server can invoke a transaction on the application server. These methods are detailed in the following subsections.

CGI (Common Gateway Interface)

CGI (Common Gateway Interface) is a specification for transferring information between a web server and a CGI program. The CGI script (sometimes called a *CGI program)* runs on either the web server or application server. CGI defines how scripts communicate with web servers. The URL points to the CGI script, and the server launches it. The actual script can be written in a variety of languages, such as Perl and Visual Basic. In essence, instead of the URL in the incoming request pointing directly to an HTML document, it points to a script. This script is run, and the output from the script is an HTML document that is then returned to the client in response to the request.

The advantages of CGI include the following:

- Simplicity
- Language and web server independence
- Wide acceptance

Here are the disadvantages:

- The web server is always between the client and the database.
- No transaction support (stateless).
- Not intended for long exchanges.
- Each CGI execution spawns a new process (or thread), which presents resource issues.
- CGI is not inherently secure.

Server-Side Includes

Server-Side Includes (SSI) has commands embedded in the document that cause the web server to execute a program (as with CGI) and incorporate the output into the document. Essentially, SSI is in an HTML macro. The URL in the request points to an HTML document, but the web server parses the document and handles any SSI commands before returning the document to the requesting client. SSI solves some of the CGI performance issues, but it offers few other advantages or disadvantages.

Non-CGI Gateways

Non-CGI gateways work like CGI gateways, except that each is a proprietary extension to a specific vendor's web server. The two most popular choices during the "dot-com" era were the Netscape Server API and Active Server Pages (ASP), part of the Microsoft Internet Information Server (IIS) API. The Netscape Server API was subsequently acquired by Sun Microsystems and incorporated into their product line.

The advantages of non-CGI gateways include the following:

- Improved performance over CGI.
- Additional features and functions.
- They run in the server address space instead of as new processes or threads.

Here are the disadvantages:

- Proprietary solution that is not portable to another vendor's web server
- Potential instability
- Much more complex compared with CGI

Connecting Databases to Applications

Now that you have seen how the web layer interacts with the application server layer, you need to understand how applications on the application server connect to and interact with the database. Most connections between the application server and remote databases (that is, those running on another server) use a standard API.

An *API (application programming interface)* is a set of calling conventions by which an application program accesses services. Such services can be provided by the operating system or by other software products such as the DBMS. The API provides a level of abstraction that allows the application to be portable across various operating systems and vendors.

Connecting Databases via ODBC

ODBC (Open Database Connectivity) is a standard API for connecting application programs to DBMSs. ODBC is based on a Call Level Interface (CLI, a convention that defines the way calls to services are made), which was first defined by the SQL Access Group and released in September 1992. Although Microsoft was the first company to release a commercial product based on ODBC, it is not a Microsoft standard, and in fact there are now versions available for Unix, Macintosh, and other platforms.

ODBC is independent of any particular language, operating system, or database system. An application written to the ODBC API can be ported to another database or operating system merely by changing the ODBC driver. It is the ODBC driver that binds the API to the particular database and platform, and a definition known as the *ODBC data source* contains the information necessary for a particular application to connect with a database service. On Windows systems, the most popular ODBC drivers are shipped with the operating system, as is a utility program to define ODBC data sources (found on the Control Panel or Administrative Tools Panel, depending on the version of Windows).

Most commercial software products and most commercial databases support ODBC, which makes it far easier for software vendors to market and support products across a wide variety of database systems. One notable exception is applications written in Java. They use a different API known as JDBC, which is covered in the next section.

A common dilemma is that relational database vendors do not handle advanced functions in the same way. This problem can be circumvented using an escape clause that tells the ODBC driver to pass the proprietary SQL statements through the ODBC API untouched. The downside of this approach, of course, is that applications written this way are not portable to a different vendor's database (and sometimes not even to a different version of the same vendor's database).

Connecting Databases to Java Applications

Java started as a proprietary programming language (originally named Oak) that was developed by Sun Microsystems. It rapidly became the de facto standard programming language for web computing, at least in non-Microsoft environments. Java is a type-safe, object-oriented programming language that can be used to build client components (applets) as well as server components (servlets). It has a machine-independent architecture, making it highly portable across hardware and operating system platforms.

You may also run across the terms *JavaScript* and *JScript*. These are scripting languages with a Java-like syntax that are intended to perform simple functions on client systems, such as editing dates. They are not full-fledged implementations of Java and are not designed to handle database interactions, but they can perform the same function as a CGI script if desired.

JDBC (Java Database Connectivity)

JDBC (Java Database Connectivity) is an API, modeled after ODBC, for connecting Java applications to a wide variety of relational DBMS products. Some JDBC drivers translate the JDBC API to corresponding ODBC calls, and thus connect to the database via an ODBC data source. Other drivers translate directly to the proprietary client API of the particular relational database, such as the Oracle Call Interface (OCI). As with ODBC, an escape clause is available for passing proprietary SQL statements through the interface. The JDBC API offers the following features:

- **Embedded SQL for Java**   The Java programmer codes SQL statements as string variables, the strings are passed to Java methods, and an embedded SQL processor translates the Java SQL to JDBC calls.
- **Direct mapping of RDBMS tables to Java classes**   The results of SQL calls are automatically mapped to variables in Java classes. The Java programmer may then operate on the returned data as native Java objects.

JSQL (Java SQL)

JSQL (Java SQL) is a method of embedding SQL statements in Java without having to do special coding to put the statements into Java strings. It is an extension of the ISO/ANSI standard for SQL embedded in other host languages, such as C. A special program called a *precompiler* is run on the source program that automatically translates the SQL statements written by the Java programmer into pure Java. This method can save a considerable amount of development effort.

Middleware Solutions

Middleware can be thought of as software that mediates the differences between an application program and the services available on a network, or between two disparate application programs. In the case of Java database connections, middleware products such as JRB (Java Relational Binding) from O2 Technology can make the RDBMS look as if it is an object-oriented database running on a remote server. The Java programmer then accesses the database using standard Java methods, and the middleware product takes care of the translation between objects and relational database components.

Quiz

Choose the correct responses to each of the multiple-choice questions. Note that there may be more than one correct response to each question.

1. In the centralized deployment model:
   a. A web server hosts all web pages.

   b. A "dumb" terminal is used as the client workstation.
   c. Administration is quite easy because everything is centralized.
   d. There are no single points of failure.
   e. Develop costs are often very high.

2. In the distributed deployment model:
   a. The database and/or application is partitioned and deployed on multiple computer systems.
   b. Initial deployments were highly successful.
   c. Distribution can be transparent to the user.
   d. Costs and complexity are reduced compared with the centralized model.
   e. Fault tolerance is improved compared with the centralized model.

3. In the two-tier client/server model:
   a. All application logic runs on an application server.
   b. A web server hosts the web pages.
   c. The client workstation handles all presentation logic.
   d. The database is hosted on a centralized server.
   e. Client workstations must be high-powered systems.

4. In the three-tier client/server model:
   a. All application logic runs on an application server.
   b. A web server hosts the web pages.
   c. The client workstation handles all presentation logic.
   d. The database is hosted on a centralized server.
   e. Client workstations must be high-powered systems.

5. In the N-tier client/server model:
   a. All application logic runs on an application server.
   b. A web server hosts the web pages.
   c. The client workstation handles all presentation logic.
   d. The database is hosted on a centralized server.
   e. Client workstations must be high-powered systems.

6. The Internet:
   a. Began as the U.S. Department of Education's ARPANET
   b. Dates back to the late 1960s and early 1970s
   c. Always used TCP/IP as a standard
   d. Is a worldwide collection of interconnected computer networks
   e. Supports multiple protocols, including HTTP, FTP and Telnet

7. An intranet is
   a. Available to anyone on the Internet
   b. Available to authorized (internal) members of an organization

    c. Available to authorized outsiders

    d. Protected by a firewall

    e. Typically connected to the Internet

8. An extranet is

    a. Available to anyone on the Internet

    b. Available to authorized (internal) members of an organization

    c. Available to authorized outsiders

    d. Protected by a firewall

    e. Typically connected to the Internet

9. The World Wide Web:

    a. Uses a web browser to present pages

    b. Supports only static web pages

    c. Uses hyperlinks to navigate pages

    d. Uses the Telnet protocol

    e. Is a hypermedia-based system

10. A URL may contain

    a. A protocol

    b. A host name or IP address

    c. A port

    d. The absolute path to a resource on the web server

    e. Arguments

11. HTTP is

    a. The Hypertext Transmission Protocol

    b. A stateless protocol

    c. A document formatting language

    d. A protocol used to transfer web pages

    e. Used for remote database connections

12. XML is

    a. HTML on steroids

    b. A document formatting language

    c. A protocol used to transfer web pages

    d. Used for remote database connections

    e. Extensible because custom tags may be defined

13. The web "technology stack" includes

    a. A client workstation running a web browser

    b. A web server

    c. An application server

    d. A database server

    e. Network hardware (firewalls, routers, and so on)

14. The advantages of CGI are
    a. Statelessness
    b. Simplicity
    c. Inherently secure
    d. Widely accepted
    e. Language and server independent

15. Server-Side Includes (SSI):
    a. Are commands embedded in a web document
    b. Are non-CGI gateways
    c. Are HTML macros
    d. Solve some of the CGI performance issues
    e. Are inherently secure

16. The advantages of a non-CGI gateway are
    a. Known for stability
    b. Proprietary solution
    c. Improved security over CGI solutions
    d. Simpler than CGI
    e. Runs in server address space

17. ODBC is
    a. A standard API for connecting to DBMSs
    b. Independent of any particular language, operating system, or DBMS
    c. A Microsoft standard
    d. Used by Java programs
    e. Flexible in handling proprietary SQL

18. JDBC is
    a. A standard API for connecting to DBMSs
    b. Independent of any particular language, operating system, or DBMS
    c. A Microsoft standard
    d. Used by Java programs
    e. Flexible in handling proprietary SQL

19. JSQL is
    a. A Sun Microsystems standard
    b. A method of embedding SQL statements in Java
    c. An extension of an ISO/ANSI standard
    d. A middleware solution
    e. Independent of any particular language, operating system, or DBMS

20. Middleware solutions for Java connections:
    a. Use standard Java methods for access to an RDBMS
    b. Make the RDBMS look like an object-oriented database
    c. Provide a method for embedding SQL statements in Java
    d. Are independent of any particular language, operating system, or DBMS
    e. Usually run on a remote server

Database Security

Security has become an essential consideration in modern systems. Nothing can be more embarrassing to an organization than a media story regarding sensitive data or trade secrets that were electronically stolen from their computer systems. In this chapter we will discuss the need for security, the security considerations for deploying database servers and clients that access those servers, and methods for implementing database access security. We'll conclude with a discussion of security monitoring and auditing.

Why Is Security Necessary?

Murphy's Law states that anything that can go wrong will go wrong. Seasoned IT security professionals will tell you that Murphy was an optimist. Servers placed on the Internet with default configurations and passwords have been compromised within *minutes*. Default database passwords and common security vulnerabilities are widely known. In early 2003, the Slammer worm infected tens of thousands of

Microsoft SQL Server databases that had been set up with a default SA (System Administrator) account that had no password. Oddly, the worst damage done by this worm was in loss of service when infected computers sent out hundreds of thousands of packets on the network in search of other computers on the network to infect. If you think this cannot happen to you, think again. Here are some reasons why security must be designed into your computer systems:

- Databases connected to the Internet, or any other network, are vulnerable to hackers and other criminals who are determined to damage or steal the data. These include the following:
  - Spies from competitors who are after your secrets.
  - Hackers interested in a sense of notoriety from penetrating your systems.
  - Individuals interested in whatever they can obtain that has economic value.
  - Disgruntled employees. It seems odd that we never hear of gruntled employees (gruntle means "to make happy"), but only of disgruntled ones.
  - Zealots interested in making a political statement at the expense of your organization.
  - The emotionally unbalanced, and just plain evil people.
- Fraud attempts. Any bank auditor will tell you that 80 percent of fraud is committed by employees. So, don't assume your system is immune just because the database is not accessible from the Internet.
- Honest mistakes by authorized users can cause security exposures, loss of data, and processing errors.
- Security controls keep people honest in the same way that locks on homes and offices do.

Every organization should have a publication that prescribes the security policies and procedures that must be followed. In particular, the publication should define the specific rules, who is responsible for enforcing them, and what procedures should be followed when requesting exceptions to policy or when reporting and responding to expected security breaches. Each potential exposure must be analyzed and controls put in place that make practical sense and that are the most likely to be effective. It must be understood that security precautions can never completely *prevent* the most determined adversary from breaching a system. The only way to completely guarantee that a system cannot ever be penetrated is to power it down and leave it that way. However, the right precautions can *slow down* even the most determined and talented adversary enough to allow for detection and intervention. Above all, the use of *layers* of security at all system levels best protects valuable data resources. We explore these layers in the sections that follow.

Database Server Security

This section focuses on the security considerations for the database server. When you're considering security, it is best to start at one end of the network or the other (that is, at either the database user's client workstation or at the database server) and work systematically through all the components in the path. This is the only way you can be sure you don't miss something. In this case, we'll start with the database server and work out from there.

Physical Security

Physically securing the server is an essential ingredient. It should be in a locked room where only authorized personnel have access. Nothing is more embarrassing than having a database server or the disk drives that store the database information stolen or vandalized. Once a thief has made off with the hardware, they have all the time in the world and all the secrecy they need to hack away at the system until they are finally able to access the data. Moreover, systems are easier to compromise using the server console than remotely; therefore, "hands-on" access to servers must be tightly controlled. Depending on the sensitivity of the data in the database, the following additional measures might be needed:

- Video surveillance system.
- "Token" security devices, where administrators must possess the device in order to gain access. These range from cards or keys that must be inserted into the server in order to gain access, to crypto devices where a pin must be entered in order to obtain a password. Some of these devices are synchronized with satellites and change the encryption key used for generating passwords every minute or so.
- Biometric devices, where administrators must pass a fingerprint or retinal scan in order to obtain access.
- Policy provisions that always require at least two employees in the room whenever anyone is directly working on the server.
- Policy provisions regarding removal of hardware and software from the workplace. This author once worked at a financial institution where employees were searched whenever they left the premises. The removal of any hardware or materials, such as computer listings, microfilmed documents, or media such as tapes and disks was strictly prohibited. However, there was a laughable loophole. One could put *anything* in

an envelope addressed to their home (or anywhere else) and drop it in the outbound mail bins. Not only would the envelope go out without inspection, the firm would even *pay the postage*, no questions asked. Before you get the wrong idea, the only time we saw this technique used was to send computer games offsite, but the security exposure was enormous.

Network Security

It should be obvious that physical security is not enough when the database server is accessible via a network. Intruders who manage to obtain a network connection to the server can work from outside the server room or, for servers connected to the Internet, from anywhere in the world. Moreover, because clients or other servers (such as the application server) are able to connect to the database server, we must take a holistic approach to network security and not only ensure that the network is secure but also that *every* computer system attached to that network is equally secure.

Complete details in how to secure a network are well outside the scope of this book. However, the sections that follow comprise a summary of the network security issues that must be considered. Note that the term *enterprise network* is used to mean the private network that connects the computing resources for the business enterprise.

Isolate the Enterprise Network from the Internet

If the enterprise network is connected to the Internet, it must be isolated so that hackers on the Internet cannot see the internals of the enterprise network or easily gain access to it. Measures to consider include the following:

- The router that connects the enterprise network to the Internet must be properly configured. Recall that a *router* is a device that forwards data packets between networks using rules contained in a *routing table*. A *packet* is merely a piece of a message that is transmitted over a network. Network devices divide messages into uniformly sized packets for efficient handling. The router must be configured so that only appropriate packets of data are routed from the Internet to the local network. Some routers can do limited filtering of packets, but typically they do not look at the contents of data packets beyond the destination IP address, contained in the packet header, making decisions on the best way to route the packet based on the destination address and the routing table.
- Each layer in the enterprise network should be protected by a firewall, with the security rules applied by the firewall getting progressively tighter with

each layer. In Chapter 9, Figure 9-6 shows this arrangement. A *firewall* can be implemented using software on a general-purpose computer or on a specialized hardware device that comes with its own operating system and filtering software. The purpose of the firewall is to prevent unauthorized access to the network segment that it protects (that is, computer resources connected to the part of the network that is *inside* the firewall). All data packets passing from the network outside the firewall to the network segment (often called a *subnet*) inside the firewall must pass the security criteria imposed by the firewall or they are simply rejected. Here are some of the methods the firewall may use:

- **Packet filtering**   The contents of each packet entering or leaving the network are inspected to make sure user-defined rules are met. Although packet filtering is effective, it is subject to *IP spoofing*, where a hacker masquerades as a legitimate user by planting a legitimate IP address that is acceptable to the firewall in an otherwise illegitimate message. To prevent your network from being used to launch so-called *zombie attacks*, your firewall should always be configured to reject outbound packets that have a return IP address that is not a legitimate address for the enterprise network. A zombie attack occurs when an intruder plants a rogue program on one of your servers, which at an appointed time, wakes up and starts sending hundreds or thousands of packets per minute at a target system, typically the web browser of an enterprise that the attacker has some grudge against, in an attempt to clog their system, rendering it useless. This type of attack (that is, flooding the target with useless packets) is called a *denial of service* attack.

- **Application gateway**   Different network applications (HTTP, FTP, Telnet, and so on) use different default ports. For example, HTTP uses port 80 as a default. Ports that are not needed should be shut down. *Always* configure firewalls to open *only* the ports that are *absolutely required* for your normal business.

- **Circuit-level gateway**   For efficiency, this feature applies security mechanisms when a connection is established; then, after the connection is established, it allows packets to flow freely for that established connection. A firewall should normally be configured so that connections can *only* be established from *inside* the firewall—attempts made from outside the firewall to establish connections with resources inside the firewall should be rejected.

- **Proxy server**   Firewalls can translate all the IP addresses used in the protected network into different addresses as packets pass through, typically assigning each a different port so that any responses to those packets can be sorted out and passed back to the originator. This feature, known as *network address translation (NAT),* hides the internal network from the outside world.

- Employees working from home present a special risk. If they are connected to a broadband Internet service such as DSL or cable, they essentially reside on a local area network (LAN) with many other uses of that particular service. Therefore, if these employees merely plug their personal computers directly into the DSL or cable modem without other precautions, any shared devices they may have (disk drives, printers, and so forth) are now automatically shared by all their *neighbors* on the same LAN. All the intruder has to know is how to click Network Neighborhood and then Entire Network, and all the unprotected systems on the LAN will be there ripe for picking. Two precautions can circumvent the problem:

  - A security device, typically a combination router/hub/firewall, should be placed between the DSL or cable modem and any computers used in the home. A side benefit here is that the user can hook multiple computers to the high-speed service while only paying for one IP address with their ISP (some ISPs forbid this practice). The device automatically "NATs" any IP address inside the home network to the single IP address assigned by the ISP for the broadband connection, using different ports to differentiate between different connections. This author has such a device on his home Internet cable service and has seen first hand attempts by hackers to scan ports and to ping resources inside the home network. A *port scan* is a technique commonly used to by hackers where they launch a special program that tries every conceivable port on an IP address, recording which ones are active so they can try to use the active ports to break into the target system. Intrusion attempts happen with *alarming* frequency, sometimes several times in a single hour. If you install an unprotected home network, your network will likely be penetrated within *hours* of it being activated. Note that Microsoft Windows XP comes with a built-in configurable software firewall. However, most security experts prefer an external firewall on a dedicated hardware device because it offers better protection.

  - A secure network technique known as a *virtual private network (VPN)* can be used when connecting from the Internet to the enterprise network. This approach encrypts all data packets and applies other measures to make sure that the packets are useless to any unauthorized party that intercepts them, and that they cannot be altered and retransmitted by hackers. Usually, this technique is implemented using special software from a commercial software vendor in concert with a small device that the remote user employs to generate a unique password each time they connect remotely to the enterprise network. Without the device in their possession (and typically a PIN that goes with the device), the would-be hacker has no chance of penetrating the enterprise network using the VPN.

Secure Any Wireless Network Access

Wireless access points are network devices that receive radio signals from computer devices equipped with wireless network adapters, connecting them to the wired network in the office. Most wireless networks adhere to a version of the network standard protocol known as 802.11. Wireless access points have become inexpensive (less than $100) and therefore prolific because people like to be able to freely move around their home or office without having to drag a network cable with them. However, wireless access points require special attention because an intruder can access your network from outside your premises without going through the routers and firewalls that you have carefully set up to prevent such an intrusion. Horror stories abound in IT trade publications about an unknowing user bringing an unauthorized wireless access point into an office, plugging it into the nearest network jack, and giving everyone within 75 to 150 feet open access to the network. These devices, by default, have *absolutely no* encryption or other access controls enabled, thus providing access to anyone with a wireless-capable computer in a neighboring office, out in the parking lot, or even in a building across the street. Worst of all is that once the intruder connects, they are on the intranet, completely *inside* all the firewalls and other controls you so carefully implemented to protect your network from intruders.

If you think this cannot happen to you, here are just a few real-life examples:

- On a recent trip to a medical office, this author's laptop, which is equipped with an 802.11g wireless network adapter, *automatically* connected to a wireless network in an adjoining doctor's office from the waiting room. I didn't look to see what I might have been able to get to in terms of computers, shared disks, files, and the like, but the office staff in the office was totally unaware that anyone could connect to their wireless network. They didn't understand that walls don't stop wireless networks. Incidentally, a quick look at the wireless adapter's site survey showed two other vulnerable networks accessible from the same waiting room. One of those even had the default network name that comes with the wireless access point, so one can easily guess that the password to the router would also be the factory default. An intruder could reconfigure their entire network before they knew what happened.
- On a recent drive down Market Street in San Francisco, the wireless adapter in the same laptop detected an average of three wireless networks in every

block, a surprising number of them wide open to anyone who would want to connect.

- An IT manager reported to this author that after they discovered their company's network had been intruded from an unauthorized wireless access point, they went hunting for it, failing to find it in several attempts. Finally, they brought in a consultant who had a device to track down the rogue signal. (Believe it or not, a potato chip tube covered with aluminum foil makes an excellent directional antenna for "sniffing out" wireless access points.) They found it hidden in the suspended ceiling of a conference room. The person who installed it knew it was against the rules, but just didn't want to bother to cable-connect their laptop to a nearby outlet. Needless to say, that person lost their job, but who knows what the intruders got before the unauthorized access point was shut down.

In terms of wireless access points, here are some recommendations:

- **Policy**   Your organization's security policy should address wireless connections, forbidding anyone other than trained network administrators from installing them, and setting standards for their proper installation.
- **Mandatory encryption**   Standards should mandate that encryption be enabled on every wireless access point. All the access points on the market have encryption capability built into them, and it only takes a few minutes to enable the feature and to input a pass phrase that any device trying to connect must supply in order to gain access to the network.
- **MAC address list**   Every network device currently manufactured has a unique MAC (Media Access Control) address assigned to it by the manufacturer. Most wireless access points permit the entry of a MAC address list that restricts network access to *only* the devices that appear in the list. Alternatively, the MAC address list can list devices that are *not* allowed to connect.

The configuration of the wireless access point is typically done using a web page accessible from any computer on the network—all you need to know is the IP address of the wireless access point and its administrative password. For a home network, it really only takes a few minutes to get the MAC addresses from your wireless network adapters, input them into the MAC address list on the wireless access point, and then to activate encryption (typically using WEP, or Wireless Encryption Protocol) by entering a pass phrase. The pass phrase must then be entered into each device that will connect to the access point. While you are in there, don't forget to *change* the administrative password on the wireless access point—the bad guys know the default passwords for all the popular devices.

System-Level Security

Once the network is as secure as we can make it, the next area of focus is the system that will run the DBMS. A poorly secured database server can provide many unchecked paths for intruders to use. Here are some measures worth considering:

- **Installing minimal operating system software**   Particularly on a production server, install only the minimal software components to get the job done. Avoid default or "typical" installation options and use the "custom" installation option to choose only the components needed. For example, on production Unix servers, you should be in the habit of removing the "make" utility and C language compilers after you complete an installation. Hackers have a very difficult time installing things when the tools needed to perform software installations do not exist on the server.
- **Using minimal operating system services**   Shut down or remove operating system services that are not required. In particular, communications services such as FTP (File Transfer Protocol) should not be running unless they are expressly required. On Windows systems, it's a good idea to set Startup Type to "Disabled" for services that are not required. This makes it impossible to start these service unless you have Administrator privileges.
- **Installing minimal DBMS software**   The fewer the features of the DBMS that you have installed, the less exposure you'll have to problems such as buffer overflow vulnerabilities. The DBA should work with the application developers to develop a consolidated list of the DBMS functions needed. Once you have the list, use the custom installation option for the DBMS and perform only minimal installations.
- **Applying security patches in a timely manner**   Establish a program wherein security alerts are reviewed as they are announced and countermeasures, including patches and workarounds, are applied in a timely manner. Patches should be shaken down in a development environment for a finite period of time before application to a production environment.
- **Changing all default passwords**   These should be changed to new ones that are difficult to guess or discover via *brute force*, a method that repeatedly tries possibilities until access is finally achieved.

Database Client and Application Security

A *database client* is any computer system that signs on directly to the database server. Therefore, the application server is nearly always a database client, along with the client workstation of any person in the organization who has sign-on privileges with the database. Typically, the DBMS requires installation of client software on these systems to facilitate communication between the database client and the DBMS using any specialized communications mechanisms required by the DBMS.

Login Credentials

Every database user who connects to the database must supply appropriate credentials to establish the connection. Typically, this is in the form of a user ID (or login ID) and a password. Care must be taken to establish credentials that are not easily compromised. Here are some considerations:

- Credentials must not be shared by multiple database users.
- Passwords should be selected that are not easy to guess. A security policy should establish minimum standards for password security, including minimum length, the mixture of upper/lowercase letters, numbers and special characters required, avoiding words that can be found in a dictionary, and the like.
- Passwords should be changed on a regular basis, such as every 30 or 45 days.
- Any exposed password should be immediately changed.
- Passwords should never be written down and must be encrypted whenever they are electronically stored.

Data Encryption

Encryption is the translation of data into a secret code that cannot be read with the use of a password or secret key. Unencrypted data is called *plain text,* whereas encrypted data is called *cipher text*.

Some encryption schemes use a *symmetric key,* which means that a single key is used to both encrypt plain text and to decrypt cipher text. This form is considered less secure compared with the use of *asymmetric keys,* where a pair of keys is used—one called the *public* key and the other the *private* key. What the public key encrypts, the private key can decrypt, and vice versa. The names come from the expected use of the keys—the public key is given to anyone with whom an enterprise does business, and the private key remains confidential and internal to the enterprise.

Here are some guidelines to follow regarding encryption:

- Encryption keys should be a minimum of 128 bits in length. The longer the key, the more secure it is considered to be.

- The loss of an encryption key should be treated with the same seriousness as the loss of the data that it was used to encrypt.
- Sensitive data should be encrypted whenever permanently stored. Which data is considered sensitive is a judgment call that should be made by the business people who own the data, not by the DBA. In general, however, any personal data (such as social security numbers) that can be used for identity theft should be considered sensitive.
- All data not considered public knowledge should be encrypted whenever transported electronically across network connections that are not otherwise encrypted. For example, if a company sends a purchase order file to a trading partner via FTP, the file should be encrypted. There is no guarantee that the bad guys are not monitoring public networks.
- E-mail is not considered secure, so any sensitive information to be sent via e-mail should be in an encrypted attachment instead of the main body of the e-mail message.

Other Client Considerations

Database clients require special scrutiny in terms of security precautions because, if compromised, they provide an easy pathway for the intruder to gain access to data in the database. Here are some additional client considerations:

- **Web browser security level**   Modern web browsers allow the setting of a security level for the browser. For Microsoft Internet Explorer, the security settings are controlled using the Security tab on the Internet Options panel, which is accessible using the Tools option on the main toolbar. This security level should be set to the highest possible level that still permits normal use of the database applications. Here are two considerations related to the web browser:
  - *Cookies* provide the ability for the web browser to store textual information on the client, which can be automatically retrieved later by the web browser and sent to the web server that requested them. Cookies are not very secure and can be used to spy on users of the client system. Furthermore, there is no guarantee that unauthorized persons and software will have no access to information in cookies. The organization's security policy should address this issue and set a clear standard for cookie use, which is one of the facilities controlled by the web browser's security level. Also, it is not wise to design application systems that require cookies because they are not supported by all web browsers and not permitted by all users. In Microsoft Internet Explorer,

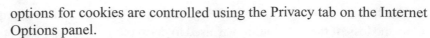

options for cookies are controlled using the Privacy tab on the Internet Options panel.

- Scripting languages such as VBScript, JavaScript, and JScript provide nice features for assisting with a user's interaction with a web page. However, they can and have been used for injecting malicious code into systems, so care should be taken when allowing such languages to be used on the client. VBScript is especially notorious for its misuse and has been used to transport viruses in e-mail attachments.

- **Minimal use of other software** Software that is not required for the normal functioning of the client should not be installed. Security policy should forbid employees from installing unauthorized software.

- **Virus scanner** All computer systems running operating systems that are susceptible to computer viruses should have appropriate virus-scanning software installed. Virus scanners that automatically update their virus profiles on a regular basis offer the most effective protection.

- **Test application exposures** Web-based applications should be thoroughly tested using a client configured just the way your real business users' client workstations will be configured. Hacker tricks such as the following should be attempted to verify that the exposures do not exist:

  - **SQL Injection** SQL statements are entered into web pages in such a way that the application server or web server hands them off to the database for processing.

  - **URL spoofing** The URL in the web browser is manually overtyped in such a way that unauthorized data is revealed. Designs where session IDs are assigned sequentially by the application server and then passed back to the web browser as an argument in the URL are especially susceptible to this approach. If you can guess another user's session ID, you can hijack their session just by overtyping the session ID in the URL.

  - **Buffer overflows** Published exposures such as buffer overflows should be thoroughly tested once the vendor's patch has been installed to ensure that the problem really was corrected.

Database Access Security

With the confidence that our clients, servers, and network are now secure, we can focus on database access. The goal here is to determine precisely the data that each database user needs to conduct their business, and what they are permitted to do with the data (that is, select, insert, update, or delete). Each database user should be given *exactly* the privileges they need—nothing more and nothing less. Recall that an application program with database access is a database user just as an employee who directly queries the database is. In terms of database security, all database users should be treated in the same way (that is, the same standards should be applied to all), whether the database user is software or "liveware." In this section, we will explore the options and challenges related to securing access to the database and its data.

Database Security Architectures

For DBAs who support databases from multiple vendors, one of the challenges is that, with the exception of Microsoft SQL Server and Sybase, no two databases have the same architecture for database security. And of course, this is a side effect of the overall database architectures being different. The only reason that Microsoft SQL Server and Sybase have such similar architectures is that the former was derived from the later. Because Microsoft SQL Server and Oracle are among the most popular databases today, let's have a quick look at how each implements database security.

Database Security in Microsoft SQL Server and Sybase

With Microsoft SQL Server and Sybase, once the DBMS software is installed on the server, a database server is created. This is a confusing term, of course, because we call the hardware a "server." In this case, the term *server* or *SQL server* is a copy of the DBMS software running in memory as a set of processes (also called *services* in Windows environments) with related control information that is stored in a special database on the SQL server. We will use the term *SQL server* to mean the DBMS software and the term *database server* to mean the hardware platform on which the database is running. In this architecture, each SQL server manages many databases, with each database representing a logical grouping of data as determined by the database designer. Figure 10-1 shows a simplified view of the security architecture for Microsoft SQL Server and Sybase.

Security in Microsoft SQL Server and Sybase may be administered using either the GUI tools provided in Enterprise Manager or the vendor-provided stored procedures invoked using SQL statements. Here's a list of the components of the security architecture:

- **Login**   This is a user account on the SQL server, also called a *user login*. This is not the same as any operating system account the user may have on the database server. However, on database servers running Microsoft Windows, the login can use Windows authentication, meaning the Windows

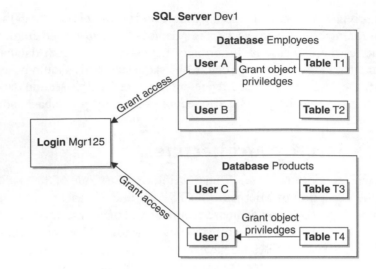

SQL Server Dev1

Figure 10-1   Security in Microsoft SQL Server and Sybase

operating system stores the credentials (login name and password) and authenticates users when they connect to the SQL server. An obvious advantage to Windows authentication is that user access to the various SQL servers in the enterprise can be centrally managed through the Windows account, rather than locally managed on each SQL server. Note that once a login is defined in the SQL server, the database user may connect to the SQL server, but a login alone does *not* give them access to any database information. There is, however, a master login called "sa" (system administrator) that, similar to root in Unix and Administrator in Microsoft Windows, has full privileges to everything in the SQL Server environment. Figure 10-1 shows only one user login, called Mgr125.

- **Database**   A database is a logical collection of database objects (tables, views, indexes, and so on) as defined by the database designer. Figure 10-1 shows two databases: Employees and Products. It is important to understand that a login is allowed to connect to a database only after it has been granted that privilege by an administrator. (See the "User" topic that follows.) In addition to databases holding system data, some special databases are created when the SQL server is created (not show in Figure 10-1) and are used by the DBMS to manage the SQL server. Among these are the following databases:
  - **master**   The master database contains system-level information, initialization settings, configuration settings, login accounts, the list of

databases configured in the SQL server, and the location of primary database data files.

- **tempdb**   The tempdb database contains temporary tables and temporary stored procedures.
- **model**   The model database contains a template for all other databases created on the system.
- **msdb**   In Microsoft SQL Server databases only, the msdb database contains information used for scheduling jobs and alerts.
- **User**   Each database has a set of users assigned to it. Each database user maps to a login, so each user is a pseudo-account that is an alias to an SQL Server login account. User accounts do not necessarily have to have the same user name as their corresponding login accounts. When an administrator grants access to a database for a particular login account, the user account corresponding to the login account is created by the DBMS. In Figure 10-1, the Mgr125 login corresponds to user A in the Employees database and to user D in the Products database. These privileges permit the login to connect to the database(s), but do not give the user any privileges against objects in those databases. We discuss how this happens in the next topic.
- **Privileges**   Each user account in a database may be granted any number of privileges (also called *permissions*). *System privileges* are general privileges applied at the database level. Microsoft SQL Server divides these into *server privileges,* which include such permissions as starting up, shutting down, and backing up the SQL server, and *statement privileges*, which include such permissions as creating a database and creating a table. *Object privileges* allow specific actions on a specific object, such as allowing select and update on table T1. Figure 10-1 contains arrows that show the granting of object privileges on table T1 to user A in the Employees database, and on Table T4 to user D in the Products database. These privileges work in much the same way across all relational databases, thanks to ANSI standards, and are therefore covered in the "System Privileges" and "Object Privileges" sections that follow a little later in this chapter.

Database Security in Oracle

Oracle's security architecture, shown in Figure 10-2, is markedly different compared to that of SQL Server. The differences between the two are highlighted as each component is introduced:

- **Instance**   This is a copy of the Oracle DBMS software running in memory. Each instance manages only *one* database.

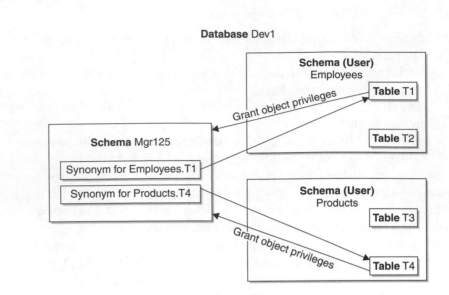

Figure 10-2   Database security in Oracle

- **Database**   This is the collection of files managed by a single Oracle instance. Taken together, the Oracle instance and database comprise what Microsoft SQL Server and Sybase call the *SQL server*. Figure 10-2 depicts the Dev1 database.
- **User**   Each database account is called a *user*. As with Microsoft SQL Server and Sybase, the user account may be authenticated externally (that is, by the operating system) or internally (by the DBMS). Each user is automatically allocated a schema (defined next), and this user is the *owner* of that schema, meaning it automatically has full privileges over any object in the schema. The following predefined users are created automatically when the database is created (not shown in Figure 10-2):
  - The SYS user is the owner of the Oracle instance and contains objects that Oracle uses to manage the instance. This user is equivalent to the "sa" user in Microsoft SQL Server and Sybase.
  - The SYSTEM user is the owner of the Oracle database and contains objects that Oracle uses to manage the database. This user is similar to the master database in Microsoft SQL Server and Sybase.
  - Many Oracle database options create their own user accounts when those options are installed.
- **Schema**   This is the collection of database objects that belong to a specific Oracle user. The Oracle schema is equivalent to what Microsoft SQL Server and Sybase call a *database*. Figure 10-2 shows the Employees, Products,

and Mgr125 schemas, which are owned by the Employees, Products, and Mgr125 users, respectively. Schema and user names are *always* identical in Oracle. Mgr125 is a workaround to a special challenge we face with Oracle's security architecture, as discussed in the "Schema Owner Accounts" section that follows.

- **Privileges**   As with Microsoft SQL Server and Sybase, privileges are divided into system and object privileges. These are covered in the "System Privileges" and "Object Privileges" sections that follow.

Schema Owner Accounts

With all databases, we want to avoid giving database users more privileges than they need to do their job. This not only prevents errors made by humans (including those contained in the application programs and database queries they write) from becoming data disasters, but it also keeps people honest.

In Microsoft SQL Server and Sybase, we want to avoid having database users connect as the "sa" user. We want to create database logins that have the minimal privileges required. Sadly, this is often not done, and applications connect as "sa" or to a database with a user account that has the DBO (database owner) or DBA (database administrator) role. Roles are a collection of privileges and are discussed in an upcoming section. Whether done out of lack of understanding or out of laziness, this practice represents a *huge* security exposure that should be forbidden as a matter of policy.

In Figure 10-2, note that the Mgr125 user owns no tables but does have some privileges granted to it by the Employees and Products users. This is to work around a fundamental challenge with Oracle's security architecture. If we allowed a database user to connect to the database using a user such as Employees or Products, the user would automatically have full privileges to every object in the schema, including insert, delete, and update against any table, and also the ability to create and alter tables without restriction. This is fundamentally the same issue as allowing use of the "sa" user or the DBO and DBA roles in Microsoft SQL Server and Sybase. The Mgr125 user mimics the behavior of the login with the same name as shown in Figure 10-1. With the right system privileges, we can prevent the Mgr125 user in Oracle from being able to create any tables of its own.

You may have noticed the synonyms for user Mgr125 in Figure 10-2. A *synonym* is merely an alias or nickname for a database object. The synonyms are for the convenience of the user so that names do not have to be qualified with their schema name. To select from the T1 tables in the Employees schema directly, user Mgr125 would have to refer to the table name as Employees.T1 in the SQL statement. This is not only inconvenient, but also can cause no end to problems if we ever decide to change the name of the Employees user. By creating a synonym called T1 in the Mgr125 schema that points to Employees.T1, the user may now refer to the table as just T1. Incidentally, you may recall that all user and object names in Oracle are case insensitive, so the use of mixed case here is only for illustration. The syntax for creating this synonym is as follows:

```
CREATE SYNONYM T1 FOR EMPLOYEES.T1;
```

System Privileges

As stated earlier, system privileges are general permissions to perform functions in managing the server and the database(s). Hundreds of permissions are supported by each database vendor, with most of those being system privileges. As with object privileges, system privileges are granted using the SQL GRANT statement and rescinded using the SQL REVOKE statement. Some of the most commonly used ones are listed in the sections that follow. Complete details may be found in vendor-supplied documentation.

Microsoft SQL Server System (Server and Statement) Privilege Examples

Here are some commonly used Microsoft SQL Server system privileges:

- **SHUTDOWN**   Provides the ability to issue the server shutdown command
- **CREATE DATABASE**   Provides the ability to create new databases on the SQL server
- **BACKUP DATABASE**   Provides the ability to run backups of the databases on the SQL server

Oracle System Privilege Examples

Here are some commonly used Oracle system privileges:

- **CREATE SESSION**   Provides the ability to connect to the database.
- **CREATE TABLE**   Provides the ability to create tables in your own schema. Similar privileges exist for other object types, such as indexes, synonyms, procedures, and so on.
- **CREATE ANY TABLE**   Provides the ability to create tables in *any* user's schema. Similar privileges are available for other object types, such as indexes, synonyms, procedures, and so on.

- **CREATE USER**   Provides the ability to create new users in the database.

Oracle permits the WITH ADMIN OPTION clause to be included when granting system permissions. When this option is included, the user(s) not only acquire the privilege but also the ability to grant the permission to other users. I do *not* recommend this practice because it opens up too many potential security exposures, especially because revocation of permissions granted in this way do not cascade.

Object Privileges

Object privileges are granted to users with the SQL GRANT statement and revoked with the REVOKE statement. The database user (login) who receives the privileges is called the *grantee.* These statements are also covered in Chapter 6. The GRANT statement may include a WITH GRANT OPTION clause that allows the recipient to then grant the privilege to others. If the privilege is subsequently revoked, a cascading revoke takes place if this user has, in turn, granted the permission to anyone else. I do *not* recommend use of the WITH GRANT OPTION clause because it is far too easy to lose control over who has which privileges.

The general syntax of the GRANT statement is shown here, along with some examples:

```
GRANT <privilege list> ON <object> TO <grantee list>
   [WITH GRANT OPTION];
GRANT SELECT, UPDATE, INSERT ON T1 TO Mgr125;
GRANT SELECT ON T2 TO User1, User2, User3;
```

The general syntax of the REVOKE statement is shown here, along with some examples:

```
REVOKE <privilege list> ON <object> FROM <grantee list>;
REVOKE SELECT, UPDATE, INSERT ON T1 FROM Mgr125;
REVOKE SELECT ON T2 FROM User1, User2, User3;
```

Roles

A *role* is a named collection of privileges that can, in turn, be granted to one or more users. Most RDBMS systems have predefined roles that come with the system, and database users with the CREATE ROLE privilege may create their own. Roles have the following advantages:

- *Roles may exist before user accounts do.* For example, we can create a role that contains all the privileges required to work on a particular development

project. When a new hire joins the project team, one GRANT statement gives their new user account all the permissions they need.

- *Roles relieve the administrator of a lot of tedium.* Many privileges may be granted with a single command when a role is used.
- *Roles survive when user accounts are dropped.* In cases where the DBA must drop and re-create a user account, it can be a lot of work to reinstate all the privileges, which is simplified if all the privileges are assembled into one role.

The only potential disadvantage of roles, especially predefined ones, is that they can be granted without sufficient attention to all the privileges contained in them, thereby giving a user more privileges than the minimum they need. For example, the CONNECT role in Oracle includes CREATE SESSION and ALTER SESSION, as you would expect, but it also includes CREATE CLUSTER, CREATE DATABASE LINK, CREATE SEQUENCE, CREATE SYNONYM, CREATE TABLE, and CREATE VIEW. This is probably a more powerful collection than you would want a business user of the database to have, so it might be better to grant CREATE SESSION instead.

For administrators, a common role is DBA, which conveys a lot of powerful privileges (over 125 separate privileges in Oracle). Obviously, such a high-powered privilege must be granted judiciously.

Views

One of the common security issues to be addressed is how to allow database users access to some rows and columns in a table while preventing access to other rows and columns. Views are an excellent way to accomplish this. Here are some of the benefits of using views to accomplish security objectives:

- *Columns that a database user does not require may be omitted from the view.* Assuming the user has been granted access to the view rather than the underlying table, this method totally prevents them from seeing the information in the columns that were omitted from the view.
- *A WHERE clause may be included in the view to limit returned rows.* Joins may be included to match to other tables as a way of limiting rows. For example, the view could limit Product table rows to only those products for a Division ID that matches the division in which the employee works.

- *Joins to "lookup" tables can be used to replace code values in a table with their corresponding descriptions.* A lookup table typically contains a list of code values (for example, department codes, transaction codes, status codes) and their descriptions, and it's used to "look up" the descriptions for the codes. Although this is a minor point, employees trying to hack database records during fraud attempts have a much more difficult time if they cannot see the codes used to categorize the transactions. Furthermore, employees trying to do their best usually have a better time reading and understanding code descriptions than the corresponding code values.

There are other ways to accomplish these objectives, however. Many modern RDBMSs, including Oracle and Microsoft SQL Server, have provisions for column-level security wherein a DBA may grant access by table column. For row-level restrictions, a feature called Virtual Private Database, available in Oracle starting with version 9*i*, can be used to accomplish the objective. Finally, some prefer to use stored procedures for all database access and thus use custom programming to control all database access.

Security Monitoring and Auditing

Security policies and controls are typically not enough to ensure compliance. There must be a monitoring system to detect security breaches so that corrective measures may be taken. Multiple intrusion-detection tools are on the market that are capable of monitoring a server and detecting unauthorized changes to files stored in the file system. Also, all the major RDBMS products have provisions for setting up auditing so that selected actions in the database are silently logged, typically into audit tables that may subsequently be used for reporting. Consult your RDBMS documentation for a full description of these auditing features.

It is also a good idea to have an independent auditor review your organization's security policies and procedures when they are initially written, and at periodic intervals thereafter. Furthermore, it is wise to have your auditors, or a consultant who specializes in information systems security, perform an onsite audit, including testing the site for vulnerabilities that have not yet been addressed. System intrusions, including fraud, can cost you many times more than a system audit, which may save you any embarrassment before your employees and customers.

Quiz

Choose the correct responses to each of the multiple-choice questions. Note that there may be more than one correct response to each question.

1. Security is necessary because:
   a. Databases connected to the Internet are vulnerable to hackers.
   b. 80 percent of fraud is committed by outside hackers.
   c. Honest people make mistakes.
   d. Security controls keep people honest.
   e. Application security controls alone are inadequate.

2. Physical security of the database server:
   a. Is unnecessary if the server is connected to the Internet
   b. Should include a locked room to contain the server
   c. Requires both physical devices and policies
   d. May include biometric controls
   e. May include surveillance equipment

3. Network security:
   a. Can be handled by routers alone
   b. Can be handled by firewalls alone
   c. Is necessary only if the database server is connected to the Internet
   d. Must include provisions for remotely located employees
   e. Is mandatory for all computer systems connected to any network

4. Firewall protection may include
   a. Packet filtering
   b. Packet selection using a routing table
   c. Network address translation
   d. Limiting ports that may be used for access
   e. IP spoofing

5. Employees connecting to the enterprise network from home, or another remote work location:
   a. Are best protected by a software firewall such as is available in Microsoft Windows XP
   b. Should have a firewall between their computer and a cable or DSL modem
   c. Should have IP spoofing implemented
   d. Are better protected when a VPN is used
   e. Should not use network address translation

6. Wireless networks need to be secured because:
   a. Inexpensive wireless access points are readily available.
   b. Anyone with a wireless network adapter can connect to an unprotected network.
   c. Employees may use the wireless network to secretly communicate with hackers.
   d. Radio waves penetrate walls to adjoining offices.
   e. Radio waves may carry to public roads outside the building.

7. Components of wireless access point security include
   a. Network address translation
   b. The organization's security policy
   c. Encryption
   d. Virtual private networks
   e. MAC address lists

8. System-level security precautions include
   a. Installing the minimal software components necessary
   b. Granting only table privileges that users require
   c. Applying security patches in a timely manner
   d. Changing all default passwords
   e. Using simple passwords that are easy to remember

9. Login credentials:
   a. May be shared by multiple users provided all of them are trustworthy
   b. Should have passwords changed periodically
   c. Need not be encrypted
   d. Should be governed by security policy
   e. Should be difficult to guess

10. Encryption:
    a. Should be used for all sensitive data
    b. Should use keys of at least 28 bits in length
    c. Should be used for sensitive data sent over a network
    d. Can use symmetric or asymmetric keys
    e. Should never be used for login credentials

11. Client security considerations include
    a. MAC address lists
    b. Web browser security level
    c. Granting only database table privileges that are absolutely necessary
    d. Use of a virus scanner
    e. Testing of application exposures

12. In Microsoft SQL Server, a login (user login):
    a. Can connect to any number of databases
    b. Automatically has database access privileges
    c. Can use Windows authentication
    d. Can be authenticated by Microsoft SQL Server
    e. Owns a database schema

13. In Microsoft SQL Server, a database:
    a. Is owned by a login
    b. May have one or more users assigned to it
    c. May contain system data (for example, master) or user (application) data
    d. May be granted privileges
    e. Is a logical collection of database objects

14. In Oracle, a user account:
    a. Can connect (log in) to any number of databases
    b. Automatically has database privileges
    c. Can use operating system authentication
    d. Can be authenticated by the Oracle DBMS
    e. Owns a database schema

15. In Oracle, a database:
    a. Is owned by a user
    b. May have one or more user accounts defined in it
    c. May contain system data (for example, system schema) and user (application) data
    d. Is the same as a schema
    e. Is managed by an Oracle instance

16. System privileges:
    a. Are granted in a similar way in Oracle, Sybase, and Microsoft SQL Server
    b. Are specific to a database object
    c. Allow the grantee to perform certain administrative functions on the server, such as shutting it down
    d. Are rescinded using the SQL REMOVE statement
    e. Vary across databases from different vendors

17. Object privileges:
    a. Are granted in a similar way in Oracle, Sybase, and Microsoft SQL Server
    b. Are specific to a database object

     c. Allow the grantee to perform certain administrative functions on the server, such as shutting it down

     d. Are rescinded using the SQL REMOVE statement

     e. Are granted using the SQL GRANT statement

18. Using the WITH GRANT OPTION when granting object privileges:

     a. Allows the grantee to grant the privilege to others

     b. Gives the grantee DBA privileges on the entire database

     c. Can lead to security issues

     d. Will cascade if the privilege is subsequently revoked

     e. Is a highly recommended practice because it is so convenient to use

19. Roles:

     a. May be assigned to only one user

     b. May be shared by many users

     c. May exist before users do

     d. May contain any number of object privileges

     e. May contain only one object privilege

20. Views may assist with security policy implementation by:

     a. Restricting the table columns to which a user has access

     b. Restricting the databases to which a user has access

     c. Restricting table rows to which a user has access

     d. Storing database audit results

     e. Monitoring for database intruders

11

Database Implementation

In this chapter, we cover some considerations regarding the implementation of a database system. These include cursor processing, transaction management, performance tuning, and change control.

Cursor Processing

Before we embark on transaction management, which includes a discussion of the locking mechanisms required to support concurrent updates of the database, we must explore the way application programs handle database queries. The collection of rows returned by the execution of a database query is called the *result set*. When you're selecting data from the database, application programming languages such as C and Java present a dilemma when the result set contains multiple rows of data. These programming languages are designed to handle one record at a time (one object instance at a time in the case of Java). So there is a mismatch that must be addressed.

To overcome the mismatch, most relational databases support the concept of a *cursor*, which is merely a pointer to a single row in the result set. In Oracle, cursor support is included in a procedural language SQL extension called PL/SQL (Procedural Language/SQL), and similarly is included in Transact-SQL in Sybase and Microsoft SQL Server. The examples in this chapter use Oracle, so some of them may require minor modification before they will work on other RDBMS products. The use of a cursor parallels the use of a traditional flat file in that the cursor must be defined and opened before it may be used, it may be read from by fetching rows in a programming loop, and it should be closed when the program no longer needs it.

Following is an example of a cursor declaration. For clarity, all the keywords are shown in uppercase and database object names in lowercase. In Oracle, this makes no difference because all database object names are case insensitive. You may, however, have a different experience with other RDBMS products.

```
DECLARE CURSOR ny_customers AS
    SELECT customer_number, name, address, city, zip_code
      FROM customer
     WHERE state = 'NY';
```

You may recognize the customer table from Chapter 8. If you ignore the first line, the statement looks like any ordinary SQL query—it selects some columns from a table and, in this case, has a WHERE clause to limit the rows returned to only those from New York state. This is very nice because it means we can test the query using any interactive SQL client tool before we paste it into a program and turn it into a cursor declaration. The DECLARE CURSOR clause defines the cursor for us, which we have named ny_customers. Cursor declarations are not executable statements, meaning that when they are processed by the RDBMS, they do nothing but set up a definition that may be subsequently referenced. The declaration is checked for syntax and some other internal details, but the database does not need to access any table rows until the cursor is opened.

The cursor must be opened before it can be used. In this example, the RDBMS may not have to retrieve any rows when we open the cursor, but for efficiency, it might decide to retrieve some number of rows and place them in a buffer for us. A *buffer* is merely an area of computer memory used to temporarily hold data. It is far more efficient to use a buffer to hold some number of prefetched rows rather than going to the database files for every single row because computers can access memory so much faster than files in the file system. In some cases, however, the RDBMS *must* fetch all the rows matching a query and sort them before the first row may be returned to the application program. You may have guessed that these are queries containing an ORDER BY to sequence the returned rows for us. If there is no index on the column(s) we use for sequencing, then the RDBMS must find and sort all of them before it knows which one is the correct one to return as the *first* row (the one that sorts first in the requested sequence). Although a lot goes on when we open a cursor, the statement itself is quite simple. Here is the OPEN CURSOR statement for our example:

```
OPEN CURSOR ny_customers;
```

Each time our program requires a new row from the result set, we simply issue a FETCH command against the cursor. This is very much like reading the next record from a file in an older flat file system. Remember that the cursor is merely a pointer into the result set. Every time a fetch is issued, the row currently pointed to is returned to the calling program (that is, the program that issued the FETCH), and the cursor is advanced one row to point to the next row to be returned. If there are no more rows in the result set, a code is returned to the calling program to indicate this. Another detail handled by the fetch is mapping the columns returned to programming language variables (called *host language variables,* or just *host variables)*. This is done with the INTO clause, and naturally the syntax of the variable names will vary from one programming language to another. Our example uses very simple names to stay away from programming language issues, but in real life you would want the names to be as descriptive as possible. It's also good programming practice to use names that are *not* exactly the same as the database column names, so as to avoid confusion when someone else reads the program. The variable names in this example are prefixed with "v_" (for *variable)* for this reason. Here is the fetch of the my_customers cursor:

```
FETCH ny_customers
  INTO v_customer_number, v_name, v_address, v_city,
      v_zip_code;
```

Notice that the FETCH statement refers only to the cursor name and the host variables. The cursor declaration ties the cursor to the table(s) and column(s) being referenced. As stated, we should always close the cursor when the program no longer needs it because this frees up any resources the cursor has used, including memory for buffers. The CLOSE statement is as simple as the OPEN statement:

```
CLOSE my_customers;
```

The topic of cursor processing has been introduced before the discussion of transaction management because cursors play a key role in some transaction events.

Transaction Management

In order to successfully support the database users, the DBMS must include provisions to manage the transactions carried out by the application systems using the database.

What Is a Transaction?

A *transaction* is a discrete series of actions that must be either completely processed or not processed at all. Some call a transaction a *unit of work* as a way of further emphasizing its all-or-nothing nature. Transactions have properties that can be easily remembered using the acronym ACID (Atomicity, Consistency, Isolation, Durability):

- **Atomicity**   A transaction must remain whole. That is, it must completely succeed or completely fail. When it succeeds, all changes that were made by the transaction must be preserved by the system. Should a transaction fail, all changes that were made by it must be completely undone. In database systems, we use the term *rollback* for the process that backs out any changes made by a failed transaction, and we use the term *commit* for the process that makes transaction changes permanent.
- **Consistency**   A transaction should transform the database from one consistent state to another. For example, a transaction that creates an invoice for an order transforms the order from a *shipped* order to an *invoiced* order, including all the appropriate database changes.
- **Isolation**   Each transaction should carry out its work independent of any other transaction that might occur at the same time.
- **Durability**   Changes made by completed transactions should remain permanent, even after a subsequent shutdown or failure of the database or other critical system component. In object terminology, the term *persistence* is used for permanently stored data. The concept of permanent here can be confusing, because nothing seems to ever stand still for long in an OLTP (online transaction processing) database. Just keep in mind that *permanent* means the change will not disappear when the database is shut down or fails—it does *not* mean that the data is in a permanent state that can never be changed again.

DBMS Support for Transactions

Aside from personal computer database systems, most DBMSs provide transaction support. This includes provisions in SQL for identifying the beginning and end of each transaction, along with a facility for logging all changes made by transactions so that a rollback may be performed when necessary. As you might guess, standards lagged behind the need for transaction support, so support for transactions varies a bit across RDBMS vendors. As examples, let's look at transaction support in Microsoft SQL Server and Oracle, followed by discussion of transaction logs.

Transaction Support in Microsoft SQL Server

Microsoft SQL Server supports transactions in three modes: autocommit, explicit, and implicit. All three modes are available when you're connected directly to the database using a client tool designed for this purpose. However, if you plan to use an ODBC or JDBC driver, you should consult the driver's documentation for information on the transaction support it provides. Here's a description of the three modes:

- **Autocommit mode** In autocommit mode, each SQL statement is automatically committed as it completes. Essentially, this makes every SQL statement a discrete transaction. Every connection to Microsoft SQL Server uses autocommit until either an explicit transaction is started or the implicit transaction mode is set. In other words, autocommit is the default transaction mode for each SQL Server connection.

- **Explicit mode** In explicit mode, each transaction is started with a BEGIN TRANSACTION statement and ended with either a COMMIT TRANSACTION statement (for successful completion) or a ROLLBACK TRANSACTION statement (for unsuccessful completion). This mode is used most often in application programs, stored procedures, triggers, and scripts. The general syntax of the three SQL statements follows:

```
BEGIN TRAN[SACTION] [tran_name | @tran_name_variable]
COMMIT [TRAN[SACTION] [tran_name | @tran_name_variable]]
ROLLBACK [TRAN[SACTION] [tran_name | @tran_name_variable |
          savepoint_name | @savepoint_name_variable]]
```

- **Implicit mode** Implicit transaction mode is toggled on or off with the command SET IMPLICIT_TRANSACTIONS {ON | OFF}. When implicit mode is on, a new transaction is started whenever any of a list of specific SQL statements is executed, including DELETE, INSERT SELECT, and UPDATE, among others. Once a transaction is implicitly started, it continues until the transaction is either committed or rolled back. If the database user disconnects before submitting a transaction-ending statement, the transaction is automatically rolled back.

Microsoft SQL Server records all transactions and the modifications made by them in the *transaction log*. The before and after image of each database modification made by a transaction is recorded in the transaction log. This facilitates any necessary roll-back because the before images can be used to reverse the database changes made by the transaction. A transaction commit is not complete until the commit record has been written to the transaction log. Because database changes are not always written to disk immediately, the transaction log is sometimes the only means of recovery when there is a system failure.

Transaction Support in Oracle

Oracle supports only two transaction modes: autocommit and implicit. As with Microsoft SQL Server, support varies when ODBC and JDBC drivers are used, so the driver vendor's documentation should be consulted in those cases. Here's a description of these two modes in Oracle:

- **Autocommit mode**   As with Microsoft SQL Server, each SQL statement is automatically committed as it completes. Autocommit mode is toggled on and off using the SET AUTOCOMMIT command, as shown here, and is off by default:

```
SET AUTOCOMMIT ON
SET AUTOCOMMIT OFF
```

- **Implicit mode**   A transaction is implicitly started when the database user connects to the database (that is, when a new database session begins). This is the default transaction mode in Oracle. When a transaction ends with a commit or rollback, a new transaction is automatically started. Unlike in Microsoft SQL Server, nested transactions (transactions within transactions) are not permitted. A transaction ends with a commit when any of the following occurs: 1) the database user issues the SQL COMMIT statement; 2) the database session ends normally (that is, the user issues an EXIT or DISONNECT command); 3) the database user issues an SQL DDL statement (that is, a CREATE, DROP, or ALTER statement). A transaction ends with a rollback when either of the following occurs: 1) the database user issues the SQL ROLLBACK statement; 2) the database sessions ends abnormally (that is, the client connection is canceled or the database crashes or is shut down using one of the shutdown options that aborts client connections instead of waiting for them to complete).

Locking and Transaction Deadlock

Although the simultaneous sharing of data among many database users has significant benefits, there also is a serious drawback that can cause updates to be lost. Fortunately, the database vendors have worked out solutions to the problem. This section presents the concurrent update problem and various solutions.

The Concurrent Update Problem

Figure 11-1 illustrates the concurrent update problem that occurs when multiple database sessions are allowed to concurrently update the same data. Recall that a session is created every time a database user connects to the database, which includes the same user connecting to the database multiple times. The concurrent update problem happens most often between two different database users who are unaware that they are making conflicting updates to the same data. However, database users with multiple connections can trip themselves up if they apply updates using more than one of their database sessions.

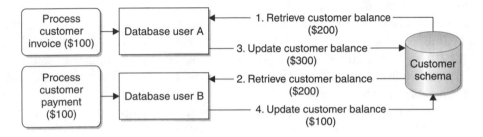

Figure 11-1   The concurrent update problem

The scenario presented uses a fictitious company that sells products and creates an invoice for each order shipped, similar to Acme Industries in the normalization examples from earlier chapters. Figure 11-1 illustrates user A, a clerk in the shipping department who is preparing an invoice for a customer, which requires updating the customer's data by adding to the customer's balance due. At the same time, user B, a clerk in the accounts receivable department, is processing a payment from the very same customer, which requires updating the customer's balance due by subtracting the amount they paid. Here is the exact sequence of events, as illustrated in Figure 11-1:

1. User A queries the database and retrieves the customer's balance due, which is $200.

2. A few seconds later, user B queries the database and retrieves the same customer's balance, which is still $200.

3. In a few more seconds, user A applies her update, adding the $100 invoice to the balance due, which makes the new balance $300 in the database.

4. Finally, user B applies his update, subtracting the $100 payment from the balance due he retrieved from the database ($200), resulting in a new balance due of $100. He is unaware of the update made by user A and thus sets the balance due (incorrectly) to $100.

The balance due for this customer should be $200, but the update made by user A has been overwritten by the update made by user B. The company is out $100 that either will be lost revenue or will take significant staff time to uncover and correct. As you can see, allowing concurrent updates to the database without some sort of control can cause updates to be lost. Most database vendors implement a locking strategy to prevent concurrent updates to the exact same data.

Locking Mechanisms

A *lock* is a control placed in the database to reserve data so that only one database session may update it. When data is locked, no other database session can update the data until the lock is released, which is usually done with a COMMIT or ROLLBACK SQL statement. Any other session that attempts to update locked data will be placed in a *lock wait* state, and the session will stall until the lock is released. Some database products, such as IBM's DB2, will time out a session that waits too long and return an error instead of completing the requested update. Others, such as Oracle, will leave a session in a lock wait state for an indefinite period of time.

By now it should be no surprise that there is significant variation in how locks are handled by different vendors' database products. A general overview is presented here with the recommendation that you consult your database vendor's documentation for details on how locks are supported. Locks may be placed at various levels (often called *lock granularity)*, and some database products, including Sybase, Microsoft SQL Server, and IBM's DB2, support multiple levels with automatic *lock escalation,* which raises locks to higher levels as a database session places more and more locks on the same database objects. Locking and unlocking small amounts of data requires significant overhead, so escalating locks to higher levels can substantially improve performance. Typical lock levels are as follows:

*   **Database**   The entire database is locked so that only one database session may apply updates. This is obviously an extreme situation that should not happen very often, but it can be useful when significant maintenance is being performed, such as upgrading to a new version of the database software. Oracle supports this level indirectly when the database is opened in exclusive mode, which restricts the database to only one user session.

- **File**   An entire database file is locked. Recall that a file can contain part of a table, an entire table, or parts of many tables. This level is less favored in modern databases because the data locked can be so diverse.
- **Table**   An entire table is locked. This level is useful when you're performing a table-wide change such as reloading all the data in the table, updating every row, or altering the table to add or remove columns. Oracle calls this level a *DDL lock,* and it is used when DDL statements (CREATE, DROP, and ALTER) are submitted against a table or other database object.
- **Block or page**   A block or page within a database file is locked. A *block* is the smallest unit of data that the operating system can read from or write to a file. On most personal computers, the block size is called the *sector size.* Some operating systems use pages instead of blocks. A *page* is a virtual block of fixed size, typically 2K or 4K, which is used to simplify processing when there are multiple storage devices that support different block sizes. The operating system can read and write pages and let hardware drivers translate the pages to appropriate blocks. As with file locking, block (page) locking is less favored in modern database systems because of the diversity of the data that may happen to be written to the same block in the file.
- **Row**   A row in a table is locked. This is the most common locking level, with virtually all modern database systems supporting it.
- **Column**   Some columns within a row in the table are locked. This method sounds terrific in theory, but it's not very practical because of the resources required to place and release locks at this level of granularity. Very sparse support for it exists in modern commercial database systems.

Locks are always placed when data is updated or deleted. Most RDBMSs also support the use of a FOR UPDATE OF clause on a SELECT statement to allow locks to be placed when the database user declares their *intent* to update something. Some locks may be considered *read-exclusive,* which prevents other sessions from even reading the locked data. Many RDBMSs have session parameters that can be set to help control locking behavior. One of the locking behaviors to consider is whether all rows fetched using a cursor are locked until the next COMMIT or ROLLBACK, or whether previously read rows are released when the next row is fetched. Consult your database vendor documentation for more details.

The main problem with locking mechanisms is that locks cause *contention*, meaning that the placement of locks to prevent loss of data from concurrent updates has the side effect of causing concurrent sessions to compete for the right to apply updates. At the least, lock contention slows user processes as sessions wait for locks. At the worst, competing lock requests call stall sessions indefinitely, as you will see in the next section.

Deadlocks

A *deadlock* is a situation where two or more database sessions have locked some data and then each has requested a lock on data that another session has locked. Figure 11-2 illustrates this situation.

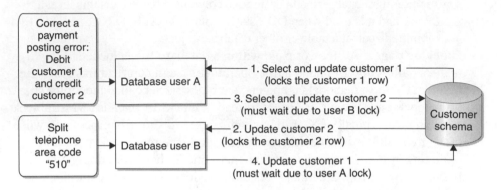

Figure 11-2   The deadlock

This example again uses two users from our fictitious company, cleverly named A and B. User A is a customer representative in the customer service department and is attempting to correct a payment that was credited to the wrong customer account. He needs to subtract (debit) the payment from Customer 1 and add (credit) it to Customer 2. User B is a database specialist in the IT department, and she has written an SQL statement to update some of the customer phone numbers with one area code to a new area code in response to a recent area code split by the phone company. The statement has a WHERE clause that limits the update to only those customers having a phone number with certain prefixes in area code 510 and updates those phone numbers to the new area code. User B submits her SQL UPDATE statement while user A is working on his payment credit problem. Customers 1 and 2 both have phone numbers that need to be updated. The sequence of events (all happening within seconds of each other), as illustrated in Figure 11-2, takes place as follows:

1. User A selects the data from Customer 1 and applies an update to debit the balance due. No commit is issued yet because this is only part of the transaction that must take place. The row for Customer 1 now has a lock on it due to the update.

2. The statement submitted by user B updates the phone number for Customer 2. The entire SQL statement must run as a single transaction, so there is no commit at this point, and thus user B holds a lock on the row for Customer 2.

3. User A selects the balance for Customer 2 and then submits an update to credit the balance due (same amount as debited from Customer 1). The request must wait because user B holds a lock on the row to be updated.

4. The statement submitted by user B now attempts to update the phone number for Customer 1. The update must wait because user A holds a lock on the row to be updated.

These two database sessions are now in deadlock. User A cannot continue due to a lock held by user B, and vice versa. In theory, these two database sessions will be stalled forever. Fortunately, modern DBMSs contain provisions to handle this situation. One method is to prevent deadlocks. Few DBMSs have this capability due to the considerable overhead this approach requires and the virtual impossibility of predicting what an interactive database user will do next. However, the theory is to inspect each lock request for the potential to cause contention and not permit the lock to take place if a deadlock is possible. The more common approach is deadlock detection, which then aborts one of the requests that caused the deadlock. This can be done either by timing lock waits and giving up after a preset time interval or by periodically inspecting all locks to find two sessions that have each other locked out. In either case, one of the requests must be terminated and the transaction's changes rolled back in order to allow the other request to proceed.

Performance Tuning

Any seasoned DBA will tell you that database performance tuning is a never-ending task. It seems there is always something that can be tweaked to make it run more quickly and/or efficiently. The key to success is managing your time and the expectations of the database users, and setting the performance requirements for an application before it is even written. Simple statements such as "every database update must complete within 4 seconds" are usually the best. With that done, performance tuning becomes a simple matter of looking for things that do not conform to the performance requirement and tuning them until they do. The law of diminishing returns applies to database tuning, and you can put lots of effort into tuning a database process for little or no gain. The beauty of having a standard performance requirement is that you can stop when the process meets the requirement and then move on to the next problem.

Although there are components other than SQL statements that can be tuned, these other components are so specific to a particular DBMS that it is best not to attempt to cover them here. Suffice it to say that memory usage, CPU utilization, and file system I/O all must be tuned along with the SQL statements that access the database. The tuning of SQL statements is addressed in the sections that follow.

Tuning Database Queries

About 80 percent of database query performance problems can be solved by adjusting the SQL statement. However, you must understand how the particular DBMS being used processes SQL statements in order to know what to tweak. For example, placing SQL statements inside stored procedures can yield remarkable performance improvement in Microsoft SQL Server and Sybase, but the same is not true at in Oracle.

A query *execution plan* is a description of how an RDBMS will process a particular query, including index usage, join logic, and estimated resource cost. It is important to learn how to use the "explain plan" utility in your DBMS, if one is available, because it will show you exactly how the DBMS will process the SQL statement you are attempting to tune. In Oracle, the SQL EXPLAIN PLAN statement analyzes an SQL statement and posts analysis results to a special plan table. The plan table must be created exactly as specified by Oracle, so it is best to use the script they provide for this purpose. After running the EXPLAIN PLAN statement, you must then retrieve the results from the plan table using a SELECT statement. Fortunately, Oracle's Enterprise Manager has a GUI version available that makes query tuning a lot easier. In Microsoft SQL Server 2000, the Query Analyzer tool has a button labeled Display Estimated Execution Plan that graphically displays how the SQL statement will be executed. This feature is also accessible from the Query menu item as the option Show Execution Plan. These items may have different names in other versions of Microsoft SQL Server.

Following are some general tuning tips for SQL. You should consult a tuning guide for the particular DBMS you are using because techniques, tips, and other considerations vary by DBMS product.

- Avoid table scans of large tables. For tables over 1,000 rows or so, scanning all the rows in the table instead of using an index can be expensive in terms of resources required. And, of course, the larger the table, the more expensive a table scan becomes. Full table scans occur in the following situations:
  - The query does not contain a WHERE clause to limit rows.
  - None of the columns referenced in the WHERE clause match the leading column of an index on the table.
  - Index and table statistics have not been updated. Most RDBMS query optimizers use statistics to evaluate available indexes, and without statistics, a table scan may be seen as more efficient than using an index.

- At least one column in the WHERE clause does match the first column of an available index, but the comparison used obviates the use of an index. These cases include the following:
  - Use of the NOT operator (for example, WHERE NOT CITY = 'New York'). In general, indexes can be used to find what *is* in a table, but cannot be used to find what is *not* in a table.
  - Use of the NOT EQUAL operator (for example, WHERE CITY <> 'New York').
  - Use of a wildcard in the first position of a comparison string (for example, WHERE CITY LIKE '%York%').
  - Use of an SQL function in the comparison (for example, WHERE UPPER(CITY) = 'NEW YORK').
- Create indexes that are selective. *Index selectivity* is a ratio of the number of distinct values a column has, divided by the number of rows in a table. For example, if a table has 1,000 rows and a column has 800 distinct values, the selectivity of the index is 0.8, which is considered good. However, a column such as gender that only has two distinct values (M and F) has very poor selectivity (.002 in this case). Unique indexes always have a selectivity ratio of 1.0, which is the best possible. With some RDBMSs such as DB2, unique indexes are so superior that DBAs often add otherwise unnecessary columns to an index just to make the index unique. However, always keep in mind that indexes take storage space and must be maintained, so they are never a free lunch.
- Evaluate join techniques carefully. Most RDBMSs offer multiple methods for joining tables, with the query optimizer in the RDBMS selecting the one that appears best based on table statistics. In general, creating indexes on foreign key columns gives the optimizer more options from which to choose, which is always a good thing. Run an explain plan and consult your RDBMS documentation when tuning joins.
- Pay attention to views. Because views are stored SQL queries, they can present performance problems just like any other query.
- Tune subqueries in accordance with your RDBMS vendor's recommendations.
- Limit use of remote tables. Tables connected to remotely via database links never perform as well as local tables.
- Very large tables require special attention. When tables grow to millions of rows in size, any query can be a performance nightmare. Evaluate every query carefully, and consider partitioning the table to improve query performance. Table partitioning is addressed in Chapter 8. Your RDBMS may offer other special features for very large tables that will improve query performance.

Tuning DML Statements

DML (Data Manipulation Language) statements generally produce fewer performance problems than query statements. However, there can be issues.

For INSERT statements, there are two main considerations:

- *Ensuring that there is adequate free space in the tablespaces to hold new rows.* Tablespaces that are short on space present problems as the DBMS searches for free space to hold rows being inserted. Moreover, inserts do not usually put rows into the table in primary key sequence because there usually isn't free space in exactly the right places. Therefore, reorganizing the table, which is essentially a process of unloading the rows to a flat file, re-creating the table, and then reloading the table can improve both insert and query performance.
- *Index maintenance.* Every time a row is inserted into a table, a corresponding entry must be inserted into every index built on the table (except null values are never indexed). The more indexes there are, the more overhead every insert will require. Index free space can usually be tuned just as table free space can.

UPDATE statements have the following considerations:

- *Index maintenance.* If columns that are indexed are updated, the corresponding index entries must also be updated. In general, updating primary key values has particularly bad performance implications, so much so that some RDBMSs prohibit it.
- *Row expansion.* When columns are updated in such a way that the row grows significantly in size, the row may no longer fit in its original location, and there may not be free space around the row for it to expand in place (other rows might be right up against the one just updated). When this occurs, the row must either be moved to another location in the data file where it will fit or be split with the expanded part of the row placed in a new location, connected to the original location by a pointer. Both of these situations are not only expensive when they occur but are also detrimental to the performance of subsequent queries that touch those rows. Table reorganizations can resolve the issue, but its better to prevent the problem by designing the application so that rows tend not to grow in size after they are inserted.

DELETE statements are the least likely to present performance issues. However, a table that participates as a parent in a relationship that is defined with the ON DELETE CASCADE option can perform poorly if there are many child rows to delete.

Change Control

Change control (also known as *change management)* is the process used to manage the changes that occur after a system is implemented. A change control process has the following benefits:

- It helps you understand when it is acceptable to make changes and when it is not.
- It provides a log of all changes that have been made to assist with troubleshooting when problems occur.
- It can manage versions of software components so that a defective version can be smoothly backed out.

Change is inevitable. Not only do business requirements change, but also new versions of database and operating system software and new hardware devices eventually must be incorporated. Technologists should devise a change control method suitable to the organization, and management should approve it as a standard. Anything less leads to chaos when changes are made without the proper coordination and communication. Although terminology varies among standard methods, they all have common features:

- **Version numbering**   Components of an application system are assigned version numbers, usually starting with 1 and advancing sequentially every time the component is changed. Usually a revision date and the identifier of the person making the change are carried with the version number.
- **Release (build) numbering**   A *release* is a point in time at which all components of an application system (including database components) are promoted to the next environment (for example, from development to system test) as a bundle that can be tested and deployed together. Some organizations use the term *build* instead. Database environments are discussed in Chapter 5. As releases are formed, it is important to label each component included with the release (or build) number. This allows us to tell which version of each component was included in a particular release.
- **Prioritization**   Changes may be assigned priorities to allow them to be scheduled accordingly.
- **Change request tracking**   Change requests can be placed into the change control system, routed through channels for approval, and marked with the applicable release number when the change is completed.

- **Check-out and Check-in**   When a developer or DBA is ready to apply changes to a component, they should be able to check it out (reserve it), which prevents others from making potentially conflicting changes to the same component at the same time. When work is complete, the developer or DBA checks the component back in, which essentially releases the reservation.

A number of commercial and freeware software products can be deployed to assist with change control. However, it is important to establish the process *before* choosing tools. In this way, the organization can establish the best process for their needs and find the tool that best fits that process rather than trying to retrofit a tool to the process.

From the database perspective, the DBA should develop DDL statements to implement all the database components of an application system and a script that can be used to invoke all the changes, including any required conversions. This deployment script and all the DDL should be checked into the change control system and managed just like all the other software components of the system.

Quiz

Choose the correct responses to each of the multiple-choice questions. Note that there may be more than one correct response to each question.

1. A cursor is
    a. The collection of rows returned by a database query
    b. A pointer into a result set
    c. The same as a result set
    d. A buffer that holds rows retrieved from the database
    e. A method to analyze the performance of SQL statements

2. A result set is
    a. The collection of rows returned by a database query
    b. A pointer into a cursor
    c. The same as a cursor
    d. A buffer that holds rows retrieved from the database
    e. A method to analyze the performance of SQL statements

3. Before rows may be fetched from a cursor, the cursor must first be
    a. Declared
    b. Committed
    c. Opened

    d. Closed
    e. Purged

4. A transaction:
    a. May be partially processed and committed
    b. May not be partially processed and committed
    c. Changes the database from one consistent state to another
    d. Is sometimes called a *unit of work*
    e. Has properties described by the ACID acronym

5. The *I* in the ACID acronym stands for:
    a. Integrated
    b. Immediate
    c. Iconic
    d. Isolation
    e. Informational

6. Microsoft SQL Server supports the following transaction modes:
    a. Autocommit
    b. Automatic
    c. Durable
    d. Explicit
    e. Implicit

7. Oracle supports the following transaction modes:
    a. Autocommit
    b. Automatic
    c. Durable
    d. Explicit
    e. Implicit

8. The SQL statements (commands) that end a transaction are
    a. SET AUTOCOMMIT
    b. BEGIN TRANSACTION (in SQL Server)
    c. COMMIT
    d. ROLLBACK
    e. SAVEPOINT

9. The concurrent update problem:
    a. Is a consequence of simultaneous data sharing
    b. Cannot occur when AUTOCOMMIT is set to ON
    c. Is the reason that transaction locking must be supported
    d. Occurs when two database users submit conflicting SELECT statements
    e. Occurs when two database users make conflicting updates to the same data

10. A lock:
    a. Is a control placed on data to reserve it so that the user may update it
    b. Is usually released when a COMMIT or ROLLBACK takes place
    c. Has a timeout set in DB2 and some other RDBMS products
    d. May cause contention when other users attempt to update locked data
    e. May have levels and an escalation protocol in some RDBMS products

11. A deadlock:
    a. Is a lock that has timed out and is therefore no longer needed
    b. Occurs when two database users each request a lock on data that is locked by the other
    c. Can theoretically put two or more users in an endless lock wait state
    d. May be resolved by deadlock detection on some RDBMSs
    e. May be resolved by lock timeouts on some RDBMSs

12. Performance tuning:
    a. Is a never-ending process
    b. Should be used on each query until no more improvement can be realized
    c. Should only be used on queries that fail to conform to performance requirements
    d. Involves not only SQL tuning but also CPU, file system I/O and memory usage tuning
    e. Should be requirements based

13. SQL query tuning:
    a. Can be done in the same way for all relational database systems
    b. Usually involves using an explain plan facility
    c. Always involves placing SQL statements in a stored procedure
    d. Only applies to SQL SELECT statements
    e. Requires detailed knowledge of the RDBMS on which the query is to be run

14. General SQL tuning tips include
    a. Avoid table scans on large tables.
    b. Use an index whenever possible.
    c. Use an ORDER BY clause whenever possible.
    d. Use a WHERE clause to filter rows whenever possible.
    e. Use views whenever possible.

15. SQL practices that obviate the use of an index are
    a. Use of a WHERE clause
    b. Use of a NOT operator
    c. Use of table joins

    d. Use of the NOT EQUAL operator

    e. Use of wildcards in the first column of LIKE comparison strings

16. Indexes work well at filtering rows when:

    a. They are very selective.

    b. The selectivity ratio is very high.

    c. The selectivity ratio is very low.

    d. They are unique.

    e. They are not unique.

17. The main performance considerations for INSERT statements are

    a. Row expansion

    b. Index maintenance

    c. Free space usage

    d. Subquery tuning

    e. Any very large tables that are involved

18. The main performance considerations for UPDATE statements are

    a. Row expansion

    b. Index maintenance

    c. Free space usage

    d. Subquery tuning

    e. Any very large tables that are involved

19. A change control process:

    a. Can prevent programming errors from being placed into production

    b. May also be called *change management*

    c. Helps with understanding when changes may be installed

    d. Provides a log of all changes made

    e. Can allow defective software versions to be backed out

20. Common features of change control processes are

    a. Transaction support

    b. Version numbering

    c. Deadlock prevention

    d. Release numbering

    e. Prioritization

12

Databases for Online Analytical Processing

Starting in the 1980s, businesses recognized the need for keeping historical data and using it for analysis to assist in decision making. It was soon apparent that data organized for use by day-to-day business transactions was not as useful for analysis. In fact, storing significant amounts of history in an *operational* database (a database designed to support the day-to-day transactions of an organization) could have serious detrimental effects on performance. William H. (Bill) Inmon participated in pioneering work in a concept known as *data warehousing*, where historical data is periodically trimmed from the operational database and moved to a database specifically designed for analysis. It was Bill Inmon's dedicated promotion of the concept that earned him the title "father of data warehousing."

The popularity of the data warehouse approach grew with each success story. In addition to Bill Inmon, others made significant contributions, notably Ralph Kimball, who developed specialized database architectures for data warehouses (covered in the "Data Warehouse Architecture" section, later in this chapter). Dr. E.F. Codd added his endorsement to the data warehouse approach and coined two important terms in 1993:

- **Online transaction processing (OLTP)** Systems designed to handle high volumes of transactions that carry out the day-to-day activities of an organization
- **Online analytical processing (OLAP)** Analysis of data (often historical) to identify trends that assist in making strategic decisions regarding the business

Up to this point, the chapters of this book have dealt almost exclusively with OLTP databases. This chapter, on the other hand, is devoted exclusively to OLAP database concepts.

Data Warehouses

A *data warehouse (DW)* is a subject-oriented, integrated, time-variant and nonvola-tile collection of data intended to support management decision making. Here are some important properties of a data warehouse:

- Organized around major subject areas of an organization, such as sales, customers, suppliers, and products. OLTP systems, on the other hand, are typically organized around major processes, such as payroll, order entry, billing, and so forth.
- Integrated from multiple operational (OLTP) data sources.
- Not updated in real time, but periodically, based on an established schedule. Data is pulled from operational sources as often as needed, such as daily, weekly, monthly, and so forth.

The potential benefits of a well-constructed data warehouse are significant, including the following:

- Competitive advantage
- Increased productivity of corporate decision makers
- Potential high return on investment as the organization finds the best ways to improve efficiency and/or profitability

However, there are significant challenges to creating an enterprise-wide data warehouse, including the following:

- Underestimation of the resources required to load the data
- Hidden data integrity problems in the source data
- Omitting data, only to find out later that it is required
- Ever-increasing end user demands (each new feature spawns ideas for even more features)
- Consolidating data from disparate data sources
- High resource demands (huge amounts of storage; queries that process millions of rows)
- Ownership of the data
- Difficulty in determining what the business really wants or needs to analyze
- "Big bang" projects that seem never-ending

OLTP Systems Compared with Data Warehouse Systems

It should be clear that data warehouse systems and OLTP systems are fundamentally different. Here is a comparison:

OLTP Systems	Data Warehouse Systems
Hold current data.	Hold historic data.
Store detailed data only.	Store detailed data along with lightly and highly summarized data.
Data is dynamic.	Data is static, except for periodic additions.
Database queries are short-running and access relatively few rows of data.	Database queries are long-running and access many rows of data.
High transaction volume.	Medium to low transaction volume.
Repetitive processing; predictable usage pattern.	Ad hoc and unstructured processing; unpredictable usage pattern.
Transaction driven; support day-to-day operations.	Analysis driven; support strategic decision making.
Process oriented.	Subject oriented.
Serve a large number of concurrent users.	Serve a relatively low number of managerial users (decision makers).

Data Warehouse Architecture

There are two primary schools of thought as to the best way to organize OLTP data into a data warehouse—the summary table approach and the star schema approach. The following subsections take a look at each approach, along with the benefits and drawbacks of each.

Summary Table Architecture

Bill Inmon originally developed the summary table data warehouse architecture. This data warehouse approach involves storing data not only in detail form, but also in summary tables so that analysis processes do not have to continually summarize the same data. This is an obvious violation of the principles of normalization, but because the data is historical—and therefore is never changed after it is stored—the data anomalies (insert, update, and delete) that drive the need for normalization simply don't exist. Figure 12-1 shows the summary table data warehouse architecture.

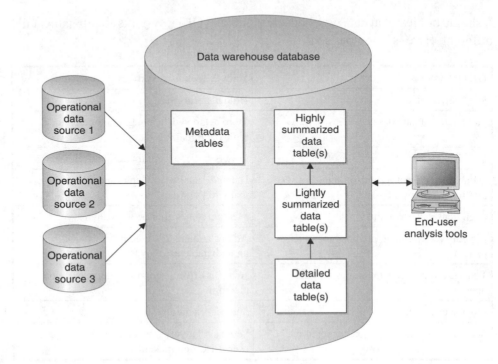

Figure 12-1   Summary table data warehouse architecture

Data from one or more operational data sources (databases or flat file systems) is periodically moved into the data warehouse database. A major key to success is determining the right level of detail that must be carried in the database and anticipating the levels of summarization necessary. Using Acme Industries as an example, if the subject of the data warehouse is sales, it may be necessary to keep every single invoice; or it may be necessary to only keep invoices that exceed a certain amount; or perhaps only those that contain certain products. If requirements are not understood, then it is unlikely that the data warehouse project will be successful. Failure rates of data warehouse projects are higher than most other types of IT projects, and the most common cause of failure is poorly defined requirements.

In terms of summarization, we might summarize the transactions by month in one summary table and by product in another. At the next level of summarization, we might summarize the months by quarter in one table and the products by department in another. An *end user* (the person using the analysis tools to obtain results from the OLAP database) might look at sales by quarter and notice that one particular quarter doesn't look quite right. The user can expand the quarter of concern and look at the months within it. This process is known as "drilling down" to more detailed levels. The user may then pick out a particular month of interest and drill down to the detailed transactions for that month.

The metadata (data about data) shown in Figure 12-1 is very important, and unfortunately, often a missing link. Ideally, the metadata defines every data item in the data warehouse, along with sufficient information so its source can be tracked all the way back to the original source data in the operational database. The biggest challenge with metadata is that, lacking standards, each vendor of data warehouse tools has stored metadata in their own way. When multiple analysis tools are in use, metadata must usually be loaded into each one of them using proprietary formats. For end user analysis tools (also called *OLAP tools)*, there are literally dozens of commercial products from which to choose, including Business Objects, BrioQuery, Powerplay, and IQ/Vision.

Star Schema Data Warehouse Architecture

Ralph Kimball developed a specialized database structure known as the *star schema* for storing data warehouse data. His contribution to OLAP data storage is significant. Red Brick, the first DBMS devoted exclusively to OLAP data storage, used the star schema. In addition, Red Brick offered SQL extensions specifically for data analysis, including moving averages, this year vs. last year, market share, and ranking. Informix acquired Red Brick's technology, and later IBM acquired Informix, so

IBM now markets the Red Brick technology as part of their data warehouse solution. Figure 12-2 shows the basic architecture of a data warehouse using the star schema.

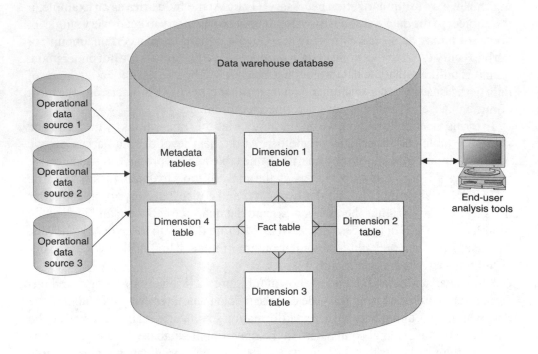

Figure 12-2   Star schema data warehouse architecture

The star schema uses a single detailed data table, called a *fact table,* surrounded by supporting reference data tables called *dimension tables,* forming a star-like pattern. Compared with the summary table data warehouse architecture, the fact table replaces the detailed data tables, and the dimension tables replace the summary tables. A new star schema is constructed for each additional fact table. Dimension tables have a one-to-many relationship with the fact table, with the primary key of the dimension table appearing as a foreign key in the fact table. However, dimension tables are not necessarily normalized because they may have an entire hierarchy, such as layers of an organization or different subcomponents of time, compressed into a single table. The dimension tables may or may not contain summary information, such as totals.

Using our prior Acme Industries sales example, the fact table would be the invoice table, and typical dimension tables would be time (months, quarters, and perhaps years), products, and organizational units (departments, divisions, and so forth). In fact, time and organizational units appear as dimensions in most star schemas. As you might guess, the key to success in star schema OLAP databases is getting the fact table right. Here's a list of the considerations that influence the design of the fact table:

- The required time period (how often data will be added and how long history must remain in the OLAP database)
- Storing every transaction vs. statistical sampling
- Columns in the source data table(s) that are not necessary for OLAP
- Columns that can be reduced in size, such as taking only the first 25 characters of a 200-character product description
- The best uses of intelligent (natural) and surrogate (dumb) keys
- Partitioning of the fact table

Over time, some variations to the star schema emerged:

- **Snowflake schema**   A variant where dimensions are allowed to have dimensions of their own. The name comes from the ERD's resemblance to a snowflake. If you fully normalize the dimensions of a star schema, you end up with a snowflake schema. For example, the time dimension at the first level could track weeks, with a dimension table above it to track months, and one above that one to track quarters. Similar arrangements could be used to track the hierarchy of an organization (departments, divisions, and so forth).
- **Starflake schema**   A hybrid arrangement containing a mixture of (denormalized) star and (normalized) snowflake dimensions.

Multidimensional Databases

Multidimensional databases evolved from star schemas. They are sometimes called *multidimensional OLAP (MOLAP)* databases. A number of specialized multidimensional database systems are on the market, including Oracle Express and Essbase. MOLAP databases are best visualized as cubes, where each dimension forms a side of the cube. To accommodate additional dimensions, the cube (or set of cubes) is simply repeated for each one.

Figure 12-3 shows a four-column fact table for Acme Industries. Product Line, Sales Department, and Quarter are dimensions, and they would be foreign keys to a dimension table in a star schema. Quantity contains the number of units sold for each combination of Product Line, Sales Department, and Quarter.

Product Line	Sales Department	Quarter	Quantity
Helmets	Corporate Sales	1	2250
Helmets	Corporate Sales	2	2107
Helmets	Corporate Sales	3	5203
Helmets	Corporate Sales	4	5806
Helmets	Internet Sales	1	1607
Helmets	Internet Sales	2	1812
Helmets	Internet Sales	3	4834
Helmets	Internet Sales	4	5150
Springs	Corporate Sales	1	16283
Springs	Corporate Sales	2	17422
Springs	Corporate Sales	3	21288
Springs	Corporate Sales	4	32768
Springs	Internet Sales	1	12
Springs	Internet Sales	2	24
Springs	Internet Sales	3	48
Springs	Internet Sales	4	48
Rockets	Corporate Sales	1	65
Rockets	Corporate Sales	2	38
Rockets	Corporate Sales	3	47
Rockets	Corporate Sales	4	52
Rockets	Internet Sales	1	2
Rockets	Internet Sales	2	1
Rockets	Internet Sales	3	6
Rockets	Internet Sales	4	9

Figure 12-3   Four-column fact table for Acme Industries

Figure 12-4 shows the multidimensional equivalent of the table shown in Figure 12-3. Note that Sales Department, Product Line, and Quarter all become edges of the cube, with the single fact Quantity stored in each grid square. The dimensions displayed may be changed by simply rotating the cube.

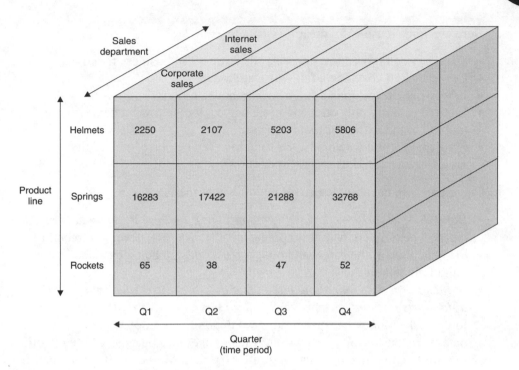

Figure 12-4   Three-dimension cube for Acme Industries

Data Marts

A *data mart* is a subset of a data warehouse that supports the requirements of a particular department or business function. In part, data marts evolved in response to some highly visible multimillion-dollar data warehouse project failures. When an organization has little experience building OLTP systems and databases, or when requirements are very sketchy, a scaled-down project such as a data mart is a far less risky approach. Here are a few characteristics of data marts:

- Focus on one department or business process
- Do not normally contain any operational data
- Contain much less information than a data warehouse

Here are some reasons for creating a data mart:

- Data may be tailored to a particular department or business function.
- Lower overall cost than a full data warehouse.
- Lower-risk project than a full data warehouse project.
- Limited (usually only one) end user analysis tool, allowing data to be tailored to the particular tool to be used.
- For departmental data marts, the database may be placed physically near the department, reducing network delays.

There are three basic strategies for building data marts:

- *Build the enterprise-wide data warehouse first, and use it to populate data marts.* The problem with this approach is that you will never get to build the data marts if the data warehouse project ends up being cancelled or put on indefinite hold.
- *Build several data marts and build the data warehouse later, integrating the data marts into the enterprise-wide data warehouse at that time.* This is a lower-risk strategy because it does not depend on completion of a major data warehouse project. However, it may cost more because of the rework required to integrate the data marts after the fact. Moreover, if several data marts are built containing similar data without a common data warehouse to integrate all the data, the same query may yield different results depending on the data mart used. Imagine the finance department quoting one revenue number and the sales department another, only to find they are both correctly quoting their data sources.
- *Build the data warehouse and data marts simultaneously.* This sounds great on paper, but when you consider that the already complex and large data warehouse project now has the data marts added to its scope, you appreciate the enormity of the project. In fact, this strategy practically *guarantees* that the data warehouse project will be the never-ending project from hell.

Data Mining

Data mining is the process of extracting valid, previously unknown, comprehensible, and actionable information from large databases and using it to make crucial business decisions. The biggest benefit is that it can uncover correlations in the data that were never suspected. The caveat is that it normally requires very large data volumes in order to produce accurate results. Most commercial OLAP tools include some data-mining features.

One of the commonly cited stories of an early success with data mining involves an NCR Corporation employee who produced a study for American Stores' Osco Drugs in 1992. The study noted that there was a correlation between beer sales and diaper sales between 5 P.M. and 7 P.M., meaning that the two items were found together in a single purchase more often than pure randomness would suggest. This correlation was subsequently mentioned in a speech, and the "beer and diapers" story quickly became a bit of an urban legend in data warehouse circles. Countless conference speakers have related the story of young fathers sent out for diapers who grab a six-pack at the same time, often embellished well beyond the facts. However, the story remains an excellent example of how unexpected the results of data mining can be.

Once you discover a correlation, the organization must decide what action to take to best capitalize on the new information. In the "beer and diapers" example, the company could either place a stack of beer next to the diapers display for that quick impulse sale, or perhaps strategically locate beer and diapers at opposite corners of the store in hopes of more impulse buys as the shopper picks up one item and heads across the store for the other. For the newly found information to be of benefit, the organization must be agile enough to take some action, so data mining itself isn't a silver bullet by any measure.

Quiz

Choose the correct responses to each of the multiple-choice questions. Note that there may be more than one correct response to each question.

1. OLTP:
   a. Was invented by Dr. E.F. Codd
   b. Was invented by Ralph Kimball
   c. Handles high volumes of transactions
   d. May use data stored in an operational database
   e. May use data stored in a data warehouse database

2. OLAP:
   a. Was invented by Dr. E.F. Codd
   b. Was invented by Ralph Kimball
   c. Handles high volumes of transactions
   d. May use data stored in an operational database
   e. May use data stored in a data warehouse database

3. Data warehousing:
   a. Involves storing data for day-to-day operations
   b. Was pioneered by Bill Inmon
   c. Involves storing historical data for analysis
   d. May involve one or more data marts
   e. Is a form of OLAP database

4. A data warehouse is
   a. Subject oriented
   b. Integrated from multiple data sources
   c. Time variant
   d. Updated in real time
   e. Organized around one department or business function

5. Challenges with the data warehouse approach include
   a. Updating operational data from the data warehouse
   b. Underestimation of required resources
   c. Diminishing user demands
   d. Large, complex projects
   e. High resource demands

6. Compared with OLTP systems, data warehouse systems:
   a. Store data that is more static
   b. Have higher transaction volumes
   c. Have a relatively smaller number of users
   d. Have data that is not normalized
   e. Tend to have shorter running queries

7. The summary table architecture:
   a. Was originally developed by Bill Inmon
   b. Includes a fact table
   c. Includes dimension tables
   d. Includes lightly and highly summarized tables
   e. Should include metadata

8. The process of moving from more summarized data to more detailed
   data is known as:
   a. Normalization
   b. Denormalization
   c. Drilling up
   d. Drilling down
   e. Data mining

9. The star schema:
    a. Was developed by Ralph Kimball
    b. Includes a dimension table and one or more fact tables
    c. Always has fully normalized dimension tables
    d. Was a key feature of the Red Brick DBMS
    e. Involves multiple levels of dimension tables

10. Factors to consider in designing the fact table include
    a. Adding columns to the fact table
    b. Reducing column sizes between the source and fact tables
    c. Partitioning the fact table
    d. How often it must be updated
    e. How long history must remain in it

11. The snowflake schema:
    a. Allows dimensions to have dimensions of their own
    b. Is a hybrid containing both normalized and denormalized tables
    c. Does not use a fact table
    d. Can be designed by fully normalizing all the dimension tables
    e. Was developed by Bill Inmon

12. The starflake schema:
    a. Allows dimensions to have dimensions of their own
    b. Is a hybrid containing both normalized and denormalized tables
    c. Does not use a fact table
    d. Can be designed by fully normalizing all the dimension tables
    e. Was developed by Bill Inmon

13. Multidimensional databases:
    a. Use a fully normalized fact table
    b. Are best visualized as cubes
    c. Have fully normalized dimension tables
    d. Are sometimes called MOLAP databases
    e. Accommodate dimensions beyond the third by repeating cubes for
       each additional dimension

14. A data mart:
    a. Is a subset of a data warehouse
    b. Is a shop that sells data to individuals and businesses
    c. Supports the requirements of a particular department or business function
    d. Can be a good starting point for organizations with no data warehouse
       experience
    e. Can be a good starting point when requirements are sketchy

15. Reasons to create a data mart include
    a. It is more comprehensive than a data warehouse.
    b. It is a potentially lower-risk project.
    c. Data may be tailored to a particular department or business function.
    d. It contains more data than a data warehouse.
    e. The project has a lower overall cost than a data warehouse project.

16. Building a data warehouse first, followed by data marts:
    a. Will delay data mart deployment if the data warehouse project drags on
    b. Has lower risk than trying to build them all together
    c. Has the lowest risk of the three possible strategies
    d. Has the highest risk of the three possible strategies
    e. May require a great deal of rework

17. Building one or more data marts first, followed by the data warehouse:
    a. May delay data warehouse delivery if the data mart projects drag on
    b. Has the potential to deliver some OLAP functions more quickly
    c. Has the lowest risk of the three possible strategies
    d. Has the highest risk of the three possible strategies
    e. May require a great deal of rework

18. Building the data warehouse and data marts simultaneously:
    a. Creates the largest single project of all the possible strategies
    b. Has the potential to take the longest to deliver any OLAP functions
    c. Has the lowest risk of the three possible strategies
    d. Has the highest risk of the three possible strategies
    e. May require a great deal of rework

19. Data mining:
    a. Is a scaled-down data warehouse
    b. Extracts previously unknown data correlations from the data warehouse
    c. Can be successful with small amounts of data
    d. Is most useful when the organization is agile enough to take action based on the information
    e. Usually requires large data volumes in order to produce accurate results

20. Properties of data warehouse systems include
    a. Holding historic rather than current information
    b. Long-running queries that process many rows of data
    c. Support for day-to-day operations
    d. Process orientation
    e. Medium to low transaction volume

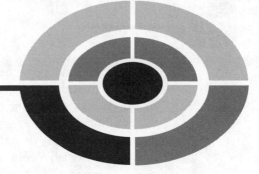

Final Exam

Choose the correct responses to each of the multiple-choice questions. Note that there may be more than one correct response to each question.

1. Properties that differentiate a database from other forms of data storage include
   a. Data items are stored in the exact same format used to display them to the database user.
   b. It provides data independence through two layers of data independence.
   c. It provides for both physical and external data independence.
   d. It provides more data independence than the file systems it replaced.
   e. It is always managed by a DBMS.

2. The benefits of user views include
   a. They may be tailored to the needs of a user department or a particular application.
   b. They provide external data independence.
   c. They always show the same current information that the base tables contain.
   d. They can always be used to apply updates to the database.
   e. They can be used to hide table rows and columns that the database user does not need to see.

3. Logical data independence:
   a. Is provided by the tables in the logical layer of the ANSI/SPARC model
   b. Is provided by the user views in the external layer of the ANSI/SPARC model
   c. Is a property that all computer systems have to some degree
   d. Allows table columns to be added without disrupting existing database queries
   e. Allows data updates applied by one user to only become visible to other users when changes are committed

4. Physical data independence:
   a. Is provided by the tables in the logical layer of the ANSI/SPARC model
   b. Is provided by the user views in the external layer of the ANSI/SPARC model
   c. Is a property that all computer systems have to some degree
   d. Allows table columns to be added without disrupting existing database queries
   e. Allows database objects to be moved from one data file (tablespace) to another without disrupting existing queries

5. The hierarchical database model:
   a. Was first proposed by Peter Chen
   b. Stores data in the form of tables
   c. Directly supports one-to-many relationships
   d. Directly supports many-to-many relationships
   e. Connects data records using physical address pointers

6. The network database model:
   a. Was first proposed by Ralph Kimball
   b. In its pure form, permits only one parent for any given record
   c. Directly supports one-to-many relationships
   d. Directly supports many-to-many relationships
   e. Connects database records using physical address pointers

7. The relational database model:
   a. Was first proposed by Dr. E.F. Codd
   b. Provides superior flexibility for ad-hoc queries
   c. Directly supports one-to-many relationships
   d. Directly supports many-to-many relationships
   e. Connects database records using physical address pointers

8. The object-oriented database model:
   a. Is newer than the relational database model
   b. Provides superior flexibility for ad-hoc queries

    c. Provides better support for complex data types than the relational model

    d. Allows access to data only through application logic modules called methods

    e. Combines concepts from the network and relational database models in an attempt to get the best from each

9. A primary key constraint is implemented using which database object?

    a. Column

    b. Index

    c. Referential constraint

    d. View

    e. Table

10. A relationship in the conceptual design is implemented using which database object?

    a. Column

    b. Index

    c. Referential constraint

    d. View

    e. Table

11. An attribute in the conceptual design is implemented using which database object?

    a. Column

    b. Index

    c. Referential constraint

    d. View

    e. Table

12. An entity in the conceptual design is implemented using which database object?

    a. Column

    b. Index

    c. Referential constraint

    d. View

    e. Table

13. Which database object appears in the external level of the ANSI/SPARC model?

    a. Column

    b. Index

    c. Referential constraint

    d. View

    e. Table

14. A referential constraint:
    a. Defines a one-to-many relationship between two tables
    b. Ensures that a primary key does not have duplicate values
    c. Ensures that a foreign key value in a child table always refers to an existing primary key value in the parent table
    d. Prevents "orphaned" foreign key values in the parent table
    e. Must have primary key and foreign key columns that are in different tables

15. A primary key constraint:
    a. Must be defined for every database table
    b. Prevents two rows in a table from having the same primary key value
    c. Must reference one or more primary key columns as well as one or more foreign key columns
    d. Must reference one or more columns in a single table
    e. Is usually implemented using an index

16. If an order may contain many products, and a product may appear on many orders, this is an example of which type of relationship?
    a. One-to-one
    b. One-to-many
    c. Many-to-one
    d. Many-to-many
    e. Recursive

17. Forms-based query languages are different from SQL because:
    a. They use a GUI (graphical user interface).
    b. They describe the desired query results rather than how to obtain the results.
    c. Queries are formed graphically rather than through typed commands.
    d. They can be used to form queries that are impossible in SQL.
    e. They were developed long before SQL.

18. A column in a database query result set can be formed from:
    a. A constant
    b. A foreign key column
    c. A calculation
    d. A table column
    e. A view column

19. The criteria line in Microsoft Access queries is used to:
    a. Order rows in a particular sequence within the result set
    b. Limit rows that will be returned in the result set
    c. Apply aggregate functions to one or more columns
    d. Form joins between multiple tables and/or views
    e. Define the circumstances under which the query is to be run

20. When sequencing is not included in a database query, the rows in the result set will be in:
    a. Primary key sequence
    b. The order in which the rows were added to the table(s)
    c. Ascending sequence by the first column in the query results
    d. Ascending sequence by the first index defined on the table(s)
    e. No particular sequence

21. In Microsoft Access:
    a. Criteria written on the same line are connected with a logical AND.
    b. Criteria written on the same line are connected with a logical OR.
    c. Criteria written on different lines are connected with a logical AND.
    d. Criteria written on different lines are connected with a logical OR.
    e. Criteria written on different lines are connected with a logical NOT.

22. The join connector between tables in a Microsoft Access query:
    a. Can cause a Cartesian product if defined incorrectly
    b. Does not support full outer joins
    c. Supports left and right outer joins in addition to standard joins
    d. May be inherited from the metadata defined on the Relationships panel
    e. Can be manually created using the Create Join dialog box

23. An aggregate function in a database query:
    a. Combines data from multiple rows together
    b. Combines data from multiple columns together
    c. Specifies how joins are to be done
    d. Requires that every column in the query be either named in the GROUP BY list for the query or formed using an aggregate function
    e. May not be applied to columns containing calculations

24. Commonly used aggregate query functions include
    a. ORDER BY
    b. AVG
    c. MIN
    d. MAX
    e. ROUND

25. SQL DML statements include
    a. INSERT
    b. CREATE
    c. UPDATE
    d. PURGE
    e. ALTER

26. An SQL DELETE statement without a WHERE clause results in:
    a. An error message
    b. Every row in the table being deleted
    c. Every column in the table being deleted
    d. The table being dropped
    e. A Cartesian product

27. An SQL UPDATE statement that omits the table name results in:
    a. An error message
    b. All tables being updated
    c. No tables being updated
    d. A Cartesian product
    e. Every row in a table being updated

28. The BETWEEN operator in SQL:
    a. Can be rewritten using the < and > operators
    b. Can be rewritten using the <= and >= operators
    c. Includes the endpoint values
    d. Results in an outer join
    e. Is used when writing subselects

29. An SQL subselect:
    a. Allows for flexible selection of rows
    b. Must be enclosed in parentheses
    c. May be used instead of a join to limit rows returned by a query
    d. Is a powerful way of calculating column values
    e. May be an inner subselect or an outer subselect

30. In SQL, a join without a WHERE clause results in:
    a. An inner join
    b. An outer join
    c. A Cartesian product
    d. An error message
    e. An empty result set (no rows returned)

31. In SQL, a self-join:
    a. Always results in a Cartesian product
    b. Can never result in a Cartesian product
    c. Resolves a recursive relationship
    d. Involves two different tables
    e. Can be a standard (inner) or outer join

32. A COMMIT in Oracle:
    a. Ends a transaction
    b. Begins a new transaction
    c. Is automatic just before any DDL statement is run
    d. Is automatic just before any DML statement is run
    e. Removes any locks held by the current transaction

33. During the conceptual design phase of the database life cycle:
    a. Normalization takes place.
    b. The conceptual data model is updated.
    c. Reports are designed.
    d. The development database is created.
    e. New entities may be discovered.

34. During the logical design phase of the database life cycle:
    a. Normalization takes place.
    b. The development database is created.
    c. Database queries are written.
    d. Program specifications are written.
    e. Database performance tuning takes place.

35. During the physical design phase of the database life cycle:
    a. Normalization takes place.
    b. The logical data model is converted to one or more physical models.
    c. DDL is written to define database objects.
    d. Application programs are written.
    e. Database indexes may be added.

36. During the construction phase of the database life cycle:
    a. Normalization takes place.
    b. Any required data conversion is tested.
    c. New entities are discovered.
    d. Application programs are written.
    e. Development and test databases are created.

37. During the implementation and rollout phase of the database life cycle:
    a. User training takes place.
    b. Users are placed on the live system.
    c. Quality assurance testing takes place.
    d. The old and new applications may be run in parallel.
    e. Enhancements are designed.

38. During the ongoing support phase of the database life cycle:
    a. Enhancements are designed and implemented.
    b. Bug fixes take place.
    c. Patches may be applied if needed.
    d. The staging environment is no longer needed.
    e. Schema changes are never required.

39. Dr. E.F. Codd invented
    a. The star schema
    b. Normalization
    c. The ERD
    d. The relational database
    e. Data warehousing

40. The purpose of normalization is to:
    a. Optimize data-retrieval performance
    b. Optimize the database design for inserts, updates, and deletes
    c. Eliminate redundant data
    d. Minimize the number of relations (tables) in the database design
    e. Remove certain anomalies from the relations

41. The insert anomaly refers to a situation where:
    a. An insert statement fails due to a duplicate primary key error.
    b. Data must be inserted before it can be deleted.
    c. A required insert cannot be done due to an artificial dependency.
    d. Too many inserts cause a performance bottleneck in the DBMS.
    e. Data must be deleted before a new row may be inserted.

42. The delete anomaly refers to a situation where:
    a. Data must be deleted before a new row may be inserted.
    b. Data deletion causes unintentional loss of another entity's data.
    c. Data must be inserted before it can be deleted.
    d. Data must be deleted before it can be inserted.
    e. A delete operation fails due to data locked by another user.

43. The update anomaly refers to a situation where:
    a. An update without a WHERE clause updates every row in a table.
    b. Data cannot be updated due to lack of privileges.
    c. A simple update requires updates to multiple rows of data.
    d. Data cannot be updated by one user because of locks held by another user.
    e. Data cannot be updated due to an existing referential constraint.

44. To be in first normal form, a relation:
    a. Must have a unique identifier
    b. Must be in Boyce-Codd normal form
    c. Must not have any repeating groups or multivalued attributes
    d. Must not have any transitive dependencies
    e. Must not have any partial key dependencies

45. To be in second normal form, a relation:
    a. Must have a unique identifier
    b. Must be in first normal form
    c. Must not have any repeating groups or multivalued attributes
    d. Must not have any transitive dependencies
    e. Must not have any partial key dependencies

46. To be in third normal form, a relation:
    a. Must be in first normal form
    b. Must be in second normal form
    c. Must not have any repeating groups or multivalued attributes
    d. Must not have any transitive dependencies
    e. Must not have any partial key dependencies

47. In general, violations of a normalization rule are resolved by:
    a. Combining relations
    b. Creating summary tables
    c. Moving attributes or groups of attributes to a new relation
    d. Denormalization
    e. Eliminating attributes

48. The elements common to all ERD formats include
    a. Rectangles or boxes representing entities
    b. Optional inclusion of attributes
    c. Ellipses representing views
    d. Lines representing relationships
    e. Line ends representing the minimum cardinality of the relationships

49. A subtype:
    a. Is a superset of the super type
    b. Is a subset of the super type
    c. Has a many-to-one relationship with the super type
    d. Has a one-to-one relationship with the super type
    e. Shows various states of the super type

50. Examples of possible subtypes for a Customer entity super type include
    a. Corporate customer
    b. Individual customer
    c. Preferred customer
    d. Former customer
    e. Commercial customer

51. The components of the CRUD matrix are
    a. Rectangles to show entities
    b. Ellipses to show attributes
    c. Major processes shown on one axis
    d. Major entities shown on the other axis
    e. Numbers to show the operations that processes carry out on entities

52. The basic components of a function hierarchy diagram are
    a. Rectangles to show process functions
    b. Diamonds to show decision points
    c. A hierarchy to show which functions are subordinate to others
    d. Ellipses to show process steps
    e. Lines connecting processes in order of execution

53. The basic components of a flowchart are
    a. Lines to show the hierarchy of functions
    b. Diamonds to show decision points
    c. Open-ended rectangles to show data stores
    d. Ellipses to show starting and ending points
    e. Rectangles to show process steps

54. The basic components of a swim lane diagram are
    a. Vertical lanes to show the organizational units that carry out process steps
    b. Rectangles to show process steps
    c. Open-ended rectangles to show data stores
    d. Lines with arrows to show the sequence of process steps
    e. Ellipses to show process steps

55. NOT NULL constraints:
    a. Are required on unique identifier columns
    b. Are required on primary key columns
    c. Are required on foreign key columns
    d. Prevent columns from being set to null values
    e. Prevent inserts from omitting mandatory columns

56. Primary key constraints:
    a. Require columns that have NOT NULL constraints
    b. Require columns that have check constraints
    c. Require column values to be unique within the table
    d. Require column values to be unique within the database
    e. Require columns that are also used as foreign keys

57. Referential constraints:
    a. Require that foreign key columns be defined as NOT NULL
    b. Require that the columns in the parent table be defined as the primary key
    c. Are always defined on the child table
    d. Must use the names automatically assigned by the DBMS
    e. Define a many-to-many relationship between two tables

58. Data types:
    a. Can restrict the maximum size of column data
    b. Can restrict the minimum size of column data
    c. Can restrict the types of characters allowed in a column
    d. Can prevent incorrect data from being inserted into a column
    e. Can be used to format dates the way users want them displayed

59. Indexes:
    a. Are often created automatically by the DBMS to assist with referential constraints
    b. May be used to improve select performance
    c. Usually improve the performance of insert, update, and delete statements
    d. Are faster to scan sequentially than the tables they index
    e. Must be refreshed manually when the tables they index are updated

60. General rules to follow regarding indexes include
    a. The larger the table, the more likely indexes will assist query performance.
    b. Columns that are frequently updated should always be indexed.
    c. Performance consequences should be evaluated carefully before more than two or three indexes are defined on the same table.
    d. Indexing foreign key columns can help with join performance.
    e. The more a table is updated, the more indexes will help overall performance.

61. Check constraints:
    a. May be used to implement a one-to-many relationship
    b. May be used to force a column to match a list of values
    c. May be used to force a column to match another column in the same row
    d. May be used to force a column to match another column in another table
    e. May be used to force a numeric column to have only positive values

62. When converting normalized relations to tables:
    a. Unique identifiers become primary key constraints.
    b. Each normalized relation becomes a table.
    c. Relationships become unique constraints.
    d. Each attribute in a relation becomes a table column.
    e. Primary key columns must be defined with check constraints.

63. JDBC:
    a. Was developed by Microsoft
    b. Can be used by C programs to connect to databases
    c. Can be used by Java programs to connect to databases
    d. Cannot handle proprietary SQL statements
    e. Is a standard API for connecting web servers to application servers

64. XML:
    a. Is a protocol used to transfer web pages
    b. Is HTML on steroids
    c. Is used for database replication
    d. Is a document formatting language
    e. Allows developers to code their own tags

65. A URL may contain
    a. A host name or IP address
    b. An SQL statement
    c. A port
    d. A web page
    e. The absolute path to a resource on a web server

66. An intranet is
    a. Usually protected by a firewall
    b. Never connected to the Internet
    c. Available to anyone on the Internet
    d. Available to authorized (internal) members of an organization
    e. A worldwide collection of interconnected computer networks

67. An extranet is
    a. A worldwide collection of interconnected computer networks
    b. Available to anyone on the Internet
    c. Available to authorized (internal) members of an organization
    d. Available to authorized outsiders such as customers of an organization
    e. Protected by a firewall

68. The N-tier client/server model:
    a. Has a database hosted on a centralized server
    b. Has all application logic running on the client workstation
    c. Uses a web browser for presentation
    d. Requires high-powered client workstations
    e. Has the client workstation handle all presentation logic

69. The three-tier client/server model:
    a. Has a database hosted on a centralized server
    b. Has all application logic running on the client workstation
    c. Uses a web browser for presentation
    d. Requires high-powered client workstations
    e. Has the client workstation handle all presentation logic

70. The two-tier client/server model:
    a. Has a database hosted on a centralized server
    b. Has all application logic running on the client workstation
    c. Uses a web browser for presentation
    d. Requires high-powered client workstations
    e. Has the client workstation handle all presentation logic

71. Database roles:
    a. May exist before users do
    b. May contain no more than 16 system privileges
    c. May contain any number of object privileges
    d. May be assigned to any number of users
    e. Are automatically dropped when users are dropped

72. Database system privileges:
    a. Are rescinded using the SQL ALTER statement
    b. Are granted using a standard SQL GRANT statement
    c. Are specific to a database object
    d. Vary considerably across different DBMS vendors and versions
    e. Automatically allow the grantee to grant the privilege to other users

73. Database object privileges:
    a. Are rescinded using the SQL DROP statement
    b. Are granted using a standard SQL ALTER statement
    c. Are specific to a database object
    d. Are included in SQL standards, so there is little variation among vendors
    e. Automatically allow the grantee to grant the privileges to other users

74. Security considerations for the client workstation include
    a. Use of a virus scanner
    b. The web browser security level
    c. The MAC address lists
    d. A properly configured firewall
    e. Packet filtering

75. Security considerations for the database server include
    a. Applying security patches in a timely manner
    b. Writing down passwords so they are not forgotten
    c. Changing all default passwords
    d. Installing every available operating system and database feature
    e. Assigning complex passwords that are difficult to guess

76. Security considerations for a wireless access point include
    a. Network address translation
    b. Encryption
    c. MAC address lists
    d. Setting a strictly enforced organization standard for its use
    e. The use of a firewall between the wireless device and the access point

77. Security considerations for access to an enterprise network from a remote
    work location include
    a. A firewall between the remote client workstation and the cable or
       DSL modem
    b. The use of a VPN
    c. Encrypting critical and sensitive data when transferred over the network
    d. The use of IP spoofing
    e. Network address translation

78. Security considerations for the enterprise network include
    a. Special considerations for any remotely connected users
    b. A firewall protecting each layer of the network
    c. Packet filtering using the routing tables in the routers
    d. Clearly written and strictly enforced standards
    e. Network address translation

79. An SQL cursor is
    a. A process that checks SQL for correct syntax
    b. A buffer that holds rows retrieved from the database
    c. A method used to determine which table columns need indexes
    d. A pointer into a result set
    e. The same as a result set

80. Properties of transactions include
    a. Must be either completely processed or not processed at all
    b. Isolation from other transactions
    c. Prevention of deadlocks
    d. Transforming the database from one consistent state to another
    e. Those described by the ACID acronym

81. The letter *A* in the acronym ACID stands for:
    a. Automated
    b. Abbreviated
    c. Atomicity
    d. Autonomous
    e. Analog

82. Database locks:
    a. Are implemented in exactly the same way by all major database vendors
    b. Are controls placed by the DBMS to reserve data so updates may be safely applied
    c. Are usually released when a COMMIT or ROLLBACK takes place
    d. May have a timeout period set by the DBMS
    e. May cause contention when other users attempt to update locked data

83. A deadlock:
    a. May be resolved automatically by the DBMS
    b. May not be resolved automatically by the DBMS
    c. Occurs when locks time out and are no longer needed
    d. Occurs when locks are deleted by the DBMS
    e. Occurs when two database users each request a lock on data that is locked by the other

84. Concurrent database updates:
    a. Are prohibited by modern DBMSs
    b. Can cause data loss when proper controls are not in place
    c. Cannot occur when AUTOCOMMIT is set to ON
    d. Can be done safely when transaction locking is supported by the DBMS
    e. Can cause contention when locking mechanisms are in place

85. An index cannot be used for a WHERE clause predicate that:
    a. Uses the LIKE operator
    b. Uses the IN operator
    c. Uses the NOT operator
    d. Uses the NOT EQUAL operator
    e. Uses an aggregate function

86. Benefits of a change control process are
    a. It provides a log of all changes made.
    b. It can allow defective software versions to be backed out.
    c. It can prevent programming errors from being placed into production.
    d. It helps to isolate performance bottlenecks.
    e. It can help with understanding when changes may be installed.

87. Data warehousing:
    a. Is a form of an OLTP database
    b. Was pioneered by Bill Inmon
    c. Involves storing historical data for analysis
    d. May involve one or more data marts
    e. Involves storing data required for day-to-day operations of the organization

88. Data marts:
    a. Support the requirements of a particular department or business function
    b. Can be a good starting point when requirements are sketchy
    c. Are supersets of a data warehouse
    d. Are the systems from which the enterprise data warehouse loads its data
    e. Can be a good starting point for organizations with limited data warehouse experience

89. The summary table architecture:
    a. Was originally developed by Ralph Kimball
    b. Was originally developed by Bill Inmon
    c. Includes a fact table
    d. Includes dimension tables
    e. Should include metadata

90. The star schema architecture:
    a. Was originally developed by Ralph Kimball
    b. Was originally developed by Bill Inmon
    c. Includes a fact table
    d. Includes dimension tables
    e. Should include metadata

91. A data warehouse is
    a. Organized around one department or business function
    b. Subject oriented
    c. Updated periodically according to a prescribed schedule
    d. Usually loaded from only one data source
    e. Time variant

92. Data mining:
    a. Is an analysis method that finds previously unknown data correlations
    b. Is a subset of a data warehouse
    c. Can be successful with small amounts of data
    d. Can only be successful with large amounts of data
    e. Is a scaled-down data warehouse

93. Compared with OLTP systems, data warehouse systems:
    a. Have short-running queries that process limited amounts of data
    b. Have a medium to low transaction volume
    c. Hold current rather than historic data
    d. Provide information for strategic decision makers
    e. Have many more regular users

94. Normalization:
    a. Was developed by Dr. Codd
    b. Was first introduced with five normal forms
    c. First appeared in 1972
    d. Provides a set of rules for each normal form
    e. Provides a procedure for converting relations to each normal form

95. When implemented, a third normal form relation becomes
    a. An index
    b. A referential constraint
    c. A table
    d. A view
    e. A database

96. The roles of unique identifiers in normalization are
    a. They are unnecessary.
    b. They are required once you reach third normal form.
    c. All normalized forms require designation of a primary key.
    d. You cannot normalize relations without first choosing a primary key.
    e. You cannot choose a primary key until relations are normalized.

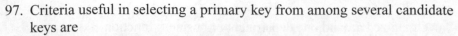

97. Criteria useful in selecting a primary key from among several candidate keys are
    a. Choose the simplest candidate.
    b. Choose the shortest candidate.
    c. Choose the candidate most likely to have its value change.
    d. Choose concatenated keys over single attribute keys.
    e. Invent a surrogate key if that is the best possible key.

98. First normal form resolves anomalies caused by:
    a. Transitive dependencies
    b. Multivalued attributes
    c. Partial dependency on the primary key
    d. Repeating groups
    e. Join dependencies

99. Second normal form resolves anomalies caused by:
    a. Transitive dependencies
    b. Multivalued attributes
    c. Partial dependency on the primary key
    d. Repeating groups
    e. Join dependencies

100. Third normal form resolves anomalies caused by:
    a. Transitive dependencies
    b. Multivalued attributes
    c. Partial dependency on the primary key
    d. Repeating groups
    e. Join dependencies

Answers to Quizzes and Final Exam

Chapter 1

1. **a, d, e**	2. **a, b, d**	3. **b, d, e**	4. **a, c, d, e**	5. **a, c ,d**
6. **b, c, d**	7. **c, e**	8. **a, b, c, d, e**	9. **c, d**	10. **b, d**
11. **a, b, c, e**	12. **a, d, e**	13. **b, e**	14. **b, d**	15. **a, d, e**
16. **a, b, d**	17. **b, c, d, e**	18. **a, b, e**	19. **a, c, e**	20. **c, d**

Chapter 2

1. **a, c**	2. **b, e**	3. **b**	4. **a, b, d**	5. **d**
6. **a, c**	7. **b, d, e**	8. **a, c, e**	9. **a, b, e**	10. **b, c, d, e**
11. **a, d, e**	12. **d**	13. **a, b**	14. **c, d**	15. **a, c, d**
16. **b**	17. **c**	18. **a**	19. **d**	20. **e**

Chapter 3

1. d	2. a, b	3. e	4. a, d	5. c
6. a, b, c, d, e	7. c	8. a	9. b	10. a, e
11. a, b, e	12. e	13. b, d, e	14. b, d	15. c, e
16. b, d	17. b	18. a, c, d, e	19. a	20. a, d

Chapter 4

1. b, d	2. a, e	3. b, c, d	4. a	5. b, c
6. a, d	7. b, e	8. c, e	9. d	10. b, e
11. b, d, e	12. b, d	13. a, b, c, d, e	14. c, d	15. c
16. a	17. c, d, e	18. a, b, e	19. b	20. b, e

Chapter 5

1. a, b, d, e	2. b, c	3. a, c, d, e	4. b, c	5. a
6. c, e	7. a, b, e	8. b, c, d	9. a, b, e	10. a, c, d
11. a, b	12. a, c, e	13. b, d, e	14. a, b, d	15. d
16. a	17. e	18. c	19. b, d	20. a

Chapter 6

1. a, c, d, e	2. b, e	3. c	4. d	5. c
6. a	7. c, d	8. b, c, d	9. a, b, e	10. b, d
11. c	12. a	13. b	14. a, b, d	15. d
16. a	17. c	18. e	19. c	20. e

Chapter 7

1. d, e	2. a, b, d	3. c	4. a, b	5. b, d
6. a, b, c	7. a, c	8. c, e	9. a, b, d	10. c, e
11. b, d, e	12. a, b, e	13. b, d	14. c, e	15. a, c, d
16. a, c, e	17. b, d	18. a, c, e	19. b, c, e	20. a, c, d

Chapter 8

1. c, d	2. a, b, e	3. b, d	4. b, c, d	5. c, e
6. b, d	7. b, c, e	8. b, c	9. a, b, d, e	10. a, d
11. b, d	12. a, d	13. b, e	14. a, b, c	15. b, e
16. a, c, d	17. b, c, d, e	18. a, b, c, d, e	19. a, b, d	20. a, b, e

Chapter 9

1. b, c	2. a, c, e	3. c, d, e	4. a, c, d	5. a, b, c, d
6. b, d, e	7. b, d, e	8. b, c, d, e	9. a, c, e	10. a, b, c, d, e
11. b, d	12. a, b, c, e	13. a, b, c, d, e	14. b, d, e	15. a, c, d
16. c, e	17. a, b, e	18. a, d, e	19. b, c	20. a, b, e

Chapter 10

1. a, c, d, e	2. b, c, d, e	3. d, e	4. a, c, d	5. b, d
6. a, b, d, e	7. b, c, e	8. a, c, d	9. b, d, e	10. a, c, d
11. b, d, c	12. a, c, d	13. b, c, e	14. b, c, d, e	15. b, c, e
16. a, c, e	17. a, b, e	18. a, c, d	19. b, c, d	20. a, c

Chapter 11

1. b	2. a	3. a, c	4. b, c, d, e	5. d
6. a, d, e	7. a, e	8. c, d	9. a, c, e	10. a, b, c, d, e
11. b, c, d, e	12. a, c, d, e	13. b, e	14. a, b, d	15. b, d, e
16. a, b, d	17. b, c	18. a, b	19. b, c, d, e	20. b, d, e

Chapter 12

1. c, d	2. e	3. b, c, d, e	4. a, b, c	5. b, d, e
6. a, c, d	7. a, d, e	8. d	9. a, d	10. b, c, d, e
11. a, d	12. a, b	13. b, d, e	14. a, c, d, e	15. b, c, e
16. a, b	17. b, c, e	18. a, b, d	19. b, d, e	20. a, b, e

Answers to Final Exam

1. b, d, e	2. a, c, e	3. b, d	4. a, c, e	5. c, e
6. c, d, e	7. a, b, c	8. c, d	9. b	10. c
11. a	12. e	13. d	14. a, c	15. b, d, e
16. d	17. a, c	18. a, b, c, d, e	19. b	20. e
21. a, d	22. a, b, c, d	23. a, d	24. b, c, d	25. a, c
26. b	27. a, c	28. b, c	29. a, b, c	30. a, c
31. c, e	32. a, b, c, e	33. b, c, e	34. a, d	35. b, c, e
36. b, d, e	37. a, b, d	38. a, b, c	39. b, d	40. b, e
41. c	42. b	43. c	44. a, c	45. a, b, c, e
46. a, b, c, d, e	47. c	48. a, b, d	49. b, d	50. a, b, e
51. c, d	52. a, c	53. b, d, e	54. a, d, e	55. b, d, e
56. a, c	57. b, c	58. a, c	59. b, d	60. a, c, d
61. b, c, e	62. a, b, d	63. c	64. b, d, e	65. a, c, e
66. a, d	67. c, d, e	68. a, c, e	69. a, e	70. a, b, d, e
71. a, c, d	72. b, d	73. c, d	74. a, b	75. a, c, e
76. b, c, d	77. a, b, c, e	78. a, b, d, e	79. d	80. a, b, d, e
81. c	82. b, c, d, e	83. a, b, e	84. b, d, e	85. c, d, e
86. a, b, e	87. b, c, d	88. a, b, e	89. b, e	90. a, c, d, e
91. b, c, e	92. a, d	93. b, d	94. a, c, d, e	95. c
96. c, d	97. a, b, e	98. b, d	99. c	100. a

INDEX

INTERNATIONAL CONTACT INFORMATION

AUSTRALIA
McGraw-Hill Book Company
Australia Pty. Ltd.
TEL +61-2-9900-1800
FAX +61-2-9878-8881
http://www.mcgraw-hill.com.au
books-it_sydney@mcgraw-hill.com

CANADA
McGraw-Hill Ryerson Ltd.
TEL +905-430-5000
FAX +905-430-5020
http://www.mcgraw-hill.ca

**GREECE, MIDDLE EAST, & AFRICA
(Excluding South Africa)**
McGraw-Hill Hellas
TEL +30-210-6560-990
TEL +30-210-6560-993
TEL +30-210-6560-994
FAX +30-210-6545-525

MEXICO (Also serving Latin America)
McGraw-Hill Interamericana Editores
S.A. de C.V.
TEL +525-1500-5108
FAX +525-117-1589
http://www.mcgraw-hill.com.mx
carlos_ruiz@mcgraw-hill.com

SINGAPORE (Serving Asia)
McGraw-Hill Book Company
TEL +65-6863-1580
FAX +65-6862-3354
http://www.mcgraw-hill.com.sg
mghasia@mcgraw-hill.com

SOUTH AFRICA
McGraw-Hill South Africa
TEL +27-11-622-7512
FAX +27-11-622-9045
robyn_swanepoel@mcgraw-hill.com

SPAIN
McGraw-Hill/
Interamericana de España, S.A.U.
TEL +34-91-180-3000
FAX +34-91-372-8513
http://www.mcgraw-hill.es
professional@mcgraw-hill.es

**UNITED KINGDOM, NORTHERN,
EASTERN, & CENTRAL EUROPE**
McGraw-Hill Education Europe
TEL +44-1-628-502500
FAX +44-1-628-770224
http://www.mcgraw-hill.co.uk
emea_queries@mcgraw-hill.com

ALL OTHER INQUIRIES Contact:
McGraw-Hill/Osborne
TEL +1-510-420-7700
FAX +1-510-420-7703
http://www.osborne.com
omg_international@mcgraw-hill.com